Peace Psychology

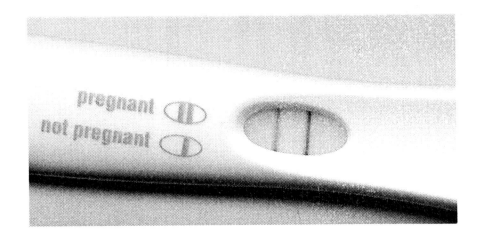

Perspectives on Abortion

Edited by Rachel M. MacNair

Published by
Feminism & Nonviolence Studies Association
811 Cleaver II Boulevard
Kansas City, MO 64110
USA

Web Page: www.fnsa.org

ISBN: 1530838266

EAN: 978-1530838264

Peace Psychology
Perspectives on Abortion

Table of Contents

Part 2.
Post-abortion Aftermath

Part 3.
Other Contentious Topics

Part 4.
The Constructive Program

Introduction

by Rachel M. MacNair, Ph.D.

Understanding Perspectives

Back when I was in college, pursuing a major in Peace and Conflict Studies at Earlham (a Quaker college, I being a Quaker), several of us activists offered a program to educate about what was wrong with nuclear energy. We did so well that a student asked how it could possibly be that anyone would support it. I immediately offered a three-minute pro-nuclear diatribe. My fellow activists started getting uncomfortable, wanting me to explain what was wrong with what I was saying.

I regard this as a crucial skill for all those interested in peace and therefore in conflict resolution. For effective debating, for proper listening, for the opportunity to fashion creative solutions not otherwise thought of, for the ability to get along with people with whom one disagrees, it is important to be able to understand and articulate a view different from one's own.

In another incident from college days, we were preparing for a program arguing against nuclear weapons. A friend said these were so horrid and dangerous that we only needed to explain this, with no further information needed. When the program came, I watched as an audience member asked this simple question: "What about the Soviets? How can we give up nuclear weapons as long as they still have them?" This was not an unusual question and should have been anticipated. Yet my friend had no answer. It is indeed important to be familiar with all points of view when the goal is to be effective in presenting one's own.

Stereotypes of differing perspectives abound in most conflicts where debates are heated. This is especially so with abortion, where partisan and "left-wing/right-wing" political and religious divides cause people to choose sides, often on criteria other than the merits of the case. Yet whatever position a person takes, it is important for that person to have a clear understanding of what the other common positions are.

This book will accordingly consider a variety of perspectives, but it is not simply a book about what perspectives are. Coming from an over-arching peace psychology perspective, it will consider psychological theories and empirical evidence. Going well beyond unsubstantiated viewpoints, it will take an approach suitable not just for psychology but for academic scholarship in general.

Abortion: Option, Violence, or Tragedy

The philosophical perspectives on abortion in contemporary controversies can be understood on a continuum from support to opposition, and as with most continuums more people are likely somewhere along the middle rather than at either extreme. Here we will call the two extremes *abortion-as-option* and *abortion-as-violence*, with the continuum between called *abortion-as-tragic-necessity*.

<u>Continuum of Positions</u>

Option   <-   Tragic   ->   Violence

The term "pro-choice" is commonly used for abortion-as-option, and is insisted upon by any peace advocates who favor abortion availability. Their reasoning is for the liberation of women and perhaps also for the alleviation of poverty. Groups that favor this view include the Women's International League for Peace and Freedom (WILPF), the War Resister's League, and magazines of wide circulation and long history such as *The Progressive* and *Mother Jones*.

However, this extreme is also occupied by men who wish the women they impregnate to take this option whether or not the women themselves actually desire it. Similarly, there are those interested in eugenics or who take a racist attitude. For purposes of this book, we are only interested in aspects of interest to *peace psychology*, and therefore will not be considering the views of those whose reasoning is not for women's benefit.

Similarly, the term "pro-life" is commonly used for the abortion-as-violence perspective, but this view is held by many for whom sensitivity to a right-to-life concern is narrow and does not extend to opposing war or the death penalty or favoring effective anti-poverty programs. This has been particularly true in recent partisan politics in several countries.

In the same way, this book is only considering the views of those who oppose all these forms of violence across the board, in what is commonly called the "consistent life ethic" (MacNair & Zunes, 2008). This view is officially held by many Catholic documents and the Mennonite church (Mennonites are a traditionally pacifist church) as well as a large number of people of varying religions and of secular orientation in the peace movement. The philosophies of pro-life feminism (Derr, MacNair, & Naranjo-Huebl, 2006) and the literature of the Pro-life Alliance of Gays and Lesbians (www.plagal.org) will also be of more appeal to peace movement activists.

In both cases, those who hold views not consistent with the actual meanings of the terms "choice" or "life" are not of interest because this book is focused on perspectives of peace psychology. We simply acknowledge at the beginning that both extremes hold adherents that are not of a peace orientation. We therefore often use more descriptive, neutral terminology for the views; this should also help us focus on the meaning of the terms without reference to wording which has accrued a great deal of emotional meaning due to current debates.

The "tragic necessity view" has at one end of its continuum people who are strong advocates of abortion availability and may even be abortion providers. An example is the title of the book, *In Necessity and Sorrow*, in which Magda Denes (1976) discusses abortion as an unfortunate need. Another is the statement of a woman abortion doctor: "Sorrow, quite apart from the sense of shame, is exhibited in some way by virtually every woman for whom I've performed an abortion, and that's 20,000 as of 1995. The sorrow is revealed by the fact that most women cry at some point during the experience . . . The grieving process may last from several days to several years" (Poppema, 1996, pp. 125-126). These are people who use the pro-choice label but nevertheless recognize in various degrees that abortion is more difficult than a tooth extraction. On the other end are people who might use the term "pro-life" to describe themselves, but only because they believe it wise to discourage abortion as a matter of persuasion, while still accepting that abortion be legal or readily available for extreme cases.

Why the Difference?

The fact that peace advocates can be found on both sides and in the middle of the continuum has much to do with understanding the status of the human embryo and fetus.

- If the status is one of "products of conception" or tissue, then removing the growth is nothing more than ending an unwanted pregnancy, and the understanding that this is entirely a decision for the pregnant woman would be determinative; this goes with the "abortion-as-option" view.

- If the embryo or fetus has the status of a human baby, a human being entitled to the same rights all human beings have to be protected from being killed, then abortion is an act of violence subject to all the problems that using violence as a problem-solver commonly has, as would be understood in the "abortion-as-violence" view.

- If the embryo or fetus is understood to be a living organism but one with a status similar to an animal, then killing an animal is to be avoided when possible but allowed when really needed. Persuasive abortion reduction programs are a good idea, but not legal bans; hence, abortion-as-tragic-necessity.

Most of the theoretical orientations in this book will only use the two extremes, because that is where the theorizing is. Those who do not really fit either end of the continuum should still be able to find much insight here.

To illustrate how these different perspectives lead to different discussions, take the impact on women's equality. To the abortion-as-option view, it is exceedingly obvious that women's control of their own reproductive lives is foundational for women's equality. From the abortion-as-violence perspective, telling women we must have surgery to be treated equally is disparaging female biology, and therefore a form of privileging male characteristics. From the abortion-as-option view, forcing women to continue pregnancies is itself a form of gender discrimination. From the abortion-as-violence perspective, when pregnancies are regarded as optional rather than a condition to be accommodated, then those employers and schools who understand themselves to be inconvenienced are more likely to discriminate against pregnant women.

Outline of Book

We start with points on which all positions on the peace-oriented continuum agree: the dynamics of abortion as it relates to violence against women. This includes intimate partner violence, coercion, sex trafficking, war-related violence, and abortion targeted at female fetuses only because they are female. I have received complaints from those of the abortion-as-option position that this is unbalanced; it presents abortion's negative aspects without mentioning positive ones. Yet mentioning positive aspects is no longer offering points common to both sides. Similarly, those who hold the abortion-as-violence position could complain this section ignores violence to the unborn child, leaving out what they regard as a crucial aspect. Hence, the section actually is balanced, but achieves balance by ignoring points each position regards as fundamental. The purpose is to start with points on which there is agreement, even if uncomfortable to those who chafe at what is missing.

Additionally, of course, violence against women is a major area of interest in the field of peace psychology. Any insight on its psychological dynamics which allows for avenues of research and prevention strategies is welcome. Such strategies will be addressed in each chapter of this section.

The second section deals with a highly contentious area, post-abortion aftermath. We cover the basics of methodology, especially the peculiarities of this field in particular. We go over what all researchers from all positions have agreed are risk factors for negative aftermath, showing where there is consensus. We then do a multi-perspective chapter on therapy, since those of different positions have had different approaches, and a basic overview of all of them is needed. Finally, we do pro-and-con chapters focused on the empirical case for different positions. Then there are two other populations dealt with in the context of abortion aftermath: the impregnating men, and the doctors and staff who provide abortions.

The third part consists of multi-perspective chapters on several other contentious issues; various different perspectives, usually both ends of the continuum, will best articulate their understanding. We have one chapter asking: what is the impact of abortion on child abuse? Another addresses how specific populations see abortion – those with disabilities, ethnic minorities, people in developing countries, and LGBT people, along with opposite positions on conscientious objectors among medical personnel. Finally, we cover not only what abortion itself does, but also the consequences of legal regulations related to abortion, since these are seen as harmful restrictions by those of an abortion-as-option view. There have been many empirical studies done by critics of the regulations.

The final section turns positive: what is the Constructive Program? This term was coined by Mohandas Gandhi as part of his practice of nonviolence. It is all very well to protest the objectionable, but what positive actions will replace it? The most obvious is the observation that no abortion happens when no pregnancy exists. This solution is agreeable to all sides, so the empirical studies on pregnancy prevention are covered. This is outside the context of violence-associated pregnancies in which the prevention strategy is to prevent the violence. Then, because prevention is no more a 100% effective strategy than is preventing all conflict a method of preventing all war (both sex and conflict being entrenched in the human condition), we discuss how to deal with pregnancies for those women who want to continue them but must surmount obstacles. Finally, we have two chapters on the basics of conflict transformation (that is, the idea of conflict resolution whereby conflicts are not merely settled but can be used for more creative outcomes). One is written by an expert in the field of conflict transformation, and another deals with the history of what has already been done and includes suggestions for future action and research.

The goal is to be thorough about covering as many aspects and viewpoints on the topic of abortion as would fit under the umbrella of peace psychology. This book can be used as a supplementary textbook in a variety of courses. It may also be of interest to anyone interested in an academic approach. This approach moves beyond the shouting matches and into what the empirical data show. It also offers the possibility of having a more accurate understanding of the different ways of viewing that empirical data. Finally, it allows us to discover what effective actions are substantiated, and what further research is needed.

Note: each author is responsible for her or his own chapter(s) only, and has not necessarily reviewed or contributed to other chapters.

APA style is used (American Psychological Association), meaning that rather than footnotes, references are listed by author's name and can be found at the end of the chapter in the reference list alphabetically under that name.

References

Denes, M. (1976). *In necessity and sorrow: Life and death in an abortion hospital.* New York: Basic Books.

Derr, M. K., MacNair, R. M. & Naranjo-Huebl, L. *Prolife feminism: Yesterday and today.* Kansas City, MO: Feminism & Nonviolence Studies Association.

MacNair, R. M. & Zunes, S. (2006). *Consistently opposing killing: From abortion to assisted suicide, the death penalty, and war.* Westport, CT: Praeger.

Poppema, S. & Henderson, M. (1996). *Why I am an abortion doctor.* New York: Prometheus Books.

Chapter 1

Intimate Partner Violence

by Catherine Coyle, Ph.D.
Co-director of the Alliance for Post-Abortion Research & Training

Incidence and Prevalence

Intimate Partner Violence (IPV) is a form of domestic violence (which also includes child abuse and elder abuse). IPV may be inflicted as physical or sexual violence and is often accompanied by emotional abuse (Watts & Zimmerman, 2002). Although IPV may be perpetrated by both men and women and either sex may be victims of IPV, the focus here is on violence against women.

According to the U.S. Department of Justice (Tjaden & Thoennes, 2000), "Violence against women is primarily intimate partner violence; 64.0% of the women who reported being raped, physically assaulted, and/or stalked since age 18 were victimized by a current or former husband, cohabiting partner, boyfriend, or date. In comparison, only 16.2% of the men who reported being raped and/or physically assaulted since age 18 were victimized by such a perpetrator" (p. 2). In North America, 40-60% of the murders of women have been perpetrated by their intimate partners (Crawford, Gartner & Dawson, 1997; Brock & Stenzel, 1999). It has been estimated that 20-25% of adolescent and adult women in the United States are victims of IPV (Silverman, Raj, Mucci & Hathaway, 2001; Tjaden & Thoennes, 1998). Globally, "35% of all women worldwide have experienced either physical and/or sexual intimate partner violence or non-partner sexual violence" (Garcia-Moreno & Pallitto, 2013, p. 2). Looking at IPV by WHO region, the highest incidence was found in South-East Asia where lifetime prevalence of IPV among ever-partnered women was found to be 37.7%, followed by the Eastern Mediterranean with 37%, Africa with 36.6%, the Americas with 29.8%, Europe with 25.4%, and the Western Pacific with 24.6% (Garcia-Moreno & Pallitto, 2013, p. 17).

While most intimate partner relationships do not include physical or emotional abuse, for those affected, the effects are serious and potentially life-threatening. The large number of women exposed to IPV represents a serious public health crisis in the United States and around the world.

Consequences

"Intimate partner violence has long-term negative health consequences for survivors, even after the abuse has ended" (Campbell, 2002, p. 1331). The potential physical consequences of IPV are multiple and include the obvious such as bruises, broken bones, lacerations, and concussions as well as sexually transmitted infections and sexual dysfunction (Coker, 2007) and HIV infection and immunocompromised states (Campbell et al., 2008). Even when abuse is exclusively psychological, it has been found to be associated with a variety of physical problems, including: arthritis, migraine, chronic pain, chronic pelvic pain, stomach ulcers, and spastic colon (Coker, Smith, Bethea, King & McKeown, 2000). In fact, "Psychological IPV was as strongly associated with the majority of adverse health outcomes as was physical IPV" (Coker, et al., 2000, p. 451). Mental health has also been found to be negatively impacted by IPV with depression, substance use, anxiety, PTSD and suicidal ideation being correlated with IPV (Chandra,

Satyanarayana, and Carey, 2009; Coker, Davis, et al., 2002,; Coker, Smith, et al., 2002; Mechanic, Weaver & Resick, 2008; Porcerelli et al., 2003).

IPV, Pregnancy, and Induced Abortion

In a violent and/or abusive relationship, the victim may experience reproductive coercion and denied control of her own fertility. The notion of "reproductive coercion" has been defined by Miller and Silverman (2010) as "male partners' attempts to promote pregnancy in their female partners through verbal pressure and threats to become pregnant (pregnancy coercion), direct interference with contraception (birth-control sabotage), and threats and coercion related to pregnancy continuation or termination (control of pregnancy outcomes)" (p. 2).

Pregnant women are also vulnerable to IPV.

> Intimate partner violence during pregnancy is more common than some maternal health conditions routinely screened for in antenatal care. Global initiatives to reduce maternal mortality and improve maternal health must devote increased attention to violence against women, particularly violence during pregnancy. (Devries et al., 2010, p. 158)

Some clinicians have observed that batterers often beat their pregnant partners' bellies and display regressions that seem to indicate rage at the fetus they believe competes for their partner's love. Such observations appear to be supported by women who were queried about their beliefs as to why their partners beat them during pregnancy (Campbell, Oliver, & Bullock, 1993).

Incidence estimates of IPV during the perinatal period are reported to range from 3% to 17% in the United States (McMahon & Armstrong, 2012) and from 1.2% to 51% in Ghana (Pool, Otupiri, Owusu-Dabo, de Jonge, & Agyemang, 2014).

IPV occurring during pregnancy is associated with serious health consequences for maternal and infant health (Bailey & Daugherty, 2007; Campbell, Garcia-Moreno, & Sharps, 2004). While IPV during pregnancy has been found to predict violence post pregnancy (Charles & Perreira, 2007), a study of adolescents revealed that 78% of teens who experienced IPV during the first three months of the postpartum period did not report IPV prior to delivery (Harrykissoon, Rickert, & Wiemann, 2002). Pregnancy may be a catalyst for violence, it may be protective from violence, or it may not be directly associated with violence. IPV that occurs during pregnancy may be best predicted by the severity and frequency of IPV that occurs over the course of a relationship (Campbell et al., 1993).

Research findings indicate that women with a history of IPV are significantly more likely to experience unintended pregnancy (Campbell & Soeken, 1999; Pallitto et al., 2013) as well as rapid repeat pregnancy (Cripe et al., 2008; Jacoby, Gorenflo, Black, Wunderlich, & Eyler, 1999; Kaye, Miremba, Bantebya, Johanssen, & Ekstrom, 2006). Since unplanned and unwanted pregnancy are common reasons for choosing abortion, it is not surprising that IPV has been found to be associated with elective abortion (Fanslow, Silva, Whitehead, & Robinson, 2008; Hall, Chappell, Parnell, Seed, & Bewley, 2014; Pallitto et al. 2013; Saftlas et al., 2010; Taft & Watson, 2007). In one study (Leung, Leung, Chan, & Ho, 2002), 27.3% of women stated their experience of abuse influenced their decision to abort. Following their analysis of 31 studies, Garcia-Moreno & Pallitto (2013) found "strong evidence that women with a history of intimate partner violence are more likely to report having had an induced abortion" (p. 23). Two other studies (Glander, Moore, Michielutte, & Parsons, 1998; Woo, Fine, & Goetzl, 2005) reported that women who experience IPV are less inclined to discuss abortion with abusive partners due to fear, and Silverman et al. (2010) observed that men who perpetrated IPV were more likely to report conflicts with their female partners concerning abortion.

Men who are determined to control partners may insist on abortions their partners do not want (as in the famous case of Lorena Bobbit). Women who opt for abortion willingly or under threat may be experiencing multiple assaults from partners before and immediately after undergoing the procedure, putting their physical and emotional health at risk. Given the consistently observed association between IPV and abortion, there have been calls to screen women for a history of abuse during abortion counseling (Glander et al., 1998; Saftlas et al., 2010; Silverman et al., 2010; Wiebe & Janssen, 2001).

Repeat abortion is associated with a history of physical and sexual abuse (Fisher et al., 2005) and it is estimated that half of U.S. women obtaining abortion have had at least one previous abortion (Jones, Finer, & Singh, 2010). Steinberg and Russo (2008) reported that "multiple abortions were found to be associated with much higher rates of PTSD and social anxiety; this relationship was largely explained by pre-pregnancy mental health disorders and their association with higher rates of violence" (p. 238). Fisher et al. (2005) have suggested "Presentation for repeat abortion may be an important indication to screen for a current or past history of relationship violence and sexual abuse" (p. 637).

Implications for Meeting Women's Needs and Rights

It has been determined that "reducing IPV by 50% could potentially reduce unintended pregnancy by 2%-18% and abortion by 4.5%-40%, according to Population Attributable risk estimates," (Pallitto et al., 2013, p. 3). All methods of preventing IPV will of course be beneficial, but two that are especially important in the abortion context are:

- **Screening**
Therefore, routine screening for current or past abuse of women seeking abortion may be an effective means of reducing violence against them (Glander et al., 1998; Saftlas et al., 2010; Silverman et al., 2010; Wiebe & Janssen, 2001).

- **Social support**

  Consistent with other research noting the positive value of social support, Coker, Smith et al., (2002) reported that "Among women experiencing IPV, and controlling for IPV frequency, higher social support scores were associated with a significantly reduced risk of poor perceived mental health" (p. 465). This suggests that along with screening, women may benefit from help in rallying social support.

Research Needs

- **Longitudinal studies**

  While research findings are consistent concerning the association between IPV and women's physical and mental health problems, most studies have been cross-sectional. Therefore, longitudinal research is needed to determine the degree of causality that appears to exist between IPV and health outcomes.

- **Cultural differences**

  Current research has not attended to political and cultural differences. It has been suggested that "individual countries need their own data, and that extrapolating one country's prevalence estimates to another is not necessarily appropriate for policy and programmatic decision-making" (Garcia-Moreno & Pallitto, 2013, p. 34).

- **Clarifying conflicting results**

  Research is needed to clarify the wide range of reported incidence of IPV during pregnancy, which may be explained by differences in study designs, definitions and study populations (Shah & Shah, 2010).

- **Identifying factors**

  In addition, new studies may identify specific intermediate factors that may explain the association between IPV and abortion (e.g. fear, unintended pregnancy, pressure or coercion from male partners, pressure from others, stigma, shame, or other pressures related to being an IPV victim).

- **Qualitative studies of women**
  While multiple methodological approaches are available, qualitative research may be especially useful in identifying the influence of these intermediate factors.

- **Qualitative studies of men**
  In addition, future studies may identify the characteristics of male partners that may contribute to induced abortion among victims of IPV (Hall et al., 2014).

- **Development of screening programs**
  Clearly, there is a need to develop and evaluate screening programs for victims of IPV (Wathen & MacMillan, 2003) in terms of success in identifying victims and in protecting them from further violence including coerced abortion.

- **Evaluation of treatment programs**
  Systematic evaluations of treatment programs for victims and/or perpetrators of IPV (Ellsberg & Heise, 2005; Hall et al., 2014; Stover, Meadows & Kaufman, 2009) are also needed as well as large-scale, long-term studies to evaluate interventions aimed at reducing unintended pregnancy among women exposed to IPV (Miller et al., 2011)

References

Bailey, B. A. & Daugherty, R. A. (2007). Intimate partner violence during pregnancy: Incidence and associated health behaviors in a rural population. *Maternal Child Health Journal, 11*, 495-503.

Brock, K. & Stenzel, A. (1999). When men murder women: An analysis of 1997 homicide data. Washington, DC: Violence Policy Center.

Campbell, J. C. (2002). Health consequences of intimate partner violence. *The Lancet, 359*(9314), 1331-1336.

Campbell, J. C., Baty, M. L., Ghandour, R. M., Stockman, J. K., Francisco, L. & Wagman, J. (2008). The intersection of intimate partner violence against women and HIV/AIDS: A review. *International Journal of Injury Control and Safety Promotion, 15*(4), 221-231.

Campbell, J. C., Garcia-Moreno, C. & Sharps, P. (2004). Abuse during pregnancy in industrialized and developing countries. *Violence against Women, 10*(7), 770-789.

Campbell, J. C., Oliver, C., & Bullock, L. (1993). Why battering during pregnancy? *AWHONN's Clinical Issues in Perinatal and Women's Health Nursing, 4*(3), 343-349.

Campbell, J. C. & Soeken, K. L. (1999). Forced sex and intimate partner violence: Effects on women's risk and women's health. *Violence against Women, 5*(9), 1017-1035.

Chandra, P. S., Satyanarayana, V. A., & Carey, M. P. (2009). Women reporting intimate partner violence in India: Associations with PTSD and depressive symptoms. *Archives of Women's Mental Health, 12*, 203-209.

Charles, P. & Perreira, K. M. (2007). Intimate partner violence during pregnancy and 1-year post-partum. *Journal of Family Violence, 22*(7), 609-619.

Coker, A. L. (2007). Does physical intimate partner violence affect sexual health? A systematic review. *Trauma, Violence and Abuse, 8*(2), 149-177.

Coker, A. L., Davis, K. E., Arias, I., Desai, S., Sanderson, M., Brandt, H. M., & Smith, P. H. (2002). Physical and mental health effects of intimate partner violence for men and women. *American Journal of Preventive Medicine, 23*(4), 260-268.

Coker, A. L., Smith, P. H., Bethea, L., King, M. R. & McKeown, R. E. (2000). Physical health consequences of physical and psychological intimate partner violence. *Archives of Family Medicine, 9*(5), 451-457.

Coker, A. L., Smith, P. H., Thompson, M. P., McKeown, R. E., Bethea, L., & Davis, K. E. (2002). Social support protects against the negative effects of partner violence on mental health. *Journal of women's health & gender-based medicine, 11*(5), 465-476.

Crawford, M., Gartner, R. & Dawson, M. (1997). *Woman killing: Intimate femicide in Ontario, 1991-1994: A report prepared for the Women we Honour Action Committee.* Toronto, Ontario: Women We Honour Action Committee.

Cripe, S. M., Sanchez, S. E., Perales, M. T., Lam, N., Garcia, P., & Williams, M. A. (2008). Association of intimate partner physical and sexual violence with unintended pregnancy among pregnant women in Peru. *International Journal of Gynaecology and Obstetrics, 100*(2),104–108.

Devries, K. M., Kishor, S., Johnson, H., Stockl, H., Bacchus. L. J., Garcia-Moreno, C. & Watts, C. (2010). Intimate partner violence during pregnancy: Analysis of prevalence data from 19 countries. *Reproductive Health Matters, 18*(36), 158-170.

Ellsberg, M. C. & Heise, L. (2005). *Researching violence against women: A practical guide for researchers and activists.* Washington DC: World Health Organization and Program for Appropriate Technology in Health.

Fanslow, J., Silva, M., Whitehead, A., Robinson, E. (2008). Pregnancy outcomes and intimate partner violence in New Zealand. *Australian and New Zealand Journal of Obstetrics and Gynaecology, 48*(4), 391-397.

Fisher, W. A., Singh, S. S., Shuper, P. A., Carey, M., Otchet, F., MacLean-Brine, D., Bello, D. D. & Gunter, J. (2005). Characteristics of women undergoing repeat induced abortion. *CMAJ, 172*(5), 637-641.

Garcia-Moreno, C. & Pallitto, C. (2013). Global and regional estimates of violence against women: prevalence and health effects of intimate partner violence and non-partner sexual violence. Geneva: Switzerland: World Health Organization.

Glander, S. S., Moore, M. L., Michielutte, R. & Parsons, L. H. (1998). The prevalence of domestic violence among women seeking abortion. *Obstetrics and Gynecology, 91*(6), 1002-1006.

Hall, M., Chappell, L. C., Parnell, B. L., Seed, P. T. & Bewley, S. (2014). Associations between intimate partner violence and termination of pregnancy: A systematic review and meta-analysis. *PLOS Medicine, 11*(1), doi: 10.1371/journal.pmed.1001581

Harrykissoon, S. D., Rickert, V. I., & Wiemann, C. M. (2002). Prevalence and patterns of intimate partner violence among adolescent mothers during the postpartum period. *Archives of Pediatrics & Adolescent Medicine, 156*(4), 325-330.

Jacoby, M., Gorenflo, D., Black, E., Wunderlich, C., & Eyler, A. E. (1999). Rapid repeat pregnancy and experiences of interpersonal violence among low-income adolescents. *American Journal of Preventive Medicine, 16*(4), 318–321.

Jones, R. K., Finer, L. B. & Singh, S. (2010). *Characteristics of U.S. abortion patient,s 2008.* New York: Guttmacher Institute.

Kaye, D. K., Mirembe, F. M., Bantebya, G., Johansson, A., Ekstrom, A. M. (2006). Domestic violence as risk factor for unwanted pregnancy and induced abortion in Mulago hospital, Kampala, Uganda. *Tropical Medicine and International Health, 11*(1), 90-101.

Leung, T. W., Leung, W. C., Chan, P. L. & Ho P. C. (2002). A comparison of the prevalence of domestic violence between patients seeking termination of pregnancy and other general gynecology patients. *International Journal of Gynecology and Obstetrics 77*(1), 7-54.

McMahon, S. & Armstrong, D. Y. (2012). Intimate partner violence during pregnancy: Best practices for social workers. *Health & Social Work, 37*(1), 9-17. doi: 10.1093/hsw/hls004

Mechanic, M. B., Weaver, T. L., & Resick, P. A. (2008). Mental health consequences of intimate partner abuse: A multidimensional assessment of four different forms of abuse. *Violence Against Women, 14,* 634-654.

Miller, E., Decker, M. R., McCauley, H. L., Tancredi, D. J., Levenson, R. R., Waldman, J., Schoenwald, P. & Silverman, J. G. (2011). A family planning clinic partner violence intervention to reduce risk associated with reproductive coercion. *Contraception, 83*(3), 274-280.

Miller, E. & Silverman, J. (2010). Reproductive coercion and partner violence: Implications for clinical assessment of unintended pregnancy. *Expert Review of Obstetrics and Gynecology, 5*(5), 511-515.

Pallitto, C. C., Garcia-Moreno, C., Jansen, H., Heise, L., Ellsberg, M. & Watts. C. (2013). Intimate partner violence, abortion, and unintended pregnancy:

Results from the WHO multi-country study on women's health and domestic violence. *International Journal of Gynecology and Obstetrics, 120,* 3-9.

Pool, M. S., Otupiri, E., Owusu-Dabo, E., de Jonge, A. & Agyemang, C. (2014). Physical violence during pregnancy and pregnancy outcomes in Ghana. *BMC Pregnancy and Childbirth, 14* (71). doi:10.1186/1471-2393-14-71.

Porcerelli, J. H., Cogan, R., West, P. P., Rose, E. A., Lambrecht, D., Wilson, K. E., . . . & Karana, D. (2003). Violent victimization of women and men: physical and psychiatric symptoms. *The Journal of the American Board of Family Practice, 16*(1), 32-39.

Saftlas, A. F., Wallis, A. B., Shochet, T., Harland, K. K., Dickey, P., & Peek-Asa, C. (2010). Prevalence of intimate partner violence among an abortion clinic population. *American Journal of Public Health, 100*(8), 1412-1415. doi: 10.2105/AJPH.2009.178947

Shah, P. S. & Shah, J. (2010). Maternal exposure to domestic violence and pregnancy and birth outcomes: A systematic review and meta-analyses. *Journal of Women's Health, 19*(11), 2017-2031.

Silverman, J. G., Decker, M. R., McCauley, H. L., Gupta, J., Miller, E., Raj, A. & Goldberg, A. B. (2010). Male perpetration of intimate partner violence and involvement in abortions and abortion-related conflict. *Research and Practice, 100*(8), 1415-1417.

Silverman, J. G., Raj, A., Mucci, L. A. & Hathaway, J. E. (2001). Dating violence against adolescent girls and associated substance use, unhealthy weight control, sexual risk behavior, pregnancy, and suicidality. *JAMA, 286*(5), 572–579.

Steinberg, J. & Russo, N. (2008). Abortion and anxiety: What's the relationship? *Social Science & Medicine, 67,* 238-252.

Stover, C. S., Meadows, A. L & Kaufman, J. (2009). Interventions for intimate partner violence: Review and implications for evidence-based practice. *Professional Psychology: Research and Practice, 40*(3), 223-233.

Taft, A. J. & Watson, L. F. (2007). Termination of pregnancy: associations with partner violence and other factors in a national cohort of young Australian women. *Australian and New Zealand Journal of Public Health, 31*(2), 135-142.

Tjaden, P. & Thoennes N. (1998). *Prevalence, incidence and consequences of violence against women: Findings from the National Violence Against Women Survey.* Washington, DC: Department of Justice, National Institute of Justice.

Tjaden, P. & Thoennes N. (2000). Full report of the prevalence, incidence and consequences of violence against women. Washington, DC: Department of Justice, National Institute of Justice and the Centers for Disease Control and Prevention. Retrieved from https://www.ncjrs.gov/txtfiles1/nij/183781.txt

Wathen, C. N., & MacMillan, H. L. (2003). Interventions for violence against women: scientific review. *JAMA, 289*(5), 589-600.

Watts, C. & Zimmerman, C. (2002). Violence against women: Global scope and magnitude. *The Lancet, 359,* 1232-1237.

Wiebe, E.R. & Janssen, P. (2001). Universal screening for domestic violence in abortion. *Women's Health Issues, 11*(5), 436-441.

Woo J., Fine, P., & Goetzl, L. (2005). Abortion disclosure and the association with domestic violence. *Obstetrics and Gynecology 105* (6), 1329-34.

Chapter 2

Coercion and/or Pressure

by Catherine Coyle

While women may be coerced to continue an unwanted pregnancy as well as to abort, the focus of this chapter is on the role of coerced abortion in violence against women and therefore on what is generally agreed about coerced abortion. That is that women who are coerced to abort experience a form of violence, as it denies their free will and puts them at risk of physical and/or psychological harm (Brown, Elkins & Larson, 1993). Forced abortion has been condemned as a "violation of our human rights" by the International Community of Women Living with HIV/AIDS (ICW, 2008) and by the United Nations Commission on the Status of Women (2013).

To the extent a woman's abortion decision is coerced, she cannot provide voluntary and informed consent for the procedure. When a patient proceeds with a procedure in the absence of informed consent, this constitutes battery and is a chargeable cause of action in medical malpractice cases.

"Reproductive control," a concept similar to "reproductive coercion," is defined by Moore, Frohwirth, & Miller (2010) as occurring when partners, parents, peers, or the medical establishment "demand or enforce their own reproductive intentions whether in direct conflict with or without interest in the woman's intentions, through the use of intimidation, threats, and/or actual violence" (p. 2). Forcing a woman to become pregnant or complete a pregnancy against her wishes or forcing her to abort a pregnancy she desires to continue are forms of reproductive control. While these other forms of reproductive control warrant serious attention and more research, this chapter, as noted previously, will only address the relationship between violence and coerced abortion. Coerced child bearing is a separate subject deserving of its own attention and research agenda.

In a retrospective study involving both American and Russian women who had experienced one or more abortions, 64% of the Americans and 37.2% of the Russians felt "pressured by others" to abort (Rue, Coleman, Rue & Reardon, 2004). Research findings suggest that coercion and pressure to abort are not uncommon (Broen, Moum, Bodtker & Ekeberg, 2005; Hathaway, Willis, Zimmer & Silverman, 2005; Rue et al., 2004; Williams, 2000). However, studies report differing rates of coercion or pressure. For example, Williams (2001) reported only 11%; Pope, Adler and Tschann (2001), 17%; Hathaway et al. (2005), 18% and Williams (2000), 24.1%; while others have reported as great as 32% (Sihvo et al., 2003), 35% (Campbell, Franco & Jurs, 1988) and 64% (Rue et al., 2004). Clearly, more research is needed to establish accurate prevalence.

Coercion or pressure to abort has been associated with a number of negative psychological outcomes, including guilt (Brown et al., 1993), dysphoria (Franco, Tamburrino, Campbell, Pentz & Jurs, 1989), despair, anger, sleep disturbance, loss of appetite, and grief (Williams, 2001). Furthermore, researchers have found that coercion or pressure to abort was the strongest predictor of emotional distress at both 6 months and 2 years post-abortion (Broen et al., 2005). Likewise, Pope et al. (2001) and Williams (2001) reported more negative responses to abortion among women who were coerced or pressured. "The effects of feeling coerced into having an abortion cannot be underestimated in connection with later emotional trauma" (Turrel, Armsworth & Gaa, 1990, p. 61). In fact, "perceived coercion" is listed as a risk factor for post-abortion difficulty in two textbooks of the National Abortion Federation (Baker, Beresford, Halvorson-Boyd & Garrity, 1999; Baker & Beresford, 2009).

Coercion via Government Policy

In some countries forced abortion is official governmental policy. China provides the most prominent example through its one-child policy, established in 1978. Parents who violated the one-child limit have been punished with a financial penalty of nearly $10,000. In 2012, "more than $3.3bn in similar fines were paid by families" (Hatton, 2014). In addition, children born illegally are not provided with the government documents needed for access to healthcare and education.

A more violent outcome of the one-child policy is the occurrence of both forced abortion and forced sterilization (Sills et al., 1998; Watts, 2005). "Reports of coercive and compulsory intrauterine device (IUD) insertions, abortions, and sterilizations have emanated from China over the last few decades" (Hampton, 2003, p. 322) and "Women who proceed with an unapproved pregnancy are known to be reluctant to use antenatal and obstetric services because they fear they will face pressure to have an abortion or fines for violating the one-child policy" (Hesketh, Lu & Xing, 2005, p. 1172).

Since the "Population and Family Planning Policy" of 1978, Chinese couples are required to obtain "birth permits" to have children. Women without the required permit, or who are pregnant for the second or third time "have been required, persuaded, and even forced by the authorities to abort fetuses no matter how much they want to give birth" (Nie, 2011, p. 463). Cases of women being forced to abort even in extremely advanced stages of pregnancy have been documented by an organization called Women's Rights without Frontiers ("Cases," n.d.) and reported in Congressional testimony (*Consequences of Coercion*, 2009).

Reggie Littlejohn stated "The one-child policy is an issue about which pro-life people and pro-choice people can agree. No one supports forced abortion, because it is not a choice" (*Consequences of Coercion*, 2009, p. 1). The Chinese government's one-child policy has been implemented "at the cost of threatening Chinese women emotionally, physically, socially, and economically" (Keng, 1996, p. 205). "Many Chinese nationals have fled to the United States since the late 1980's with the hope that they will be granted political asylum" (Strawn, 2009, p. 205) and some have written in support of the United States granting asylum to those who are fleeing persecution in China due to its coercive population control policy (Brown, 1995; Sills et al., 1998).

Former Secretary of State Hillary Clinton condemned forced abortion at the Fourth World Conference on Women in Beijing (Clinton, 1995). Felice Gaer, pro-choice director of the Jacob

Blaustein Institute for the Advancement of Human Rights, labeled coerced abortion as fitting "into the definition of torture" (Starr, 2009) and Krug, Dahlberg, Mercy, Zwi & Lozano (2002) have identified forced abortion as a form of "sexual violence."

In June of 2012, a photograph of a Chinese woman, Feng Jianmei, lying with her forcibly aborted fetus was posted on the internet, shocking viewers. "Media reports from China said that Feng was seriously traumatised by what had happened" (Li, 2012, p. 804).

The Chinese government announced a new policy in October of 2015 allowing two children per couple. Women's rights advocate Reggie Littlejohn (2015) in her writing has argued that this will not end forced abortion or gendercide in China.

Coercion or Pressure by Partners

If legal abortion has given women more choice, it has given men more choice as well. They now have a potent new weapon in the old business of manipulating and abandoning women. For if women can have abortions, then there is no compelling leverage for women to use in demanding that men take responsibility for the children they procreate. That men have long coerced women into unwanted abortion when it suits their purposes is well-known but rarely mentioned. Data reported by the Alan Guttmacher Institute indicate that some 30 percent of women have an abortion because someone else, not the woman, wants it (Callahan, 1993, p. 27-28).

Male partners are frequently cited as the source of coercion in research (Broen et al., 2005; Hathaway, et al., Moore, et al., 2010). Men may coerce women by threatening abandonment or even violence (Chamberlain & Levenson, 2012; Miller & Silverman, 2010).

When women are pressured to abort by partners, they are at greater risk for mental health problems (Academy of Medical Royal Colleges, 2011; Broen et al., 2005; Moore et al., 2010; Needle & Walker, 2008; Pope et al., 2001). There have been a number of reports concerning women who were assaulted or murdered by the impregnating man because they would not submit to abortion (for example, Blair, 2013; Clark, 2006; Dempsey, 2013; Jungen, 2013; Larrubia, 1998).

Speckhard and Mufel (2003) assert that pre-abortion counseling:

> needs to address the decision-making process to ensure that the abortion decision has not been arrived at under coercion or in despair. In the former instance, the coercing partner must be stopped or the woman protected as in any other cases of battery, as a forced abortion is essentially a type of battery. (p. 33-34)

Coercion or Pressure by Parents

In one U.S. study of parental involvement with adolescent pregnancy, "among the minors whose parents found out without being told by the minor, 18% said their parents were forcing them to have an abortion and 6% reported physical violence" (Henshaw & Kost, 1992, p. 196). Adolescent females may be especially vulnerable to coercion by parents, partners, or peers due to their dependency needs and developmental immaturity. "Pressure from parents, sexual partners, and peer group members were particularly influential with younger adolescents. Such factors totally dominated the decisions of adolescents who had failed to establish relative independence from parental objects or to achieve some degree of object constancy" (Barglow & Weinstein, 1973, p. 339). Similarly, Zakus & Wilday (1987) state that "Adolescents, who are still dependent in their social situations, are particularly vulnerable to this feeling that this choice is not their own. Their decision to have an abortion may reflect their need to comply with the wishes of someone else" (p. 86). Like adult women, adolescent females are more vulnerable to negative post-abortion sequelae when they feel pressured to abort (Bhatia & Bohra, 1990; Dagg, 1991).

Coercion or Pressure by Abusers, Traffickers, or Providers

Coerced abortion has been used by adult men to hide incest or other sexual relationships with minor females. For example, in Washington state, Luis Gonzales-Jose raped and impregnated a 12 year old girl and forced her to abort to conceal his crime (Hutton, 2013).

There have also been reports of women who are trafficked being forced to submit to induced abortion (Lederer & Wetzel (2014). In fact, it is not uncommon for trafficked women to be subjected to multiple abortions (Cwikel, Chudakov, Paikin, Agmon, & Belmaker, 2004). See Chapter 3 for a fuller discussion.

Some women, who sought abortion but then changed their minds, have been forced to abort by a provider who refused to stop the procedure. For example, the much publicized case against Dr. Kermit Gosnell included reports of such cases. The official grand jury report stated: "Gosnell began an abortion on a 29-week pregnant woman and then refused to take dilators out when the woman changed her mind" (Williams, 2011, p. 86). The patient sought treatment at a hospital and prematurely delivered a baby girl. Two other patients, a 15-year old girl and an adult woman who did not want to go through with the abortion procedure were physically restrained, forcibly drugged, and then subjected to abortion against their will (DiFilippo, 2011). It is unknown how often women are coerced or pressured by either abusers or providers.

Economic Coercion

"Many women feel coerced economically into having an abortion" (Callahan, 1993, p. 28). Abortion is not always coerced by another individual but also by circumstances, particularly economic circumstances. Women who believe they cannot support a child or yet another child may feel enormous pressure to abort. The policies of any given society may well contribute to economic coercion, particularly when prenatal care, child health services, and other forms of public aide are not deemed worthy of that society's resources.

Coercion vs. Pressure

Some authors consider it important to distinguish between "coercion" and "pressure." However, that distinction is not always obvious. For example, in a study of male perpetrators of IPV, abusive men were significantly more likely to be involved in pregnancies ending in abortion than non-abusive men (Silverman et al., 2010). The extent to which this increase is due to actual coercion or to women feeling pressured remains to be determined. Coercion may be thought of as an overt directive to abort, while pressure may be more subtle and related to another's urging or advice or to a woman's perception that abortion is her only choice given her circumstances. The distinction between coercion and pressure is not often clear and these constructs may be conceptualized more accurately as a continuum.

What is clear on both sides of the abortion debate is that both *coercion* (Allanson & Astbury, 1995; Franco, et al., 1989; Gibbons, 1984; Kero, Hogberg & Lalos, 2004; Moniq & Moron, 1982; Paul et al., 2009; Stotland, 2001, 2003; Turell, et al., 1990; Zakus & Wilday, 1987) and *pressure* (Academy of Medical Royal Colleges, 2011; Broen et al., 2005; Dagg, 1991; Kimport, Foster & Weitz, 2011; Major et al., 2009; Needle & Walker, 2008; Olson, 1980; Pope et. al, 2001; Stotland, 1997; Williams, 2001) are risk factors for women's psychological adjustment to abortion.

Implications for Meeting Women's Needs and Rights

- **Screening**

Women who are screened for coercion and pressure are more likely to make autonomous decisions, receive needed support, and experience better outcomes. Screening is also likely to help identify women being exploited by traffickers and minors being sexually abused by adult males. The National Abortion Federation's current textbook for abortion providers includes "coercion" in a pre-abortion screening tool (Baker & Beresford, 2009).

- **Protective interventions**

Once identified, these women can be offered protection from further violence in a variety of available programs in their vicinity.

Research Needs

- **Documentation**

Future studies need to document the extent and incidence of forced or coerced abortion globally.

- **Coercion vs. pressure**

An exploration of the concept of *pressure* that identifies specific factors or conditions (e.g., economic, cultural, relational, intrapersonal, societal pressures from war or environmental disaster) that women perceive as causing them pressure to abort would also be useful. Currently, little is known about the long-term effects of coercion and pressure related to abortion on women's mental health.

- **Screening tools**

Systematic research may be useful in the development, implementation, and evaluation of screening tools to protect women from coerced and pressured abortion, and to provide evidenced-based support after abortion. Specifically, research needs to focus on how women should be screened, including (a) timing of screening, (b) method of screening, (c) questions aimed at uncovering coercion, and (d) the context in which screening occurs.

- **Sex trafficking**

Given the association between coercion and sex trafficking, evaluations of legal interventions aimed at reducing sex trafficking and thereby reducing the number of sex-trafficked women who are coerced into abortion would be beneficial to women's health and welfare.

- **Evaluation of programs**

Evaluations of programs that train medical workers in general clinics and in abortion clinics to identify victims of sex trafficking may serve to protect women from further violence and victimization.

- **Therapy needs**

Finally, explorations of the therapy needs of women who have been pressured into abortion and evaluations of therapy protocols developed for them may prevent long-term mental health consequences for women.

Each of these research suggestions has the potential to end women's exposure to violence, to restore their physical and psychological health, and to prevent their further exposure to violence.

References

Academy of Medical Royal Colleges (2011). *Induced abortion and mental health –A systematic review of the mental health outcomes of induced abortion, including their prevalence and associated factors.* London: Academy of Medical Royal Colleges/National Collaborating Center for Mental Health.

Allanson, S. & Astbury, J. (1995). The abortion decision: Reasons and ambivalence. *Journal of Psychosomatic Obstetrics and Gynaecology, 16*(3), 123-136.

Baker, A. & Beresford, T. (2009). Informed consent, patient education and counseling. In M. Paul, T. S. Lichtenberg, L. Borgatta, D. A. Grimes, P. G. Stubblefield, & M. D. Creinin, (Eds.) *Management of unintended and abnormal pregnancy.* Chichester, UK: Wiley-Blackwell.

Baker, A., Beresford, T., Halvorson-Boyd, G. & Garrity, J. M. (1999). Chapter 3, Informed consent, counseling, and patient preparation. In M. Paul, T. S. Lichtenberg, L. Borgatta, D. A. Grimes & P. G. Stubblefield (Eds.) *A clinician's guide to medical and surgical abortion.* Philadelphia, PA: Churchill Livingstone.

Barglow, P. & Weinstein, S. (1973). Therapeutic abortion during adolescence: Psychiatric observations. *Journal of Youth and Adolescence, 2*(4), 331-342.

Bhatia, M. S. & Bohra, N. (1990). The other side of abortion. *The Nursing Journal of India, 81*(2), 66-70.

Blair, L. (2013). Man charged with murder after allegedly tricking girlfriend into taking abortion pill. *The Christian Post.* Retrieved from http://www.christianpost.com/news/man-charged-with-murder-after-allegedly-tricking-girlfriend-into-taking-abortion-pill-96123/

Broen, A. N., Moum, T., Bodtker, A. S. & Ekeberg, O. (2005). Reasons for induced abortion and their relation to women's emotional distress: A prospective, two-year follow-up study. *General Hospital Psychiatry, 27*(1), 36-43.

Brown, T. A. (1995). Forced abortions and involuntary sterilization in China: Are the victims of population coercive control measures eligible for asylum in the United States? *San Diego Law Review, 32,* 745.

Brown, D., Elkins, T. E. & Larson, D. B. (1993). Prolonged grieving after abortion: A descriptive study. *The Journal of Clinical Ethics, 4*(2), 118.

Callahan, D. (1993). 1. An ethical challenge to prochoice advocates. *Bioethics: Basic Writings on the Key Ethical Questions that Surround the Major, Modern Biological Possibilities and Problems*, 21-35.

Campbell, N., Franco, K, & Jurs, S. (1988). Abortion in adolescence. *Adolescence, 23*(92), 813-823.

Cases (n.d.). Retrieved from http://www.womensrightswithoutfrontiers.org/index.php?nav=cases

Chamberlain, L. & Levenson, R. (2012). Addressing intimate partner violence, reproductive coercion and sexual coercion: A guide for obstetric, gynecologic and reproductive health care settings. *The American College of Obstetricians and Gynecologists.* Retrieved from http://www.futureswithoutviolence.org/userfiles/file/HealthCare/reproguidelines_low_res_FINAL.pdf

Clark, V. (2006). Mothers-to-be's killer gets life terms. *The Inquirer.* Retrieved from http://articles.philly.com/2006-10-18/news/25418065_1_life-terms-search-la-toyia- Figueroa

Clinton, H. (1995). Remarks for the United Nations fourth world conference on women. Retrieved from http://www.un.org/esa/gopher-data/conf/fwcw/conf/gov/ 950905175653.txt

Consequences of Coercion: China's One Child Policy and Violence against Women and Girls: Hearing before the Tom Lantos Congressional Human Rights Caucus, 111th Congress (November 10, 2009).

Cwikel, J., Chudakov, B., Paikin, M., Agmon, K. & Belmaker, R. H. (2004). Trafficked female sex workers awaiting deportation: Comparison with brothel workers. *Archives of Women's Mental Health, 7,* 243–9.

Dagg, P. K. (1991). The psychological sequelae of therapeutic abortion – denied and completed. *American Journal of Psychiatry, 148*(5), 578-585.

Dempsey, C. (2013). Warrant: Man had girlfriend killed because she was pregnant. *The Courant.* Retrieved from http://articles.courant.com/2013-06-07/community/hc-hartford-bryan-murder-arraignment-0608-2-20130607_1_girlfriend-killed-magnolia-street-police

DiFilippo, D. (2011). Victims say abortion doctor scarred them for life. *Philly.com.* Retrieved from http://articles.philly.com/2011-01-21/news/27041098_1_abortion-doctor-abortion-clinic-one-treatment-room

Franco, K., Tamburrino, M., Campbell, N., Pentz, J., Jurs, S. (1989). Psychological profile of dysphoric women postabortion. *Journal of the American Medical Women's Association, 44*(4), 113-115.

Gibbons, M. (1984). Psychiatric sequelae of induced abortion. *Journal of the Royal College of General Practitioners, 34*(260), 146-150.

Hampton, A. (2003). Population control in China: Sacrificing human rights for the greater good. *Tulsa Journal of Comparative and International Law , 11,* 321-361. Retrieved from http://digitalcommons.law.utulsa.edu/tjcil/vol11/iss1/9/

Hathaway, J., Willis, G., Zimmer, B., & Silverman J. (2005). Impact of partner abuse on women's reproductive lives. *Journal of the American Medical Women's Association 60*(1), 42-45.

Hatton, C. (2014). Children denied an identity under China's one-child policy. *BBC News.* January 17, Beijing.

Henshaw, S. & Kost, K. (1992). Parental involvement in minors' abortion decisions. *Family Planning Perspectives, 25*(4), 196-204.

Hesketh, T., Lu, L., & Xing, Z. W. (2005). The effect of China's one-child family policy after 25 years. *New England Journal of Medicine, 353*(11), 1171-1176.

Hutton, C. (2013). Everson rapist gets prison for impregnating girl, making her get abortion. Retrieved from http://www.bellinghamherald.com/2013/05/16/3012333/ everson-rapist-gets-prison-for.html

ICW / International Community of Women Living with HIV/AIDS. (2008). *Addressing the needs of HIV-positive women for safe abortion care.* London, ICW.

Jungen, A. (2013). Man charged with threatening woman who refused abortion. *The LaCrosse Tribune.* Retrieved from http://lacrossetribune.com/news/local/man-charged-with-threatening-woman-who-refused-abortion/article_69045fr32-8551-11e2-9aad-0019bb2963f4.html

Keng, E. (1996). Population control through the One-Child Policy in China; Its effects on women. *Women's Rights Law Reporter, 18*(2), 205.

Kero, A., Hogberg, U. & Lalos, A. (2004). Well-being and mental growth—long-term effects of legal abortion. *Social Science and Medicine, 58*(12), 2559-2569.

Kimport, K., Foster, K, & Weitz, T. (2011). Social sources of women's emotional difficulty after abortion: Lessons from women's abortion narratives. *Perspectives on Sexual and Reproductive Health, 43*(2), 103-109.

Krug, E. G., Dahlberg, L. L., Mercy, J. A., Zwi, A. B., & Lozano, R. (Eds.). (2002). *World report on violence and health.* Geneva, Switzerland: World Health Organization.

Larrubia, E. (1998). Jury convicts man in ex-girlfriend's slaying. *The Los Angeles Times.* Retrieved from http://articles.latimes.com/1998/may/21/local/me-52107

Lederer, L. & Wetzel, C. (2014). The health consequences of sex trafficking and their implications for identifying victims in health care facilities. *Annals of Health Law, 23*(1), 61-91.

Li, Y. (2012). Reflections on the causes of forced abortion in China. *The Lancet, 380,* 804.

Littlejohn, R. (2015). China's new two child policy will not end forced abortion or gendercide. Retrieved from: http://www. womensrightswithoutfrontiers. org/blog/?p=2082

Major, B., Applebaum, M., Beckman, L. Dutton, M., Russo, N. & West, C. (2009). Abortion and mental health: Evaluating the evidence. *American Psychologist, 64*(9), 863-890.

Miller, E. & Silverman, J. (2010). Reproductive coercion and partner violence: Implications for clinical assessment of unintended pregnancy. *Expert Review of Obstetrics and Gynecology, 5*(5), 511-515.

Moniq, C. & Moron, P. (1982). Psychological aspects of induced abortion. *Psychologie Medicale, 14*(8), 1181-1185.

Moore, A.M., Frohwirth, L. & Miller E. (2010). Male reproductive control of women who have experienced intimate partner violence in the United States. *Social Science and Medicine, 70* (11), 1737-44. doi: 10.1016/j.socscimed.2010.02.009.

Needle, R. & Walker, L. (2008). *Abortion counseling: A clinician's guide to psychology, legislation, politics, and competency.* New York: Springer Publishing Company.

Nie, J. B. (2011). Non-medical sex-selective abortion in China: Ethical and public policy issues in the context of 40 million missing females. *British Medical Bulletin, 98*(1), 7-20.

Olson, J. (1980). Social and psychological correlates of pregnancy resolution among adolescent women: A review. *American Journal of Orthopsychiatry, 50,* 432-445.

Paul, M., Lichtenberg, E., Borgatta, L., Grimes, D., Stubblefield, P. & Creinen, M. (2009*). Management of unintended and abnormal pregnancy: Comprehensive abortion care.* West Sussex, UK: Blackwell Publishing.

Pope, L. M., Adler, N. E., & Tschann, J. M. (2001). Postabortion psychological adjustment: are minors at increased risk? *Journal of Adolescent Health, 29*(1), 2-11.

Rue, V. M., Coleman, P. K., Rue, J. J. & Reardon, D. C. (2004). Induced abortion and traumatic stress: A preliminary comparison of American and Russian women. *Medical Science Monitor, 10*(10): SR5-16.

Sihvo, S., Bajos, N., Ducot, B, Kaminski, M., & the Cocon Group. (2003). Women's life cycle and abortion decision in unintended pregnancies. *Journal of Epidemiological Community Health, 57,* 601-605.

Sills, E. S., Strider, W., Hyde, H. J., Anker, D., Rees, G. J., & Davis, O. K. (1998). Gynaecology, forced sterilisation, and asylum in the USA. *The Lancet, 351*(9117), 1729-1730.

Silverman, J. G., Decker, M. R., McCauley, H. L., Gupta, J., Miller, E., Raj, A. & Goldberg, A. B. (2010). Male perpetration of intimate partner violence and involvement in abortions and abortion-related conflict. *Research and Practice, 100*(8), 1415-1417.

Speckhard, A. & Mufel, N. (2003). Universal responses to abortion? Attachment, trauma and grief responses in women following abortion. *Journal of Prenatal & Perinatal Psychology & Health, 18*(1), 3-37.

Starr, P. (2009). Prochoice human rights activists call Chinese abortion practices torture. Retrieved from http://www.cnsnews.com/news/article/pro-choice-human-rights-activists-call-chinese-abortion-practices-torture

Stotland, N. L. (1997) Psychosocial aspects of induced abortion. *Clinical Obstetrics and Gynecology, 40*(3), 673-686.

Stotland, N. L. (2001). Psychosocial aspects of induced abortion. *Archives of Women's Mental Health, 4,* 27-31.

Stotland, N. L. (2003). Abortion and psychiatric practice. *Journal of Psychiatric Practice, 9*(2), 139-149.

Strawn, K. M. (2009). Standing in her shoes: Recognizing the persecution suffered by spouses of persons who undergo forced abortion or sterilization under China's coercive population control policy. *Wisconsin Journal of Law, Gender and Society, 24,* 205.

Turell, S. C., Armsworth, M. W. & Gaa, J. P. (1990). Emotional response to abortion: A critical review of the literature. *Women and Therapy, 9*(4), 49-68.

United Nations Commission on the Status of Women. (2013). Elimination and prevention of all forms of violence against women and girls: 2013 Commission on the Status of Women, Agreed Conclusions. New York: UN Women. Retrieved from: http://www.unwomen.org/~/media/headquarters/attachments/sections/csw/57/csw57-agreedconclusions-a4-en.pdf?v=1&d=20140917T100700

Watts, J. (2005). Chinese officials accused of forcing abortions in Shandong. *The Lancet, 366*(9493), 1253.

Williams, G. (2000). Grief after elective abortion: Exploring nursing interventions for another kind of perinatal loss. *Association of Women's Health, Obstetric and Neonatal Nurses Lifelines, 4*(2), 37-40.

Williams, G. (2001). Short –term grief after an elective abortion. *Journal of Obstetric, Gynecologic and Neonatal Nursing, 30*(2), 174-183.

Williams, S. (2011). *Report of the Grand Jury.* First Judicial District of Pennsylvania, Criminal Trial Division. Retrieved from: http://www. phila.gov/districtattorney/pdfs/grandjury_womensmedical.pdf

Zakus, G. & Wilday, S. (1987). Adolescent abortion option. *Social Work in Health Care, 12*(4), 77-91.

Chapter 3

Sex Trafficking

by Catherine Coyle

Terminology from the past era of the slave trade has been widely applied to contemporary human trafficking which has been referred to as "modern day slavery" or "21st century slavery" (Picarelli, 2007; Schaeffer-Gabriel, 2010). "Disparate political, economic, and legal conditions provide the traffickers with both the ready supply of workers and demanding customers" (Diep, 2006, p. 310). It is estimated that 80% of those trafficked are female and 70% of those women are trafficked for the purpose of sexual exploitation (U.S. Department of State, 2005). The widespread international trafficking of humans for sex has resulted in the illegal sex trade becoming the third fastest growing economic activity in the world (Nelson, 2002). Furthermore, the pervasive preference for sons and consequent abortion of millions of female fetuses has directly contributed to the trafficking of women in countries such as China (Tiefenbrun & Edwards, 2008) and Vietnam (Giang, 2002) where the sex ratio balance has been disrupted leaving more males unable to find female mates.

The sex trafficking industry poses serious health risks. Researchers have identified three broad categories of health consequences as applying globally to women and girls who are trafficked:

1. direct health consequences of commercial sex such as sexually transmitted diseases and sexual trauma that may result in infertility or malignancies;

2. threats to mental health such as depression, substance abuse, and post-traumatic stress disorder (PTSD);

3. difficulties relating to health care access (Beyrer & Stachowiak, 2003, p. 105-106).

Still another health hazard of trafficking is coerced abortion, which has been reported and confirmed among women who are trafficked. According to Lederer and Wetzel (2014), "The prevalence of forced abortions is an especially disturbing trend in sex trafficking" (p. 73). Women and girls who are forced into sex trafficking, as well as those who choose to work as prostitutes, may experience forced abortion (Abdulraheem & Oladipo, 2010; Acharya, 2008; Diep, 2006; Hoyle, Bosworth, & Dempsey, 2011; Zimmerman, Hossain & Watts, 2011). As noted by Lederer and Wetzel:

> [T]he phenomenon of forced abortion as it occurs in sex trafficking transcends the political boundaries of the abortion debate, violating both the pro-life belief that abortion takes innocent life and the pro-choice ideal of women's freedom to make their own reproductive choices. (Lederer & Wetzel, 2014, p. 74)

In spite of the evidence of coerced abortion and the logical assumption of agreement between those on both sides of the abortion debate, little progress has been made in reducing the incidence of both sex trafficking and coerced abortion among women who are trafficked. The American Psychological Association (APA), in 2011, established a task force on sex trafficking. Its report acknowledged a need for research on the long-term effects of "forced abortions on survivors' sexual and reproductive health," (American Psychological Association, 2013, p. 19). However, this is a monumental task, given the obstacles in obtaining accurate data concerning victims of trafficking (U.S. Department of Justice, 2007).

Women trafficked for sex are often subjected to multiple abortions, risking health problems (Cwikel, Chudakov, Paikin, Agmon, & Belmaker, 2004; Zimmerman et al., 2003) and infertility (U.S. Justice Department, n.d.). Of 67 trafficked women who responded to a question concerning abortion experience, 29.9% reported having multiple abortions (Lederer & Wetzel, 2014).

Furthermore, "While only thirty-four respondents answered the question whether their abortions were of their own volition, more than half (eighteen) of that group indicated that one or more of their abortions was at least partly forced upon them" (p. 73). Some women are forced to abort during late pregnancy and to resume sex work only days later (Getu, 2006).

According to a sex trafficking expert in Wichita, Kansas in the United States, pregnant women are in demand due to consumer fetishes. As a result, they carry their pregnancies nearly to term and are then forced to abort (personal communication, March 2014). Another expert in human trafficking confirmed this claim that forced abortion is directly related to pregnancy fetishes (personal communication, July 2014).

As noted, trafficking of humans for sex has numerous serious public health implications (Huda, 2006; Lederer & Wetzel, 2014) including "sexually transmitted diseases, pelvic inflammatory disease, hepatitis and tuberculosis. Unwanted pregnancy, forced abortion, and abortion-related complications are other causes of health problems among trafficked persons," (Getu, 2006, p. 149). Despite the increased risk for life-threatening health consequences, "Traffickers typically do not allow victims to seek health care—unless it is for an abortion, in which case, the cost of the abortion is added to any outstanding debt the woman owes," (Riegler, 2007, p. 243). Nonetheless,

> Despite their abusive situations . . . 87.8% had contact with a healthcare provider while they were being trafficked. By far the most frequently reported treatment site was a hospital/emergency room, with 63.3% being treated at such a facility. Survivors also had significant contact with clinical treatment facilities, most commonly Planned Parenthood clinics, which more than a quarter of survivors (29.6%) visited. More than half (57.1%) of respondents had received treatment at some type of clinic (urgent care, women's health, neighborhood, or

Planned Parenthood). (Lederer & Wetzel, 2014, p. 77)

Sadly, of those women who did report having seen a health care provider while being trafficked, only about one-half of them believed the doctor recognized they were sex workers. Even then, doctors did not understand that the women were being trafficked (Lederer & Wetzel, 2014). Similarly, previous research found that doctors were not adequately prepared to identify victims of trafficking (Chisolm-Straker & Richardson, 2007; Wong, Hong, Leung, Yin & Stewart, 2011).

Alissa Perrucci (2012) is the author of *Decision, Assessment and Counseling in Abortion Care: Philosophy and Practice* which is listed as a respected resource in the National Abortion Federation Clinical Policy Guidelines (2015). In her book, Perrucci observes that women who are victims of trafficking present themselves at clinics "under complex coercive conditions" (p. 160).

According to Stephen Wagner, former director of the Human Trafficking Program at the Department of Health and Human Services:

> The mortality rate for someone in commercial sexual exploitation is 40 times higher than for a non-exploited person of the same age. Helping a victim return to exploitation more quickly by terminating a pregnancy increases the odds of death. (Wagner, 2011)

Therefore, coerced abortion among sex-trafficked women poses significant health risks and may threaten their lives.

Coerced abortion among victims of trafficking may be particularly traumatic given other concurrent risk factors affecting those who are trafficked. For example, the very nature of trafficking involves forced and repetitive sexual exploitation. The lack of consent makes this exploitation the equivalent of repeated rape. It is well known that rape and sexual trauma pose a significant risk for Post-Traumatic Stress Disorder (Brewin, Andrews & Valentine,

2000; Kessler, Sonnega, Bromet, Hughes & Nelson, 1995; Resnick, Kilpatrick, Dansky, Saunders & Best, 1993). Furthermore, trafficked women are often subjected to other forms of abuse, including both physical and psychological violence (Oram, Stockl, Busza, Howard & Zimmerman, 2012). These other forms of abuse may add to the potential for trauma and mental illness among trafficking victims.

> Injuries and sexual violence during trafficking were associated with higher levels of PTSD, depression, and anxiety. Sexual violence was associated with higher levels of PTSD. More time in trafficking was associated with higher levels of depression and anxiety. More time since trafficking was associated with lower levels of depression and anxiety but not of PTSD. (Hossain, Zimmerman, Abas, Light & Watts, 2010).

Still other factors that increase the risk for poor mental health among trafficked females after abortion include:

1. the fact that abortions occur due to pressure or coercion;

2. age of the trafficking victim;

3. the occurrence of abortion during the second or third trimester.

Evidence that coercion increases risk for post-abortion psychological problems is readily available (Broen, Moum, Bodtker & Ekeberg, 2005; Brown, Elkins & Larson, 1993; Rue, Coleman, Rue & Reardon, 2004; Williams, 2001). Age has also been found to predict psychological difficulty after abortion with adolescents being at greater risk than adults (Coleman, 2006; Cougle, Reardon & Coleman, 2005; Franz & Reardon, 1992; Gissler, Berg, Bouvier-Colle & Buekens, 2005; Hope, Wilder & Watt, 2003).

Finally, abortion performed during the second or third trimester increases the risk for poor psychological outcome (Brewer, 1978; Coleman, Coyle & Rue, 2010; Söderberg, Janzon & Sjöberg,

1998). The respected text book, *Management of Unintended and Abnormal Pregnancy: Comprehensive Abortion Care,* edited by Paul et al. (2009) acknowledges the following as risk factors for adverse outcome after abortion: perceived coercion, advanced stage of pregnancy, past or present sexual, physical, or emotional abuse, and preexisting experience of trauma. Therefore, one would expect abortion providers who have utilized this text to be aware of the multiple traumas and increased risks faced by trafficked women who undergo induced abortion.

Implications for Women's Needs and Rights

Since health care workers are likely to be the only professionals that have direct contact with women being trafficked, those professionals are in a unique position to identify and assist victims (Dovydaitis, 2010). This includes professionals who are employed in abortion clinics, women's clinics, urgent care clinics, and emergency rooms.

In the United States, a valuable resource for medical and other professionals is the Rescue and Restore Victims of Human Trafficking campaign which is "primarily focused on outreach to those individuals who most likely encounter victims on a daily basis, but may not recognize them as victims of human trafficking" (U.S. Dept. of Health and Human Services, 2012). Another critical component of the campaign is the National Human Trafficking Resource Center or NHTRC (1-888-3737) which provides information by which victims can contact local organizations to help them. This is an example of the kind of programs needed world-wide.

Research Needs

Those on all sides of the abortion debate can agree that there is an immediate and unmet need to identify and support victims of trafficking and to engage in research that informs the means by which to successfully do so. Examples of needed studies include the following:

- Evaluations of legal interventions aimed at reducing sex trafficking and thereby reducing the number of sex-trafficked women who are coerced into abortion (e.g. Diep, 2006 notes that Sweden's criminalization of paying for sex services has dramatically reduced the number of women trafficked into Sweden).

- Evaluations of programs that train medical workers in general clinics and in abortion clinics to identify victims of sex trafficking.

- Explorations of the therapy needs of trafficked women who have been pressured or coerced into abortion and evaluations of therapy protocols developed for them.

- Further examination of the long-term effects of coercion and pressure related to abortion on trafficked women's mental health.

References

Abdulraheem, S. & Oladipo, A. R. (2010). Trafficking in women and children: A hidden healthand social problem in Nigeria. *International Journal of Sociology and Anthropology, 2*(3), 034-039.

Acharya, A. K. (2008). Sexual violence and proximate risks: A study on trafficked women in Mexico City. *Gender, Technology and Development, 12*(1), 77-99.

American Psychological Association, (2013). *Report of the task force on trafficking of women and girls.* Washington, DC. Retrieved from http://www.apa.org/pi/women/programs/trafficking/executive-summary.pdf

Beyrer, C. & Stachowiak, J. (2003). Health consequences of trafficking of women and girls in Southeast Asia. *Brown Journal of World Affairs, X*(1), 105-117.

Brewer, C. (1978). Induced abortion after feeling fetal movements: Its causes and emotional consequences. *Journal of Biosocial Science, 10*, 203-208.

Brewin, C. R., Andrews, B., & Valentine, J. D. (2000). Meta-analysis of risk factors for posttraumatic stress disorder in trauma-exposed adults. *Journal of Consulting and Clinical Psychology, 68*(5), 748-766.

Broen, A. N., Moum, T., Bodtker, A. S. & Ekeberg, O. (2005). Reasons for induced abortion and their relation to women's emotional distress: A prospective, two-year follow-up study. *General Hospital Psychiatry, 27*(1), 36-43.

Brown, D., Elkins, T. E. & Larson, D. B. (1993). Prolonged grieving after abortion: A descriptive study. *The Journal of Clinical Ethics, 4*(2), 118.

Chisolm-Straker, M., & Richardson, L. (2007). Assessment of Emergency Department (ED) Provider Knowledge about Human Trafficking Victims in the ED. *Academic Emergency Medicine, 14*(5S), S134-S134.

Coleman, P. K. (2006). Resolution of unwanted pregnancy during adolescence through abortion versus childbirth: Individual and family predictors and psychological consequences. *The Journal of Youth and Adolescence, 35*, 903-911.

Coleman, P. K., Coyle, C. T. & Rue, V. M. (2010). Late-term elective abortion and susceptibility to posttraumatic stress symptoms. *Journal of Pregnancy.* doi: 10.1155/2010/130519.

Cougle, J. R., Reardon, D. C. & Coleman, P. K. (2005). Generalized anxiety following unwanted pregnancies resolved through childbirth and abortion: A cohort study of the 1995 National Survey of Family Growth. *Journal of Anxiety Disorders, 19*(1), 137-142.

Cwikel, J., Chudakov, B., Paikin, M., Agmon, K. & Belmaker, R. H. (2004). Trafficked female sex workers awaiting deportation: Comparison with brothel workers. *Archives of Women's Mental Health, 7*, 243-9.

Diep, H. (2006). We pay—The economic manipulation of international and domestic laws to sustain sex trafficking. *Loyola University Chicago International Law Review, 2*(2), 309-331.

Dovydaitis, T. (2010). Human trafficking: The role of the health care provider. *Journal of Midwifery and Women's Health, 55*(5), 462-467.

Franz, W. & Reardon, D. (1992). Differential impact of abortion on adolescents and adults. *Adolescence, 27*(105), 161-172.

Getu, M. (2006). Human trafficking and development: The role of microfinance. *Transformation, 23*(3), 142-156.

Giang, T. T. (2002 September 27). Vietnamese women fall prey to traffickers. *Asia Times*. Retrieved from http://tinyurl.com/47k3jbx.

Gissler, M., Berg, C., Bouvier-Colle, M. & Buekens, P. (2005). Injury deaths, suicides, and homicides associated with pregnancy, Finland 1997-2000. *European Journal of Mental Health, 5,* 469-453.

Hope, T. L., Wilder, T. I. & Watt, T. T. (2003). The relationships among adolescent pregnancy, pregnancy resolution and juvenile delinquency. *The Sociological Quarterly, 44* (4), 461-472.

Hossain, M., Zimmerman, C., Abas, M., Light, M., & Watts, C. (2010). The relationship of trauma to mental disorders among trafficked and sexually exploited girls and women. *American Journal of Public Health, 100*(12), 2442-2449.

Hoyle, C., Bosworth, M. & Dempsey, M. (2011). Labelling the victims of sex trafficking: Exploring the borderland between rhetoric and reality. *Social and Legal Studies, 20*(3), 313-329. doi: 10.1177/0964663911405394.

Huda, S. (2006). Sex trafficking in south Asia. *International Journal of Gynecology and Obstetrics, 94,* 374-381.

Kessler, R. C., Sonnega, A., Bromet, E., Hughes, M., & Nelson, C. B. (1995). Posttraumatic stress disorder in the National Comorbidity Survey. *Archives of General Psychiatry, 52,* 1048–1060.

Lederer, L. & Wetzel, C. (2014). The health consequences of sex trafficking and their implications for identifying victims in health care facilities. *Annals of Health Law, 23* (1), 61-91.

National Abortion Federation (2015). *Clinical Policy Guidelines.* Retrieved from: http://5aa1b2xfmfh2e2mk03kk8rsx.wpengine.netdna-cdn.com/wp-content/uploads/2015_NAF_CPGs.pdf

Nelson, K. E. (2002) Comment, *Sex Trafficking and Forced Prostitution: Comprehensive New Legal Approaches, Houston Journal of International Law, 4,* 551, 574.

Oram, S., Stöckl, H., Busza, J., Howard, L. M., & Zimmerman, C. (2012). Prevalence and risk of violence and the physical, mental, and sexual health problems associated with human trafficking: systematic review. *PLoS Medicine, 9*(5), e1001224. doi:10.1371/journal.pmed.1001224

Paul, M., Lichtenberg, E., Borgatta, L., Grimes, D., Stubblefield, P. & Creinen, M. (2009). *Management of unintended and abnormal pregnancy: Comprehensive abortion care.* West Sussex, UK: Blackwell Publishing.

Perrucci, A. C. (2012). *Decision, assessment and counseling in abortion care: Philosophy and Practice.* Lanham, MD: Rowman & Littlefield.

Picarelli, J. (2007). Historical approaches to the trade in human beings. In M. Lee (Ed.). *Human trafficking.* Collumpton: Willan, pp. 26-48.

Rue, V. M., Coleman, P. K., Rue, J. J. & Reardon, D. C. (2004). Induced abortion and traumatic stress: A preliminary comparison of American and Russian women. *Medical Science Monitor, 10*(10): SR5-16. PMID: 15448616.

Resnick, H. S., Kilpatrick, D. G., Dansky, B. S., Saunders, B. E., & Best, C. L. (1993). Prevalence of civilian trauma and posttraumatic stress disorder in a representative national sample of women. *Journal of Consulting and Clinical Psychology, 61,* 984–991.

Riegler, A. (2007). Missing the mark: Why the trafficking victims protection act fails to protect sex trafficking victims in the United States. *Harvard Journal of Law &Gender, 30,* 231.

Schaeffer- Gabriel, F. (2010). Sex trafficking as the "new slave trade". *Sexualities, 13*(2), 153-160.

Söderberg, H., Janzon, L., & Sjöberg, N-O. (1998). Emotional distress following induced abortion: A study of its incidence and determinants among abortees in Malmo, Sweden. *European Journal of Obstetrics & Gynecology and Reproductive Biology, 79,* 173-178.

Tiefenbrun, S. & Edwards, C. J. (2008). Gendercide and the cultural context of sex trafficking in China. *Fordham International Law Journal, 32*(3), 730-780.

U.S. Department of Health and Human Services. (2012). Rescue and restore victims of human trafficking, Retrieved from www.acf.hhs.gov/programs/orr/resource/about-rescue-restore

U.S. Department of Justice, Attorney General's Annual Report to Congress on U.S. Government Activities to Combat Trafficking in Persons: Fiscal Year 2006 1 (2007). Retrieved from www.usdoj.gov/ag/annualreports/tr2006/agreporthumantrafficing2006.pdf

U.S. Department of State. (2005)Trafficking in persons: Report 6. Retrieved from www.state.gov/documents/organization/47255.pdf

U.S. Justice Department. Resources (n.d.) Common health issues seen in victims of human trafficking. Retrieved from http://www.justice.gov/usao/ian/htrt/health_problems.pdf

Wagner, S. (2011). Kathleen Sebelius' gruesome moral calculus. *National Catholic Register.* Retrieved from http://www.ncregister.com/daily-news/kathleen-sebelius-gruesome-moral-calculus

Williams, G. (2001). Short –term grief after an elective abortion. *Journal of Obstetric, Gynecologic and Neonatal Nursing, 30*(2), 174-183.

Wong, J. C., Hong, J., Leung, P., Yin, P., & Stewart, D. E. (2011). Human trafficking: an evaluation of Canadian medical students' awareness and attitudes. *Education for Health, 24*(1), 501.

Zimmerman, C., Hossain, M. & Watts, C. (2011). Human trafficking and health: A conceptual model to inform policy, intervention and research. *Social Science & Medicine, 73*(2), 327-335.

Zimmerman, C., Yun, K., Shvab, I., Watts, C., Trappolin, L., Treppete, M. (2003). *The health risks and consequences of trafficking in women and adolescents: Findings from a European study.* London: London School of Hygiene and Tropical Medicine.

Chapter 4

War

by Rachel M. MacNair and Catherine Coyle

While peace psychology covers all forms of violence, the practice of war is at the foundation of what is studied, the main motivation for the very establishment of the field.

Infliction of Unchosen Abortion

In the medical literature "spontaneous abortion" is the technical term for what is more commonly called a miscarriage – a premature ending of the pregnancy that happened for reasons outside anyone's control. "Induced abortion," the topic of this book, means that the ending was deliberately arranged by medical means. When miscarriages happen because of women being subjected to horrific violence, this is one of a long list of outrageous effects of war on innocent civilian populations. It does not often make such lists, but as a matter of clear reproductive justice and a focus on women's needs in particular, it is a major area of concern for large groups of women.

War as an Instrument of Unchosen Abortion

In an article entitled "Abortion and War," Emanuel Charles McCarthy (2011) points out what is obvious upon paying attention to the point:

> As I read the triumphant headlines in the newspapers day after day—"U.S. Pounds Iraq from Air"—and saw the pictures of missiles streaking into Iraq, I could not help but hear the silent screams of all the little Iraqi children *in utero* who were having their lives ripped from them. The lucky ones were the ones who took a direct hit. The ones, who were aborted because of percussion, vibration or because of the terror, trauma, malnourishment and/or exhaustion visited upon their mothers by war, would probably have suffered less agonizing deaths at the wrong end of a suction machine in an abortion clinic. . . . Modern industrial war, once unleashed, produces an instant Auschwitz for the unborn—that's fact, not conjecture. Mass abortions are the necessary and one hundred per cent inevitable consequence of modern war. (McCarthy, 2011, p. 1-2)

The thesis of McCarthy's article is that those in the pro-life movement should oppose the war. This point about war's effects is still obvious from a pro-choice perspective, since the brutal and violent ending of wanted pregnancies is anti-choice.

To cite a specific case to show how this works within the dynamics of war, Jon Lee Anderson, a writer for *The New Yorker*, said in a March 24, 2003 interview with Charlie Rose on Rose's PBS show: "My driver, a sweet Iraqi man, was bitter today because one of his daughters suffered what he called an involuntary abortion during last night's bombing due to fright. She was 3 to 4 months pregnant." This was by way of illustrating how Iraqis who opposed Saddam Hussein might nevertheless turn against the United States if the destruction became too great.

Another experience is offered in a report from the organization Save the Children:

> My husband was killed during the fighting and I had to leave my village with my four children. I was five months pregnant and it took me two months to get to this shelter. Throughout my entire journey my children and I were bitterly cold and hungry. When I arrived I went into early labour in my seventh month. There was no hospital or medical staff nearby so the other women helped me. My baby was born so prematurely and there was no special care to help him survive. He lived just two hours [after birth]. (Save the Children, 2014, p. 6)

The actual prevalence of fetal loss by induced or spontaneous abortion or prematurity in war is not known, and probably varies by the war and how it is carried out. That it is widespread is therefore speculation from an empirical point of view, but those familiar with how wars are normally experienced are not likely to argue about whether or not it is a common problem.

From another aspect, the BBC News (2015) reported that the Revolutionary Armed Forces of Colombia, known by its Spanish-language acronym of FARC, is being investigated for approximately 150 forced abortions on its own soldiers, with one man being extradited from Spain for performing about a hundred of them. About a third of its fighting force was women, and being pregnant impeded their fighting ability.

War on the Environment

The smaller the size and the less developed an organism is, the more sensitive to environmental toxins it will be. Accordingly, human fetuses are extremely sensitive to nuclear radiation and to toxic chemicals. In milder form, this means they are born with birth defects, which will last all of their lives. In more severe form, the toxins will kill them.

Farmworkers are especially subjected to pesticides in close range. The original president of the U.S. union called the United Farmworkers, Cesar Chavez, commented:

> So we accept decades of environmental damage these poisons have brought upon the land. The growers, the chemical companies and the bureaucrats say these are acceptable levels of exposure.
>
> Acceptable to whom? . . .
>
> There is no acceptable level of exposure to any chemical that causes cancer. There can be no toleration of any toxin that causes miscarriages, still births, and deformed babies. (Chavez, 1989)

There is a possible aspect of racism involved here as well: ethnic minorities and indigenous peoples tend to be placed closer to where pesticides are used in farming and to toxins emitted from such activities as mining.

This is a matter of insensitivities of large corporations, rather than actual intent to harm. Their war on the environment is a side-effect of profit-making rather than a declared assault. War itself is of course another major source of environmental contamination – sometimes as a callous side-effect of other activities, and other times quite deliberately used as a weapon. In either case, the exposure to poisons from industry or war events may cause spontaneous abortions or birth defects.

Use of nuclear weapons, even if limited rather than world-ending, would be especially catastrophic in environmental effects. One nuclear strategist, Herman Kahn, in the early days discounted the impact this way:

> Probably of limited significance to us are the so-called embryonic deaths. These are conceptions which would have been successful if it had not been for radiation that damaged the germ cell and thus made the potential conception result in a failure.

There will probably be five million of these in the first generation, and one hundred million in future generations . . . On the whole, the human race is so fecund that a small reduction in fecundity should not be a serious matter even to individuals. It is almost completely misleading to include the "early deaths" or embryonic deaths in the same total with the major and minor defects, but this is sometimes done by scientists who have overemphasized the abstraction "genetic death" and thus lost sight of the difference in terms of human tragedy of a serious defect or an embryonic death. (Kahn, 1960, p. 50)

Women with wanted pregnancies that "would have been successful if it were not for radiation" may have a different opinion as to whether it is "a serious matter even to individuals."

Abortion Induced Because of Women Trapped in War

War as a Pressure for Abortion

There is very little empirical study of war as a pressure for women to abort pregnancies that would have been desired in the absence of war. There has been some documentation in news reports that indicate this has occurred; for example, *The Washington Post* (Pomfret, 1993) reported that Srecko Simic, chief of obstetrics at Kosevo hospital, did a study there and found that during the siege of Sarajevo there were three abortions for every pregnancy carried to term, with rates of prematurity, stillbirth, and death within seven days of birth also skyrocketing.

Mary Meehan (2012) wrote a magazine article with cases indicating how this dynamic works:

> In 2007, Iraq's Red Crescent Society reported that over one million Iraqis had been displaced by violence or the threat of it. *ABC News*, covering the Red Crescent report, said many pregnant women in that situation were having abortions "because they are unable to get medical care for themselves and their unborn." (Meehan, 2012)

She also points to a case reported in *The Washington Post*:

> [A] 33-year-old woman . . . said she struggled for weeks, trying to decide between her religion and her love for children on the one hand and her inability to support a newborn baby on the other. Finally she went ahead with the abortion.
>
> The Catholic mother of two said she spent the night crying and praying . . . "I would never do this in peacetime and God knows I wanted that child, but there is no food for him in my house," she said. "There is nothing. What could I do?" (Pomfret, 1993).

Another plausible method by which war might lead to an increase in abortion is that wars make common contraceptive methods of pregnancy prevention less available. The *Washington Post* story, for example, reported that in the siege of Sarajevo, condoms had become a black-market item as scarce as gasoline (Pomfret, 1993).

Environmental Destruction as Pressure for Abortion

Following the Chernobyl nuclear accident in 1986, there were reports that induced abortion increased in the most contaminated areas (Pershagen, 1988). In Greece, it was estimated that 23% of pregnancies were aborted due to fears of fetal harm from radiation (Trichopoulos et al., 1987). Denmark also saw an increase in the rate of induced abortion in the months following the accident: "anxiety among the pregnant women and their husbands caused more fetal deaths in Denmark than the accident" (Knudsen, 1991, p. 229).

Rape as a Weapon of War

Rape of thousands of women has been used as a weapon of war throughout history – a strategic decision to spread terror and humiliation (Moore, 2010). As Jina Moore summarizes:

> Rape has been a consequence of military defeat for millennia. But in the last 20 years — from Bosnia to Rwanda, from Colombia to the Democratic Republic of Congo — sexual violence against women, and sometimes even against men, has become a strategic military tactic designed to humiliate victims and shatter enemy societies. And increasingly, governments presiding over peaceful countries are using mass rape in deliberate and targeted campaigns to spread terror and humiliation among political dissenters, often during election seasons. The strategic use of rape has been recognized by international courts as an act of genocide and ethnic cleansing . . . silence and shame shroud the issue, and some governments that deny wartime rape occurs in their countries have banned international aid groups that treat their citizens who have been victimized. (Moore, 2010)

Massive rapes will likely lead to feticides and infanticides, both voluntary and pressured, among those impregnated. There will also be numerous suicides among such women. The whirlwind of war harms many people who are never counted in the battle casualties.

One study investigating the psychological consequences of rape in the wars following the break-up of Yugoslavia in the early 1990s contained quite a bit of information about women who were impregnated by the rapes (Loncar, Medved, Jovanovic, & Hotujac, 2006). Out of a very large population of refugees (n = 1,926), they focused on the 55 women who confirmed having been raped. This was a mixed-methods study in which they used both a qualitative method with interviews and a quantitative survey.

Unsurprisingly, they did find that there were many negative and intense aftereffects. Rape normally has such an impact. Additionally, in the case of rapes within war, the normal kinds of post-rape therapeutic interventions were rendered unavailable by the war itself.

Of the 55 women, 29 got pregnant; this rate of over half is well out of bounds of the portion of women who get pregnant by rape outside of war circumstances. The authors have no explanation for this, but one possibility is that those rape victims who get pregnant may be much more likely to admit to being raped. The pregnancy makes the rape harder to deny and makes the event much more firmly established as a completed trauma.

Of the 29 impregnated, 17 had an induced abortion, which means that 12 did not. In logistic regression, authors found that the strongest predictor of the outcome of deciding on an abortion was suicidal thoughts and impulses. This was a powerful predictor, with an odds ratio of 25.8.

Implications for Meeting Women's Needs and Rights

The most obvious implication for anyone in the field of peace psychology is that we should prevent all wars. Falling short of that, however, there are still things that can be done.

- **UN Resolution 1820**

  People active in the United Nations have succeeded in having the body address this issue with some firmness, as shown in the resolution from which we quote an excerpt (emphasis in the original):

> *Reaffirming* the important role of women in the prevention and resolution of conflicts and in peacebuilding, and *stressing* the importance of their equal participation and full involvement in all efforts for the maintenance and promotion of peace and security, and the need to increase their role in decision-making with regard to conflict prevention and   resolution,
>
> *Deeply concerned* also about the persistent obstacles and challenges to women's participation and full involvement in the prevention and resolution of conflicts as a result of violence, intimidation and discrimination, which erode women's capacity and legitimacy to participate in post-conflict public life, and acknowledging the negative impact this has on durable peace, security and reconciliation, including post-conflict   peacebuilding   .   .   .
>
> *Demands* that all parties to armed conflict immediately take appropriate measures to protect civilians, including women and girls, from all forms of sexual violence, which could include, inter alia, enforcing appropriate military disciplinary measures and upholding the principle of command responsibility, training troops on the categorical prohibition of all forms of sexual violence against

civilians, debunking myths that fuel sexual violence, vetting armed and security forces to take into account past actions of rape and other forms of sexual violence, and evacuation of women and children under imminent threat of sexual violence to safety . . . and *stresses* the importance of ending impunity for such acts as part of a comprehensive approach to seeking sustainable peace, justice, truth, and national reconciliation. (United Nations, 2008)

This does give governments, legal counsel, and grassroots activists a basis upon which to act. As with all high-sounding rhetoric, it does require much work on the ground to make it happen.

- **United Nations peacekeepers**
  United Nations peacekeepers in theory help prevent wars, or prevent further outbreaks after wars have mainly wound down. Accordingly, they get immunity from prosecution, to keep local governments from interfering with their work by bringing unfair charges. However, women and girls in war-torn areas are vulnerable. Sometimes, because of extreme poverty, they sell sexual favors. There is also outright rape. As a result, a campaign has been launched with the specific goal of removing legal immunity for sexual exploitation and assaults committed by U.N. Peacekeepers, called Code Blue (see http://www.codebluecampaign.com).

- **Direct support for women**
  All women who have been sexually exploited are traumatized and need psychological support ranging from tender loving care to professional counseling. Some of the women will have had abortions or go to the extreme of infanticide, and their reactions to this will vary according to cultural beliefs and individual predilections. Some of the women will give birth to the children and place them for adoption, and their psychological aftermath can vary depending on whether this was a well-facilitated

international adoption (there are an ample supply of eager adoptive parents) or whether government blocking of adoption is part of the war situation. Yet others will choose to give birth to and raise their own children. However, the background of hatred in which the child was conceived may require special attention for compassionate care of both mother and child.

- **Post-war reconciliation**

The need to ease tensions after a war, both for the people involved and to prevent another round of war, is always especially difficult. It is even more complicated if rape was used by one ethnic group against another. When people regard "rape-babies" or "scum-babies" as worthy targets of their prejudice, it adds fuel to the ethnic tensions commonly causing the problem in the first place. Emotions will be raw on this point, whatever options the women and their families choose. They will need to be taken into account in the post-war reconciliation efforts in which peace psychology excels.

Research Needs

- **Prevalence**

Studies establishing the prevalence of inflicted miscarriages and rises in the rates of induced abortion associated with war can help us understand this crucial aspect of the human condition, and can inform us as to what kind of therapeutic interventions may be necessary. Findings from such studies may also have an impact on public opinion by emphasizing yet again the real-world impact that war has on innocent civilian populations.

- **Practices**

As always, studies of techniques to mitigate the damage of war by helping people cope with its impact with minimal harm, to avoid fright and toxins and displacement, and to prevent rape, will help establish what practices work best. Of course, this will always be less than satisfactory since the major effort and primary focus of peace psychology is to prevent war itself.

- **Efficacy of post-war reconciliation**

The best practices to promote healing in post-war reconciliation, taking all this chapter's considerations into account, could be a very fruitful area of research.

- **Therapeutic needs**

Pregnant women and their entire families who have been traumatized by war and who, because of war, are receiving inadequate medical care, will have specific therapeutic needs related to miscarriages, induced abortions, stillbirths, birth defects, or very frightened newborns. Once such women and families arrive at a safe place, by being refugees or by the end of the war, help from psychologists may be paramount for many. Research that identifies their particular needs would be critical in meeting those needs and helping them to recover.

References

BBC News. (2015, December 12). Colombia: FARC rebels "abortions nurse" arrested in Spain. Retrieved from http://www.bbc.com/news/world-latin-america-35085941

Chavez, C. (1989). Address by Cesar Chavez. Tacoma, WA: Pacific Lutheran University. Retrieved from http://www.ufw.org/_page.php? menu=research&inc=history/10.html

Kahn, H. (1960). *On thermonuclear war.* Princton, NJ: Princeton University Press

Knudsen, L. B. (1991). Legally induced abortions in Denmark after Chernobyl. *Biomedicine & Pharmacotherapy, 45*(6), 229-231.

Loncar, M., Medved, V., Jovanovic, N. & Hotujac, L. (2006). Psychological consequences of rape on women in 1991-1995 war in Croatia and Bosnia and Herzegovina. *Croatian Medical Journal, 47*(1), 67-75.

McCarthy, E. C. (2011). *Abortion and war.* Retrieved from http://www.centerforchristiannonviolence.org/data/Media/Abortion_and_War.pdf

Meehan, M. (2012, January 16). In harm's way: Children, born and unborn, trapped in wartime. *America.* Retrieved from http://americamagazine.org/issue/5126/article/harms-way

Moore, J. (2010). Confronting rape as a war crime: Will a new U.N. campaign have any impact? *CQ Researcher, 4*(5). Retrieved from http://photo. pds.org:5012/cqresearcher/document.php?id=cqrglobal2010050000

Pershagen, G. (1988). Health effects of Chernobyl. *British Medical Journal, 297*(6662), 1488-1489.

Pomfet, J. (1993, August 12). Besieged Sarajevo, no place for a baby. *The Washington Post*, A-18.

Save the Children (2014). *A devastating toll: The impact of three years of war on the health of Syria's children*, page 6. Retrieved from http://www.savethechildren.org/atf/cf/%7B9def2ebe-10ae-432c-9bd0-f91d2eba74a%7D/SAVE_THE_CHILDREN_A_DEVASTATING_TOL L.PDF

Trichopoulos, D., Zavitsanos, X., Koutis, C., Drogari, P., Proukakis, C. & Petridou, E. (1987). The victims of Chernobyl in Greece: Induced abortions after the accident. *British Medical Journal (Clinical Research Edition), 295* (6606), 1100.

United Nations (2008). Resolution 1820. Retrieved from http://www.securitycouncilreport.org/atf/cf/%7B65BFCF9B-6D27-4E9C-8CD3-CF6E4FF96FF9%7D/CAC%20S%20RES%201820.\

Chapter 5

Gendercide: Sex-Selection Abortions

by Catherine Coyle

In 1793, the Marquis Nicolas de Condorcet questioned

> what might be [the effect] on humankind [of] the discovery of a means of producing a male or female child according to the will of the parents . . . Supposing that this is likely to become a common practice . . . would it [not] lead to [changes] in the social relations of human beings, whose consequences could be harmful to the peaceable development of that indefinite perfectibility with expectations of which we have flattered humankind? (Brian & Jaisson, 2007, p. 189).

The Marquis's question has been answered. It has been estimated that more females have been killed solely because they are female in the last fifty years than the total number of men killed in all the wars of the 20th century (DeReus, 2010). As a result, countries such as Pakistan, India, and Bangladesh are missing 11%, 9.4%, and 8.9% of their women respectively (Grech & Mamo, 2014, p. 8-9) and it has been estimated that as many as 163 million women are missing in Asia (Guilmoto, 2007).

Prevalence

Sex-selection abortions are common throughout the world and nearly always victimize unborn females. The term "gendercide," referring to the deliberate killing of members of a specific sex, was first used in 1985 (Warren, 1985). *Feticide* refers to the killing of a fetus or unborn human being and female feticide has become widespread in countries such as India and China where male offspring are preferred.

> Female foeticide is an extreme manifestation of violence against women. Female foetuses are selectively aborted after pre-natal sex determination, thus avoiding the birth of girls. As a result of selective abortion, between 35 and 40 million girls and women are missing from the Indian population. (Goel, 2014, p. 77)

In China, "sex selective abortion after ultrasonography undoubtedly accounts for a large proportion of the decline in female births" (Hesketh, Lu & Xing, 2005, p. 1173). With the advent of ultrasound technology in many countries, it has become routine to identify sex prior to birth. Sex-selection abortion then enables parents to eliminate their unborn children who happen to be an unwanted sex.

As a result of sex-selective abortion, many countries are experiencing a skewed sex-ratio. The issue of sex ratio imbalance was addressed at the Fourth World Conference on Women of the

UN Commission on the Status of Women in the Beijing Declaration (United Nations, 1995). Delegates included both "prenatal sex selection" and "female infanticide" in their official definition of "violence against women." Former U.S. President Jimmy Carter (2014), in his recent book concerning women's rights, observed that 160 million fetuses have been aborted because they were female. To date, little progress has been made in deterring the practice of gendercide or feticide through prenatal sex-selective abortion.

In an official report accepted by the European Parliament, Liisanantti & Beese (2012) noted the skewed sex ratios in many countries around the world including India, China, Vietnam, Albania, Azerbaijan, Georgia, Armenia, and among children of Asian parents in Great Britain, the United States, and Canada. A skewed sex ratio among migrant Asians in England, Italy, Norway, and the U.S. has also been reported by Guilmoto and Duthe (2013) who state that the

> existence of these preferences in the Asian diaspora populations, far from their countries of origin, shows that sex selection is linked more to the cultural attitudes brought by migrants to their host country than to the circumstances of the origin country (such as restrictive birth control policies like those enforced in China). (Guilmoto & Duthe, 2013, p. 3).

However, Mohapatra (2015) has argued against the claim that sex-selective abortion occurs among women in the United States, be they citizens or immigrants. Rather, Mohapatra observes that the

> data shows there is not a son preference within the Asian population of the United States. A recent comprehensive report by University of Chicago researchers entitled "Replacing Myth with Facts: Sex Selective Abortion Laws in the United States" found that foreign born Chinese, Korean, and Indian parents actually have *more* daughters than white Americans do. (Mohapatra, 2015, p. 271)

The contradictory claims concerning the occurrence of sex-selective abortion in the U.S. raise interesting questions about the availability of accurate data concerning women's reasons for their choice to abort and immigrants' motivations for coming to the United States. On the first point, women who elect to undergo an induced abortion may be hesitant to admit or disclose that they did so because of the sex of their fetuses. On the second point, however, some immigrants may choose to live in the U.S. because they perceive that country to place a higher value on females than their home countries do. However, they are not specifically asked questions that would reveal such a motivation.

Focusing on India and China, Liisanantti & Beese (2012) identified three main factors to explain the skewed sex ratios in those countries: (a) falling fertility;(b) wide availability of ultrasound, allowing parents to learn the sex of their fetuses: and (c) a deeply entrenched preference for sons. In India, when ultrasound reveals a female fetus:

> it is a societal norm that the family, particularly the mother-in-law and husband force the pregnant woman (to abort) and if she does not cooperate, she faces domestic violence and kicking on the abdomen. This is rampant in rich and poor, illiterate and educated. (personal communication, Vinita Shaw of the Disha Foundation, 2014).

Similarly, "Confucian values and patriarchal family systems" in China have contributed to son preference, which has led to neglect of girls as well as to infanticide and feticide of females (Hesketh et al., 2011). Investigators continue to study the problem of distorted sex ratios in various countries including China, where the ratio is "alarmingly skewed" in favor of males (Nie, 2011, p. 3); India, where males outnumber females by almost 40 million (Goldberg & Dooley, 2011); Vietnam (Becquet & Ceped, 2013); and several countries in Eastern Europe (Guilmoto & Duthe, 2013).

Connection to Military Strategy

In her book, *Unnatural Selection,* Mara Hvistendahl (2011), who has a pro-choice position on abortion, recounts how gender imbalances came about.

During the 1970s, South Korea and Taiwan were both dependent on American military protection and financial aid, and people in the US presidential administrations of Nixon and Ford indicated in the archives which Hvistendahl reviewed that they were terrified that countries with many poor Asian peasants would "go communist." Therefore, rather than offering programs that might help prevent the peasants from being poor, they were determined to see that there were fewer poor people by drastically reducing their birth rate.

However, families wanted sons, a minimum of two – an heir and a spare. If every family tried for two sons, accepting whatever daughters come naturally in addition, steady population growth is assured.

If the number of girls is reduced, this has a far greater impact in reducing future population growth. One man can impregnate several women during the same time period, but the number of women is an absolute constraint on the number of births.

Yet this would require widespread acceptance of abortion as a routine tool, rather than as a rare emergency procedure. So the US government pressured Korea and Taiwan to move toward a system where abortion was the typical means of birth control.

In commentary on Hvistendahl's book, Douthat (2011) states, "For many of these anti-population campaigners, sex selection was a feature rather than a bug, since a society with fewer girls was guaranteed to reproduce itself at lower rates." Douthat also noted Hvistendahl's depiction of the "unlikely alliance between Republican cold warriors worried that population growth would fuel the spread of Communism and the left-wing scientists and activists who believed that abortion was necessary."

In an article called "Global Demographic Trends to the Year 2010: Implications for U.S. Security," Foster (1989) commented on population control as military strategy: "policymakers must . . .

employ all the instruments of statecraft at their disposal (development assistance and population planning every bit as much as new weapon systems)" (p. 24). Abortion aimed at female fetuses may be considered by some as an acceptable and effective weapon.

Gender Imbalance Leads to Violence against Women

An article in *The Economist* (Gendercide, 2010) discussed societal consequences of gender imbalance. In China and India, rising crime rates are correlated with the increase in the ratio of males to females. Specifically, crimes against women such as rape, prostitution, and sex trafficking are becoming more prevalent.

Both the United States Department of State (Lagon, 2008) and the Chinese Academy of Social Sciences have identified gender imbalance as a contributing factor to trafficking and forced prostitution (*China Faces Growing Gender Imbalance*, 2010). In China:

> the scarcity of females has resulted in kidnapping and trafficking of women for marriage and increased numbers of commercial sex workers, with a potential resultant rise in human immunodeficiency virus infection and other sexually transmitted diseases. There are fears that these consequences could be a real threat to China's stability in the future. (Hesketh et al., 2005, p. 1173)

As cross-cultural studies demonstrate, "the overwhelming majority of violent crime is perpetrated by young unmarried, low status males, [and] it is expected that these men are more prone to violent and anti-social behaviour and crime" (Liisanantti & Beese, 2012, p. 27).

Current sex imbalances indicate that more men than women are available for relationships, which increases the likelihood of marriage for higher status males. As more men have been unable to find wives, thousands of Vietnamese women have been forcibly taken to China, compelled to work in brothels or sold as wives for Chinese men (Giang, 2002; Linh, n.d.). Women who are trafficked in India may be required to sleep with not just one man but "with his brothers as well" (Hvistendahl, 2011, p. 190). This was confirmed by Vinita Shaw who stated that in Haryana, India, it is a common practice for many brothers to share one woman as their wife (personal communication, July, 22, 2014).

Child marriage is also increasing as adult women become increasingly scarce (Burns, 1998; Hvistendahl & Lindquist, 2008) and women sold to be brides often find themselves in abusive marriages. Among foreign wives living in Korea, 25% stated they felt physically threatened by their husbands (*Foreign Brides Rejuvenate Korea's Aging Society,* 2009). Forced marriage has become so common in Asia that it is now recognized as a valid reason to petition for political asylum in the United States (Gao v. Gonzales, 2006).

Still another consequence of sex-selection abortion is reflected by the "High female suicide rates, particularly in China, [that] have also been partially attributed to the sex imbalance, pressure on women for having male offspring and preferential treatment of males in the society" (Liisanantti & Beese, 2012, p. 5). In countries where abortion is a form of discriminatory violence against unborn females, it appears to have precipitated even more violence, often self-inflicted, against adult women and girls.

Implications for Meeting Women's Needs and Rights

Several government programs have attempted to address this problem.

- **India**

The Pre-Natal Diagnostic Techniques (PDNT) Act was passed in 1994 to combat gender imbalance. "The main challenge seems to be that the parties seeking (prospective parents) and parties offering (physicians) the illegal service of determining the sex of a foetus have no other incentive than moral conscience to comply with the PNDT Act" (Liisanantti & Beese, 2012, p. 18).

Another program instituted in India in 1997 provides financial incentives for the education of girls from poor families (Liisanantti & Beese, 2012).

On January 29, 2015, the Supreme Court of India ordered internet search engines to stop all ads for sex determination of fetuses, a common preparation for female feticide. The drop in sex-selection abortions in India and in neighboring Nepal was immediate and dramatic in the first week (Sharma, 2015). Whether this effect is long-lasting, of course, awaits the passage of time and further study.

- **China**

To promote gender equality in China, the government passed a number of laws and regulations supporting equal rights and, in 1995, outlawed sex-selective abortions (Li, 2007). In 2000, China initiated the "Care for Girls," a campaign which aimed to "improve the environment for girls' survival and development" (Liisanantti & Beese, 2012, p. 22). The program provides economic and educational aid for families with daughters and has been evaluated. "Since the introduction of the program in Chaohu (a city in Anhui province), the local SRB [Sex Ratio Balance] went from 125 in 1999 to 114 in 2002.

In response to this apparent success, the government expanded the program to 24 counties with high SRB rates in 2003-2004, and saw the average SRB in those counties drop from 133.8 in 2000 to 119.6 in 2005. Stipulation and initiation of a national "Care for Girls" campaign occurred in January 2006 - July 2006, with the goal of bringing the national SRB average to normal levels within 15 years (Liisanantti & Beese, 2012, p. 22).

However, "according to the UN inter-agency statement on gender-biased sex selection, these measures have had only limited results" (Liisanantti & Beese, 2012, p. 22). Clearly more research is needed in the coming years to evaluate the effectiveness of these government programs.

Research Needs

- **Actual prevalence**

An urgent need is for investigators to determine the prevalence and incidence of sex-selection abortion accurately. A number of challenges make that task difficult. "Female births can remain unregistered, and girls who are killed shortly after birth or given away for adoption may remain unaccounted for" (Liisanantti & Beese, 2012, p. 8). Because many countries have recently banned sex-selection abortion and made it a punishable crime, there is little motivation to acknowledge having participated in the identification of a fetus's sex or in provision of abortion or procurement of abortion due to the child's sex. Furthermore, "the relevant data relating to sex selective abortions are not easy to find especially in rural areas because the majority of these cases take place in secret" (Li, 2007).

- **Prevalence in different countries and cultures**

Still another challenge is the disparity in research findings concerning modern, Western countries such as the UK and the US, where some researchers have found skewed sex ratios among immigrants and others have not. Some of the contradictory findings may be explained by differences due to religious group affiliation as it has been reported that "[s]ome groups, such as Sikhs or Jains, exhibit extreme sex ratio values, while Christian and Muslim groups have sex ratios closer to normal" (Liisanantti & Beese, 2012, p. 16).

- **Psychological factors**

Future studies should also seek to identify those psychological factors which influence the practice of sex-selection abortion, utilizing both quantitative and qualitative studies of attitudes among citizens and medical professionals. Factors may include long-standing cultural values as well as more immediate economic needs.

Qualitative research which delves into moral motivations may provide knowledge to inform moral educational interventions that promote the inherent value of females as well as males.

- **Changes in attitudes over time**

Along with identifying the reasons for son-preference, it would be beneficial to compare results from older studies with current ones to determine if son-preference is changing:

> Fortunately, the younger generations already show signs of self-remedying this state of affairs in that the traditional preference for boys may be changing. The Chinese National Family Planning and Reproductive Health Survey of 2001 showed that 37% of women claimed to have no offspring gender preference, 45% stated that the ideal family consisted of one boy and one girl, and in the case of one offspring, women were slightly more in favor of having one girl than one boy (Grech & Mamo, 2014, p. 10).

- **Qualitative and quantitative**

In order to gain knowledge concerning the immediate and long-term impact of gendercide via sex-selective abortion on women, men, couples, marital relationships, and siblings, both qualitative and quantitative studies are needed. The former offers a means to gain a deeper understanding of the meanings and perceptions individuals hold while the latter is needed to determine incidence and pervasiveness of any effects.

- **Evaluation of interventions**

  Evaluations of interventions such as compliance with international human rights laws (Tiefenbrun & Edwards, 2008), educational and public campaigns to raise awareness and improve the status of females (Manhas & Banoo, 2013), and financial incentives (Liisanantti & Beese, 2012) that may mitigate the practice of sex-selective abortions, are needed to protect unborn females and restore normal sex-ratios.

- **Psychological effects**

  A most interesting research question for future studies is "How are women affected by the rejection of their own sex via a sex-selection abortion?" In-depth, qualitative studies to explore the experience of women who choose or are coerced to abort a fetus because of their shared gender may help answer that question. Such studies may be essential to recognize the effects on women's self-esteem, their sense of value as females, their mental health, and to identify women's therapeutic needs.

  Along the same lines, qualitative and quantitative studies are needed to gather data concerning how sex-selective abortion affects women's attachment to and parenting of existing and future children and whether these vary depending on the children's sex.

  Surely there is much left to learn about the consequences and prevention of sex-selection abortion. Future research may provide the knowledge to prevent that violence and meet the needs of women in non-violent ways.

References

Becquet, V. & Ceped, P. (2013). From gender inequality to prenatal sex selection: Comparative analysis of son preference in Hai Duong and Ninh Thuan provinces, Vietnam. Retrieved from the International Union for the Scientific Study of Population website at: http://www.iussp.org/sites/default/files/event_call_for_papers/From%20gender%20inequality%20to%20prenatal%20sex%20selection%20Vietnam%20_BECQUET%20LE_0.pdf

Brian, E., & Jaisson, M. (Eds.). (2007). *The descent of human sex ratio at birth: A dialogue between mathematics, biology and sociology*. New York: Springer.

Burns, J. F. (1998, May 11). Though illegal, child marriage is popular in part of India. *New York Times*. Retrieved from http://tinyurl.com/4mtcqrg.

Carter, J. E. (2014). *A call to action: Women, religion, violence, and power*. New York: Simon & Schuster.

China faces growing gender imbalance. (2010). BBC, January 11. Retrieved from http://news.bbc.co.uk/2/hi/8451289.stm

De Reus, L.A. (2010). Half the sky: Turning oppression into opportunity for women worldwide. *Journal of Family Theory & Review, 2*, 98-103.

Douthat, R. (2011). 160 million and counting. *The New York Times: The Opinion Pages*. Retrieved from http://www.nytimes.com/2011/06/27/opinion/27douthat.html?_r=0

Foreign brides rejuvenate Korea's aging society. (2009, October 28). *KI Media*. Retrieved from http://ki-media.blogspot.com/2009/10/foreign-brides-rejuvenate-south-koreas.html

Foster, G. D. (1989). Global demographic trends to the year 2010: Implications for U.S. security. *Washington Quarterly, 12*(2), 5-24.

Gao v. Gonzales, 04-1874-ag, 2nd Circuit Court of Appeals, (2006).

Gendercide: The world wide war on baby girls. (2010, May 4). *The Economist*. Retrieved from www.economist.com/node/15636231

Giang, T. T. (2002). Vietnamese women fall prey to traffickers. *Asia Times*, September 27. Retrieved from http://tinyurl.com/47k3jbx

Goel, K. (2014). Female foeticide and PNDT act. *Younker International Journal of Humanities, 1*(1), 77-82.

Goldberg, A. B. & Dooley, S. (2011, December 9). Disappearing daughters: Women pregnant with girls pressured into abortion. *ABC News 20/20*. Retrieved from http://abcnews.go.com/Health/women-pregnant-girls-pressured-abortions-india/story?id=15103950#.UaWMkr4o5Zd

Grech, V. & Mamo, J. (2014). Gendercide – A review of the missing women. *Malta Medical Journal, 26* (1), 8-11.

Guilmoto, C. Z. (2007). *Sex-ratio imbalance in Asia: Trends, consequences and policy responses.* Paris: United Nations Fund for Population Activities, 1-12.

Guilmoto, C. Z. & Duthe, G. (2013). *Masculinization of birth in Eastern Europe.* (No. 506). Institut National d'Etudes Demographiques.

Hesketh, T., Lu, L., & Xing, Z. W. (2005). The effect of China's one-child family policy after 25 years. *New England Journal of Medicine, 353*(11), 1171-1176.

Hesketh, T., Lu, L. & Xing, Z.W. (2011). The consequences of son preference and sex-selective abortion in China and other Asian countries. *CMAJ, 183*(12), 1374-1377.

Hvistendahl, M. (2011) *Unnatural selection: Choosing boys over girls, and the consequences of a world full of men.* New York: Public Affairs.

Hvistendahl, M. & Lindquist, A. (2008). Half the sky: How China's gender imbalance threatens its future. *Virginia Quarterly Review, 84*(4). Retrieved from http://www.vqronline.org/dispatch/half-sky-how-china%E2%80%99s-gender-imbalance-threatens-its-future

Lagon, M. (2008, September 17). *Missing girls in Asia: Magnitudes, implications, and possible responses.* American Enterprise Institute, Washington, D.C. Retrieved from https://www.aei.org/events/missing-girls-in-asia-magnitudes-implications-and-possible-responses/

Li, S. (2007). Imbalanced sex ratio at birth and comprehensive intervention in China. Paper prepared for the 4th Asia and Pacific Conference on Sexual and Reproductive Health and Rights, Hyderabad, India. Retrieved from: www.unfpa.org/gender/case_studies.htm

Linh, H. T. T. (n.d.). *Cross border trafficking in Quang Ninh Province,* International Organization for Migration. Hanoi, Vietnam. Retrieved from http://tinyurl.com/4okg7yx

Liisanantti, A. & Beese, K. (2012). *Gendercide: The missing women?* European Parliament, Directorate-General for External Policies. Retrieved from http://www.europarl.europa.eu/RegData/etudes/etudes/join/2012/433777/EXPO-DEVE_ET(2012)433777_EN.pdf

Manhas, S. & Banoo, J. (2013). A study of beliefs and perceptions related to female foeticide among Muslim community in Jammu, Jammu and Kashmir, India. *Studies on Home and Community Science, 7* (2), 125-130.

Mohapatra, S. (2015). False framings: the co-opting of sex selective abortion by the anti-abortion movement. *Journal of Law, Medicine and Ethics, 43,* 270-274.

Nie, J. B. (2011). Non-medical sex-selective abortion in China: ethical and public policy issues in the context of 40 million missing females. *British Medical Bulletin, 98*(1), 7-20.

Sharma, C. (2015, February 4). Female foeticides and selective abortions drop in Nepal. *Asia News.* Retrieved from http://www.asianews.it/news-en/Female-foeticides-and-selective-abortions-drop-in-Nepal-33373.html

Tiefenbrun, S. & Edwards, C.J. (2008). Gendercide and the cultural context of sex trafficking in China. *Fordham International Law Journal, 32*(3), 730-780.

United Nations. (1995). *Beijing Declaration and platform for action.* New York: Author, Retrieved from http://www.un.org/esa/gopher-data/conf/fwcw/off/a--20.en

Warren, M.A. (1985). *Gendercide: The implications of sex selection.* New Jersey: Rowman & Allanhead.

Chapter 6

Deriving Sensible Conclusions from the Scientific Literature on Abortion and Women's Mental Health

by Priscilla K. Coleman, Ph.D.
Professor of Human Development and Family Studies
Bowling Green State University

Abortion engenders strong emotion by virtue of its unique position among elective medical procedures, with two biological systems (woman and fetus) involved. Whether viewed as an actual developing human being, a potential human being in an immature state, or simply as tissue or a cluster of cells, a fetus is forever eliminated through abortion. Efforts to discern psychological meaning of abortion in women's lives are intrinsically tied to the deeper philosophical, moral, and social questions. A commitment to a dispassionate, empirically-based approach to investigation of the risks and benefits should be actively endorsed and pursued by the scientific community.

Conducting studies designed to address mental health implications of abortion has been challenging due to the inherent sensitivity of the topic, conflicting ideological perspectives and polarized socio-political initiatives. Virtually all mainstream professional organizations in the fields of psychology and medicine, including the American Psychological Association (APA) have embraced a clear political stance on abortion. In 1969 the APA adopted as part of its official policy the political position that abortion is a civil right: "WHEREAS, termination of unwanted pregnancies is clearly a mental health and child welfare issue, and a legitimate concern of APA; be it resolved, that termination of pregnancy be considered a civil right of the pregnant woman, to be handled as other medical and surgical procedures in consultation with her physician."

Despite a long history of advocacy for abortion rights by professional organizations, scientific information indicating the experience of an induced abortion increases risk for adverse psychological consequences has made its way into well-respected journals and is now being actively used in courtrooms across the U.S. as a basis for implementing legal restrictions. Many of the newly enacted laws mandate sharing information regarding potential psychological harm with women undergoing the procedure as part of the informed consent protocol. As a result, there are grave concerns that publication of findings revealing risks to women will and are eroding women's access. Since 2010, the states have instituted 282 restrictions on abortion with 51 of them occurring in 2015 (Guttmacher Institute, 2015). The current cultural dynamic naturally breeds hesitancy on the part of journal editors to publish research revealing abortion-related risks to women's psychological health, introducing a strong potential for bias in favor of null findings.

Academics in psychology, medicine, and related disciplines are relatively far from a consensus interpretation of the specific content of the studies comprising the professional literature on abortion and mental health. Nevertheless, when it comes down to the elements of a high quality study, most researchers would agree on a number of crucial parameters. Fortunately there is an emerging core of highly respected researchers determined to address the topic in an objective manner in order to provide the best available evidence to guide practice. For example, Fergusson and colleagues (2013) described the dire need to "revisit both clinical practice and the law in those jurisdictions in which mental health grounds are the principal criteria for recommending and authorizing abortion. The history of abortion law and law reforms shows that this is likely to resurrect politically uncomfortable and socially divisive debates about access to legal abortion . . . However, it is our view that the growing evidence suggesting that abortion does not have therapeutic benefits cannot be ignored indefinitely, and it is unacceptable for clinicians to authorize large numbers of abortions on grounds for which there is, currently, no scientific evidence."

Beyond a push for conducting stronger studies on the psychological experiences of women who choose abortion, there is a serious need to provide more concrete guidance to the professional community regarding how to objectively interpret an already expansive published literature. A straightforward approach to evaluation of research on the mental health implications of abortion to guide the informed consent process and serve as a foundation for evidence-based practice is greatly needed; therefore the primary objectives of this chapter are twofold: (a) to address methodological concerns, advances, and continued needs germane to this area of investigation; and (b) to provide a protocol for conducting systematic analyses of large portions of the literature for the purpose of assessing risk and causality relative to abortion and mental health.

Methodological Challenges and Progress

Given the diverse characteristics of individuals choosing abortion, as well as the highly variable and dynamic contexts in which decisions are embedded, efforts to understand abortion decisions and adjustment must by nature incorporate a wide array of variables:

- demographic factors (e.g., age, ethnicity, socioeconomic status, reproductive history, and marital history);

- history of stressful life experiences;

- personality variables, intelligence, and other cognitive variables such as personal beliefs and morals;

- psychological and physical health both past and present;

- relationship history including family of origin/attachment dynamics, present family situation, current and past intimate relationships, and experience of various forms of victimization;

- material and social challenges and supports surrounding the abortion decision;

- cultural values and norms pertaining to abortion.

Sensitivity to these multiple layers of influence is vital to arriving at a comprehensive understanding of how and why women choose abortion, as well as their prospects for adjustment in the immediate and over the long-term.

Researchers conducting investigations on this topic must also be sensitive to the fact that human psychological health outcomes, such as anxiety, depression, substance abuse, and suicidal behavior are highly complex, rendering identification of a single, precise cause applicable to all cases not possible. Every mental health problem is determined by a multitude of physical and psychological characteristics, background, and current contextual elements subject to individual variation. Moreover, any one cause (e.g. abortion) is likely to have a variety of effects (e.g., anxiety, depression, suicidal behavior) based on the variables involved.

The specificity needed to predict how a particular woman will arrive at the decision to abort and how she will fare afterwards is not possible; just as we are unable to predict at the individual level when considering a broad array of variables in the social sciences that are not suited for manipulation. Nevertheless, by studying thousands of women before and after an abortion procedure, with the methods of science available to us, we are able to identify women who are at an elevated risk for abortion-related distress and describe common ways that psychological problems tend to manifest. This is information that needs to be accurately consolidated and interpreted in order to provide women with the best available evidence as they face an unintended pregnancy. In order to achieve this objective, it is necessary to take a critical look at the major methodological challenges involved in the academic study of abortion and women's mental health. In Table 1 below, the following information is provided:

1. a description of methodological challenges;

2. an explanation of how each challenge compromises the quality of evidence;

3. an assessment of the degree to which published studies have already addressed each challenge;

4. ideas regarding how future investigators might implement procedures to reduce or eliminate the various problems and thereby enhance the quality of evidence on the topic.

Table 1
Methodological Challenges

Methodological Challenge	How the challenge compromises the quality of evidence	Progress in remedying the challenge	Suggested future innovations
1. Small, non-representative samples	Low generalizability of findings to the population of women choosing abortion and risk of inappropriate application of results to all or most women who abort.	Several record-based and other large scale studies with samples well over 100 participants (many with thousands) published over the last decade.	More widely representative samples are needed, because most of the larger studies are from a particular location limiting the generalizability. Incorporate on-going data collection into medical intake interviews and secure permission from women to use their medical history data in future scientific studies.

2. Low consent to participate rates/ biased sampling	When only a small percentage of women invited to participate in a study agree to do so, they may be systematically different from the population. For example, they may anticipate being more or less likely to be psychologically impacted by the abortion or have different background characteristics (e.g., more educated with a greater appreciation for research, fewer life stressors rendering them more open to participation)	Several studies published in recent years have avoided this problem by using record-based data wherein the focus of the study was broad and abortion was just one of many variables examined.	Better incentives for participation, emphasizing the need for data in order to develop women-friendly protocols for abortion decision-making and adjustment.
3. Concealment of an abortion experience	Approximately 50% of women who have had one or more prior abortions fail to disclose their histories, resulting in comparison groups containing women with abortion(s).	Studies using record-based data containing complete medical history information have been published in recent years. When medical claims data are employed there is a higher probability of deriving accurate reproductive histories.	Reduce the stigma associated with abortion by approaching women with possible abortion experience in a non-judgmental, supportive manner, emphasizing the need for accurate data in order to understand women's responses and develop intervention protocols.

| 4. High participant attrition in longitudinal studies | Many prospective studies have suffered from high dropout rates. When a significant portion of the sample that begins the study does not complete follow-up assessments, it is possible the participants in the remaining sample differ in systematic ways from the population from which the sample is drawn. For example, they may be more or less psychologically affected by the abortion. If women have strong adverse reactions they may find completing study materials too stressful, or those that continue participation may find interacting with the researchers and responding to questions somewhat therapeutic. Other ways they may differ from women who leave a study include the tendency to be less mobile, more conscientious, more interested in research, more oriented to helping. | When the study involves a data collection effort that is not primarily about abortion, but includes a more generalized assessment of women's lives with reproductive variables and mental health variables among many others, and women have committed to being part of a larger study, the dropout rates tend to be lower. In recent years, several studies of abortion and mental health have been of this form. | Provision of increased incentives for continued participation.

In recent years several studies of abortion and mental health have been based on large, more generalized data collection efforts.

Encourage the inclusion of more abortion-related variables in more generalized national data collection efforts.

Explore avenues to secure medical record-based data wherein all medical claims for all women in a particular population are available over an extended time period. |

| **5. Inadequate controls for confounding variables including prior psychiatric history/unmatched or no comparison groups.** | When women with abortion experience are compared to women without abortion experience, there is the possibility that there are personal, demographic, and situational factors that differ systematically between the two groups in addition to reproductive outcome, rendering it difficult to draw discernable conclusions from differences observed. | Many recently published studied have included controls for variables that may differ systematically between women who choose abortion and those who do not. Among the many control variables the literature are:
- Prior history of mental health problems
- Maternal age
- Gestational age of fetus
- Marital status
- Partner commitment to relationship
- Income
- Education
- Religion
- Planning of pregnancy
- Maternal beliefs regarding the humanity of the fetus
- Decision ambivalence
- Pressure to continue or end the pregnancy
- Past or current experience of abuse. | Continue to include potential confounding variables as controls and identify additional relevant variables to include.
Use comparison groups that have not been employed previously:

- Women who go to an abortion facility intending to abort and change their minds.

- Women who choose adoption. |

| 6. Use of simplistic measures designed to assess pre-and post-abortion outcomes without adequately established psychometric properties. Over-reliance on self-report questionnaires. | Brief self-report measures may not accurately reflect the respondents' psychological states before, during, or after an abortion experience due to memory distortions, limited introspective ability, and social desirability bias among other issues.

The possible range of mental health effects of abortion are likely not captured in brief measures lacking reliability and validity evidence.

Various aspects of the context of abortion decision-making have been demonstrated in studies to have a discernable effect on outcome measures; however contextual variables tend to be measured with single items indicators. | Many studies published over the last 20 years have stronger, multiple item instruments addressing a variety of psychological outcomes and indicators of several mental illnesses in a substantive format with psychometric data derived from many different samples.

Use of record-based data overcomes this limitation when the outcome measures are actual diagnostic codes assigned by trained clinicians. Clinician judgement of mental health variables are much richer than self-report. | Continued development of sophisticated measures, perhaps focusing on instruments to address specific aspects of the abortion decision process including level of investment in the pregnancy/ wantedness, perceptions of anticipated post-abortion adjustment.

Data gathered from significant individuals in women's lives (e.g., partners and family members) and/or behavioral assessments (possibly from counsellors and other abortion provider personnel or conducted by researchers) should enhance efforts to assess the complexity of women's positive and negative experiences before, during, and after the decision to abort. |

7. Abbreviated time frame, missing potential long-term effects	Women's emotional reactions to an abortion may change over time as the experience intersects with other life events. Negative reactions may be masked in the early weeks and months after abortion due to relief regarding having resolved the unintended pregnancy,	A few studies have been published in recent years with extended time frames; however the vast majority of studies are limited to very brief follow-up periods.	Studies with longer follow-up periods (greater than a few years) are needed to identify a range of individual trajectories across various developmental stages.

The Literature Assessing Risk and Causality

Informed consent for medical procedures occurs when patients adequately understand their condition along with the benefits, risks, and limitations of treatment alternatives (Sheridan, Harris, & Woolf, 2004). Health care professionals are responsible for educating patients in a manner that reflects the current scientific literature; however, concern raised in the medical community suggests this is a too infrequently realized ideal (Institute of Medicine Committee, 2001). Clinicians often lack the requisite skills and time to interpret the ever-expanding scientific literature necessary to optimally inform their practice and provide patients with accurate up-to-date synopses of the literature that facilitate truly informed health care choices. In a report released by the U.S. Institute of Medicine titled "Crossing the Quality Chasm" the authors noted "Medical science and technology have advanced at an unprecedented rate during the past half-century. In tandem has come growing complexity of health care, which today is characterized by more to know, more to do, more to manage, more to watch, and more people involved than ever before" (Institute of Medicine Committee, 2001, p. 1). Research which should be driving positive changes in medical practice is often ignored for many years, sometimes decades.

Sackett, Rosenberg, Gray, Haynes, and Richardson (1996) defined evidence-based medicine as a process integrating individual clinical expertise with the best external evidence and patient choice to maximize the quality and quantity of life for the individual patient. Ironically as awareness of the need for evidence-based medicine has grown over the last decade and strategies are being developed to revamp health care delivery to close the gap between knowledge and practice, the divide is greater than ever relative to conferring accurate unbiased information on risks of abortion to women considering the procedure. As described earlier, political, ideological, and social forces undoubtedly compete with efforts to conduct, publish, and disseminate straightforward appraisals of a rapidly accumulating world literature on the health consequences of abortion. The objective of this section of the chapter is not to analyze the complex context for what appears to be a significant evidence-based practice lag in the domain of reproductive health, but to describe a concrete strategy for deriving accurate and meaningful reviews of the literature. A dispassionate examination of the discrepancies between what is known and what is shared with women seeking abortions should ultimately foster accuracy in pre-abortion counseling and encourage true informed consent, thereby enhancing the quality of health care delivery.

A risk factor is any variable that has been established to increase the likelihood of an individual experiencing an adverse outcome. Risk factor data are used in medicine and psychology to understand etiology, warn patients of potential problems associated with various exposures, and develop effective prevention and intervention protocols to maximize health. In the absence of the ability to introduce strict experimental control, risk factors such as abortion for negative outcomes are established over time through the two primary scientific steps described below.

1. *Analysis of each individual study.* Each study published in a peer-reviewed journal is examined to assess the quality of evidence suggestive of a causal link between abortion and negative outcomes (Hill, 1965; Susser, 1977). Three criteria are employed for this purpose:

> a. Abortion must be shown to precede the mental health problem (time precedence). This is accomplished with prospective or longitudinal data collection.
> b. Differences in abortion history (abortion, no abortion) must be systematically associated with differences in mental health status (covariation).
> c. All plausible alternative explanations for associations between abortion and mental health must be ruled out using one or more of the methods described below.

     i. Measure and statistically control for known predictors of abortion aftermath.
    ii. Match groups on all variables known to be related to abortion.
   iii. Measure potential confounding variables and introduce them as additional variables to assess their independent effects.
   iv. Sample from homogeneous populations to eliminate potential confounds.

2. *Integrative analysis.* After evaluating individual studies for causal evidence linking abortion to mental health, scientists assess the consistency and magnitude of associations across all available studies.

    a. *Consistency* refers to repeated observation of an association between abortion and mental health revealed in several studies using different people, places, and circumstances.
    b. *Magnitude* (or strength of effect) refers to whether the associations between abortion and mental health problems are slight, moderate, or strong. Strong associations across various studies are more likely causal than slight or modest associations.

The integrated analysis may take the form of a traditional, narrative or qualitative review and/or a meta-analysis or quantitative review. Regardless of the form adopted, researchers are able to apply well-accepted, scientifically-based inclusion criteria when making decisions regarding specific studies to include in any systematic review. The strength of any review and the conclusions derived is largely based on the standards employed for selecting studies to include; however a meta-analysis is considered a higher level of evidence than a narrative review, because individual studies are weighted based on objective scientific criteria.

The process of conducting literature reviews may at first glance sound not too susceptible to researcher bias, but this is most certainly not the case. Whenever there are a wide array of potential inclusion criteria based on methodological strengths to consider, choosing particular forms will result in different subsets of studies with potentially discrepant and possibly misleading conclusions resulting. Given the fact that the investigation of abortion and women's mental health has become so highly politicized, consumers of the reviews should attend very closely to how studies are chosen and excluded from the review.

In recent years there has been a discernable emphasis in the literature on nationally representative samples, prospective designs, matched control groups, statistical controls for prior psychiatric history and a wide range of third variable, and comprehensive assessments of outcome measures, which in some cases included actual medical records. Because contemporary research on abortion and mental health has addressed a number of the shortcomings described previously, all reviews undertaken today should target only the highest quality of evidence, avoiding the studies with many methodological limitations. Table 2 below provides a suggested rating system for the purpose of evaluating individual studies based largely on the limitations of extant studies highlighted in Table 1. Potential scores would range from 9 to 45, with higher scores assigned to studies with stronger methodological features.

Table 2
<u>Scheme for Objectively Evaluating Studies</u>

Criterion	1	2	3	4	5
1. Sample size	Under 100	100-250	251-500	501-1000	1001 or more

2. Sample representativeness	Restricted to one city.	2 to 4 cities within 200 miles of each other.	2 to 4 cities in different geographical locations, over 200 miles apart.	5 or more cities in random locations without any effort to be widely represent-tative.	5 or more cities/ widely represent-tative.

3. High consent to participate rate.	Not available or under 20%	20%-39%	40%-59%	60%-79%	80% or greater

4. Low rate of abortion conceal-ment.	Sample includes women who are highly prone to conceal-ment (minors, victims of domestic violence, highly religious or conser-vative family back-ground).	Concealment likely to approximate typical studies on abortion.	Method-ology employed some effort to reduce conceal-ment.	Method-ology employed extensive strategies to encourage disclosure.	Low like-lihood of con-ceal-ment or record-based data.

5. Low attrition rate (longitudinal studies only)	High: 44% or less of sample retained.	Moderately high: 45-59% of sample retained.	Moderate: 60-74% of sample retained.	Moderately low: 75-89% of sample retained.	Low: 90-100% of sample retained.
6. High control for potentially confounding variables	No controls for potential confounds.	Incorporates a few demographic controls.	Control for several potential confounds, including prior psychiatric history.	Control for several potential confounds, including prior psychiatric history and pregnancy intended-ness or wantedness.	Control for an extensive set of potential confounds including prior psychiatric history and pregnancy intended-ness or wantedness. Groups are essentially equivalent except for the abortion history variable.
7. Inclusion of a control group	No comparison group.	Women with no repro-ductive event or women who carried to term with different demo-graphics or pregnancies delivered were likely mostly wanted.	Other form of perinatal loss (mis-carriage, stillbirth, adoption placement).	Unintended pregnancy delivered.	Unintended pregnancy delivered with women having actively considered abortion.

8. Use of strong measures of mental health outcomes.	Single item, self-report measures of outcomes.	Use of measures with under 10 items and minimal to no establish-ment of psycho-metric properties.	Use of strong multiple item well-established measures of mental health.	Use of strong multiple item well-establishe d measures of mental health and at least one form of data other than self-report.	Mental illnesses diagnosed by a trained profession-al using a well-developed assessment scale or protocol.

9. Prospective data collection over an extended time frame.	One assess-ment Point.	Two or more post-abortion assess-ments occurring at any point after the abortion.	Two or more post-abortion assess-ments, with the first occurring within a year of the procedure.	Pre and post assessment s with more than one post-assess-ment extending up to a year after the procedure.	Extensive pre and post assessments extending from at least a year before the abortion to several years after the procedure.

In addition to the need for literature reviews that adhere to a standardized and accepted methodology, more focused attention should be given to the design of individual studies to generate results that are readily translatable into useful, easily comprehended information for professionals counseling women seeking abortion. For example, future investigations should be geared toward incorporating under-used data analysis techniques, such as the Population Attributable Risk (PAR) statistic. The PAR provides an estimate of the public health impact of a particular exposure, as it is the portion of the incidence of a disease in the entire population (not just the exposed) that is directly due to the exposure or that would be eliminated if the exposure did not occur. The PAR is calculated by subtracting the incidence in the unexposed (e.g. rate of suicidal behavior in women who have not aborted) from the incidence in the total population (e.g. rate of suicidal behavior in those with and without an abortion history). When population exposure rates are not available, estimation is achieved with the basic formulas modified using the relative risk or odds ratio statistic. A concrete example of the PAR is provided in a meta-analysis I published in the *British Journal of Psychiatry* (Coleman, 2011). The results revealed a PAR of 9.9, indicating that nearly 10% of the incidence of mental health problems afflicting women is due to abortion.

Ideally future studies employing the PAR will include assessments of numerous potentially confounding third variables, with statistically adjusted measures of association employed to derive accurate estimates of the unique impact of abortion. Investigative efforts designed to examine the PAR relative to induced abortion and various mental health outcomes should also include calculation of the PAR for other widely accepted predictors of mental health problems, such as histories of abuse, exposure to other significant stressors of various forms, a family history of mental illness, etc. in order to assess the magnitude of the PAR for abortion in the etiology of psychological disorders in comparison to other well-known causes. This information could prove quite valuable as professionals offer a broader context for women engaged in abortion decision-making.

The very real needs of women before and after abortion have essentially been entangled and often buried in the socio-cultural struggles related to abortion. Substantive pre- and post-abortion counseling protocols with sensitivity to diverse women, many of whom may not adjust well, cannot be realized until there is widespread professional endorsement for stronger science wherein women's voices are clearly echoed as opposed to being filtered through a maze of agendas. Ultimately the responsibility for providing women with the factual information they need to make healthy decisions belongs to individual researchers, journal editors, professional organizations, funding agencies, legislatures, and the media. The basic rights of women and the ethics of science render such a multi-level commitment hardly optional and long overdue.

References

Coleman, P. K. (2011). Abortion and mental health: A quantitative synthesis and analysis of research published from 1995-2009. *British Journal of Psychiatry, 199*, 180-186.

Fergusson, D. M., Horwood, L. J., & Boden, J. M. (2013). Does abortion reduce the mental health risks of unwanted or unintended pregnancy? A re-appraisal of the evidence. *Australian & New Zealand Journal of Psychiatry, 47*, 819-27.

Guttmacher Institute. (2015). Laws affecting reproductive health and rights: State trends at midyear. Media Center: News in Context. Retrieved from http://www.guttmacher.org/media/inthenews/2015/07/01/

Hill, B. A. (1965). The environment and disease: Association or causation? *Proceedings of the Royal Society of Medicine, 58*, 295-300.

Institute of Medicine Committee on Quality of Health Care in America (2001). *Crossing the quality chasm: A new health system for the 21st century.* Washington, DC: National Academy Press.

Sackett, D. L., Rosenberg, W. M. C., Gray, J. A. M., Haynes, R. B., & Richardson, W. S. (1996). Evidence based medicine: what it is and what it isn't. *British Medical Journal, 312*, 71-72.

Sheridan, S. L., Harris, R. P., & Woolf, S. H. (2004). Shared decision making about screening and chemoprevention. A suggested approach from the U.S. Prevention Services Task Force. *American Journal of Preventive Medicine, 26*, 56-66.

Susser, M. (1977). Judgment and causal inference: Criteria in epidemiologic studies. *American Journal of Epidemiology, 105*, 1-15.

Chapter 7

Risk Factors

by Martha Shuping, M.D.
Psychiatrist, private practice

Everyone Agrees: Some Women are at Risk

Researchers agree that some women have mental health problems associated with abortion (Baker, Beresford, Halvorson-Boyd, & Garrity, 1999; Baker & Beresford, 2009; Wilmoth, 1992). There is also agreement on specific, pre-existing risk factors that identify subgroups of women more likely to have negative psychological outcomes (American Psychological Association, 2008; Baker et al., 1999; Baker & Beresford, 2009; Coleman, 2014; Reardon, 2003). However, there are different perspectives on the meaning of these risk factors and how their presence should inform clinical practice.

The *2015 Clinical Policy Guidelines* of the National Abortion Federation (NAF) include five references for abortion counseling; three of these provide lists of risk factors (Baker, 1995; Baker & Beresford, 2009; Needle & Walker, 2008), identified by research as "psychosocial predictors for negative emotional sequelae" after abortion (Baker & Beresford 2009, p. 57). Anne

Baker, Director of Counseling of the Hope Clinic for Women (which provides abortion), compiled a list of 18 risk factors from published studies. In her 1995 book she identified some as originating from her clinical experience. Needle and Walker (2008) cite the Hope Clinic's website as the source of their list of risk factors. For most identified risk factors, there are numerous confirming studies. No one disputes the existence of these risk factors.

A 2014 report by Coleman includes a 19-page list of "Empirical Studies Published Between 1972 and 2011 on Predictors of Adverse Post-Abortion Psychological Outcomes" (p. 160), with 119 citations to peer reviewed studies. Coleman identified 12 clusters of risk factors.

Examples of risk factors widely accepted by both pro-choice and pro-life researchers and confirmed by many empirical studies include:

- low perceived ability to cope with abortion or low self-efficacy

- belief in the humanity of the child or belief that abortion is killing a child.

- attachment to the pregnancy / child or pregnancy meaningful to woman.

- significant ambivalence or decisional distress.

- perceived pressure or coercion to abort.

- advanced stage of pregnancy

- pre-existing psychiatric illness.

- pre-existing history of sexual abuse, sexual assault, or other trauma.

Co-occurring Risk Factors

The American Psychological Association's 2008 report on abortion and mental health identified at least 18 risk factors (the exact number depends on groupings). Many are similar to those identified by other authors (Baker, 1995; Baker & Beresford, 2009; Coleman, 2014; Needle & Walker, 2008; Reardon, 2003). The APA's report includes risk factors throughout the report, rather than in a single list.

This report identifies two categories of "co-occurring risk factors": *systemic* and *personal* (American Psychological Association, 2008, pp. 12-14). Poverty is an example of a systemic risk factor. Women who are poor are more likely to experience an unintended pregnancy and are also more likely to obtain an abortion. When they do, they may be more likely to later have mental health problems due to their history of adversities associated with poverty. Given their "greater exposure to adversity, the absence of such an association would be noteworthy" (American Psychological Association, 2008, p. 13).

There are also individual risk factors such as "personality factors that diminish a person's ability to regulate negative emotion" which may "put . . . her at risk for engaging in problem behaviors . . . . Importantly, many of these personal characteristics that put women at risk for problem behaviors and unplanned pregnancy also put them at risk for mental or physical health problems, whether or not a pregnancy is aborted or carried to term" (American Psychological Association, 2008, p. 14). Thus, even with some individual risk factors, from a pro-choice perspective, while the risk factors preceding the abortion may be associated with problems afterward, these women would have had problems either way, according to this perspective.

Needle and Walker (2008), in discussing women who experience longer-term adverse emotional reactions after abortion, conclude: "It is important to remember that the research has found that most of these women probably have risk factors that would make them likely to have the same long-term effects even if they carried the pregnancy to term" (p. 146). Similarly, the report of the

American Psychological Association (2008) concludes: "Women characterized by one or more such risk factors might be equally (or more) likely to experience negative psychological reactions if they pursued an alternative course of action (motherhood or adoption)" (p. 92).

Thus, one pro-choice perspective is that some women have pre-existing adverse conditions making it more likely they will have later mental health problems, whether or not they have an abortion. Risk factors exist, but from this perspective, there may be nothing that can be done about them. The mental health outcomes may be the same regardless of the pregnancy decision. From this perspective it appears for women who ultimately have poor outcomes after abortion, the results were unavoidable. However, pro-choice authors also suggest the possibility of mitigating some of the adverse outcomes.

Mitigation of Effects of Risk Factors?

A screening form to identify risk factors, developed by the Hope Clinic for Women, is reprinted in a National Abortion Federation-approved textbook (Baker & Beresford, 2009). This form asks questions to identify common risk factors: whether the woman is being pressured by someone else, whether she prefers to deliver the baby rather than have an abortion, whether she believes abortion is the same as killing a baby already born, whether she has had one or more abortions before, and how she expects to cope (since low coping expectations are associated with coping poorly).

The fact that a screening form is recommended by abortion counselors indicates there may be value in identifying risk factors in advance of the abortion, and suggests that intervention at that point may be helpful. Baker and Beresford (2009) state: "Patients with risk factors may require more time to reconsider options or make a plan for coping strategies" (p. 57).

Having a low expectation of coping well or "low self-efficacy" is a risk factor associated with coping less well after abortion, identified by several authors (American Psychological Association, 2008; Baluk & O'Neill, 1980; Baker & Beresford,

2009; Coleman, 2014; Fingerer, 1973; Major & Cozzarelli, 1992; Major, Mueller, & Hildebrandt, 1985; Mueller & Major, 1989; Needle & Walker, 2008; Reardon, 2003). Being self-critical and blaming their characters for the pregnancy is another risk factor (Coleman, 2014; Major, et al., 1985; Reardon, 2003).

A study by Mueller and Major (1989) compared two pre-abortion counseling interventions. One helped women develop positive coping expectations. The other helped women decrease self-blame attributions prior to the abortion. Results showed the intervention was effective immediately at the time of the abortion. However, results did not persist at three-week follow-up. Needle and Walker (2008) suggest this study gives hope that it may be possible to reduce "post-abortion distress by altering cognitive mediators related to the abortion experience" (p. 132).

However, to date there are no data to support the hypothesis that risk factors can be overcome by pre-abortion counseling. An intervention that gives benefit on the day of the abortion but not afterward is not a clinically useful tool for mitigation of risk factors.

Risk Factors Intrinsic to the Abortion Decision

Belief in the humanity of the unborn child

As we have considered, systemic risk factors such as poverty or individual risk factors of personality are anticipated by some pro-choice authors to unavoidably lead to poor outcomes no matter the pregnancy decisions. From this perspective, history is destiny. However, some risk factors are unique to the abortion decision. For example: "They believe having an abortion is the same thing as murdering a newborn" (Baker, 1995, p. 718), or stated differently, "Belief that a fetus is the same as a 4-year-old human and that abortion is murder" (Baker et al., 1999, p. 29, citing Conklin & O'Connor, 1995).

It is recommended when a patient has this belief the counselor ask, "How do you think you will feel about yourself [after the abortion]?" and, "What will you do to cope?" (Baker, et al., p. 27-28). If the woman believes she is killing a child and would not be able to cope, it may be important to consider options other than abortion.

Alternatively, making a plan for coping strategies in the face of this belief seems unlikely to be successful. The data show that women who believed the fetus was human scored lower on well-being variables (Coleman, 2014; Conklin & O'Connor, 1995). There are no data available to demonstrate success in changing this belief prior to abortion, nor to show that effective coping mechanisms have ever been successfully taught with corresponding reduction of risk associated with this belief. This is a risk factor very specific to the woman at the time of her abortion.

Attachment to the Pregnancy or to the Unborn Child

Another risk factor intrinsic to abortion is "commitment to the pregnancy" (American Psychological Association, 2008, p. 92; Baker et al., 1999; Lydon, Dunkel-Schetter, Cohan, & Pierce, 1996; Major et al., 1985) or "attachment to the pregnancy" (Coleman, 2014; Mufel, Speckhard, & Sivuha, 2002; Rue, Coleman, Rue, & Reardon, 2004; Stalhandske, Makenzius, Tyden, & Larsson, 2012). Some authors include both commitment and attachment (Baker and Beresford, 2009, p. 57; Reardon, 2003).

Similarly, there is increased risk when the pregnancy is "wanted or meaningful" to the woman (American Psychological Association, 2008, p. 11; Major et al., 1985; Remennick & Segal, 2001). Coleman (2014) identified a cluster of factors including "desire for the pregnancy, psychological investment in the pregnancy, belief in the humanity of the fetus and/or attachment to fetus" (p. 51), confirmed as risk factors by 21 peer reviewed studies.

To understand the risk associated with terminating a pregnancy after attachment has occurred, we review some literature on maternal-fetal attachment (MFA), defined by Condon and Corkindale (1997) as "the emotional tie or bond that normally develops between the pregnant woman and her unborn infant" (p. 359). However, MFA was first defined by Cranley in 1981 in terms of behavior of the mother associated with affiliation and interaction with the unborn child. Thus, both emotions and behavior are involved.

Though some authors have attempted to distinguish between bonding and attachment, it is worth emphasizing that Condon and Corkindale's definition of MFA uses the word "bond" (p. 359). Many authors use the terms interchangeably (Feldman, Weller, Zagoory-Sharon, and Levine, 2007, and Levine, Zagoory-Sharon, Feldman & Weller, 2007).

A qualitative study (Kjelsvik & Gjengedal, 2011) during the first trimester while the women were considering whether to terminate or to carry to term has identified physical aspects of maternal attachment to the unborn child and emotional and behavioral components. During weeks 7-11 of pregnancy, "the women 'sensed within their bodies' that they were pregnant and this bodily sensation 'filled them day and night'" (Kjelsvik & Gjengedal, 2011, p. 173). One woman stated, "I feel that when I was about to make the decision to keep it, it was because I felt it so strongly in my body" (p. 172).

The hormone *oxytocin* plays a key role in the development of attachment, beginning in early pregnancy and continuing after the child's birth (Feldman et al., 2007; Galbally, Lewis, van IJzendoor & Permezel, 2011; Levine, et al., 2007). Results for Israeli women were similar to results in U.S. women 25 years previously, suggesting prenatal bonding is similar across cultures and a span of decades (Levine et al., 2007). Oxytocin levels have been shown to be predictive of maternal attachment, including attachment thoughts and behaviors (Feldman et al., 2007).

In studies from Australia (Allanson & Astbury, 1996) and Norway (Kjelsvik & Gjengedal, 2011) attachment was observed during the period in which abortion was being considered (prior to it taking place) without examining the mental health outcomes of those who chose abortion.

Attachment to the child even though abortion was the outcome has been reported in several different countries including Belarus (Mufel et al., 2002), Russia (Rue et al., 2004), Sweden (Stalhandske et al., 2012) and the U.S. (Major et al., 1985; Rue et al., 2004). In these studies, the mental health outcomes were more negative in those who had demonstrated attachment to the fetus prior to the abortion.

The risk factor of a pregnancy that is "wanted or meaningful" is not necessarily identical to risk associated with attachment, though it would seem likely there would be much overlap. This risk factor, pregnancy being meaningful to the woman, has been studied in women in the U.S. (Major et al., 1985), in Russian immigrants in Israel and in native Israeli women (Remennick & Segal, 2001).

A Russian woman who was an immigrant to Israel said: "I couldn't stop thinking about this, counting what week in pregnancy I'd be by now, and how the baby would have looked, and all that . . . When I saw mothers with babies in the street I winced. In my dreams, I saw this hospital, the nurses, and myself in the stirrups . . . I know I couldn't keep this baby, but I also cannot stop feeling guilty" (Remennick & Segal, 2001). Baker and Beresford (1999, pp. 28-29) describe symptoms that can occur after abortion as including "nightmares about killing or saving babies." Stalhandske et al. (2012, p. 56) quotes a woman as saying, "Immediately when I found out I was pregnant, I felt like a mother. It felt like I had some kind of affinity with the child, and now afterwards, it feels empty."

Dykes, Slade and Haywood (2010) interviewed women at the age of menopause looking back at a past abortion. The authors do not have specific data on attachment or lack of attachment at the time of the abortion, but this statement from one woman strongly suggests attachment: "this child of mine would have been [number of years] this month, it's the [date] of [month] which is the day I was given and I still think about this baby and I think about it at Christmas, it's something I don't think I'll ever forget if I live to be a hundred" (2010, p. 12).

From these reports distress and symptoms are specifically associated with the unborn child. When Elaine was drinking and having suicidal thoughts, she was thinking about the death of her "baby" (Dykes et al., 2010). When Baker et al. (1999) report nightmares about killing babies, that is an indication that something about the distress of those women is related to the unborn child and the experience of abortion. It would appear that the distress is uniquely related to the abortion, and not merely related to a history of poverty or low self-esteem. These are genuine risk factors; they may be operating in women's lives whether the pregnancy was aborted or delivered -- though there is no empirical evidence the mental health outcome would be identical regardless of which was chosen. Nonetheless, there is nothing about poverty or low self-esteem that would cause a woman to have nightmares about babies or to have her cognitions filled with thoughts about the baby lost to abortion.

If there are adverse outcomes regardless of the pregnancy decision, these would tend to be more generic; depression, anxiety, stress. But when adverse outcomes specifically include cognitions about a lost child, and nightmares about killing babies, this could be an indicator the risk was uniquely associated with the abortion decision. When a woman has attached to the child, and then places herself in a known risk group by choosing abortion, she is at increased risk for adverse reactions in which some symptoms often are intimately connected with the lost child or the abortion.

Mufel et al. (2002) demonstrated that "attachment to the fetus/embryo and recognition of life are the strongest and most prevalent predictors of adverse psychological responses to abortion for all of the variables examined" (pp. 50-51). This was viewed as clinically very significant, as "the woman's perception of pregnancy (i.e. whether she views it as a life, and is attached to it) can predict how she will fare psychologically with an abortion decision" (Mufel et al., 2002, p. 51).

This would be useful to consider during the pregnancy decision-making process. Since there is no empirically supported intervention to reduce risk after attachment has developed, and no data on successful facilitation of un-attaching after bonding, some women may prefer an option other than abortion if the risk is understood.

Mufel et al. (2002, p. 51) showed that "attachment and recognition of life were predictors of guilt and grief and attachment was also a predictor of depression." Authors point out that Belarus, part of the former Soviet Union, provides a social context in which there is complete accessibility and widespread acceptance of abortion, with "little political controversy (i.e., absence of protesters)." Thus, stigma and protests were unlikely to have been operating as risk factors in this study.

Mufel et al. suggest that assessing for attachment and recognition of life may be clinically useful with women who desire counseling after abortion; "gentle inquiries" (2002, p. 42) may reveal whether a woman experienced attachment and if there are any issues she would like to discuss.

The exact number of women impacted is unknown, but it appears a substantial number are in this risk group. Rue et al. (2004) reported 37% of Russian women and 39% of American women "felt emotionally close or attached to the pregnancy/child" (p. SR9). Stalhandske et al. (2012, p. 53) reported "67% of women thought of the pregnancy in terms of a child" and "almost 50% of women reported a need for special acts in relation to the abortion" (for example, "I lit a candle for the little one and asked for forgiveness," p. 56). Allanson & Astbury (1996) reported 40% of women endorsed the statement: "I've talked to the pregnancy out loud or in my mind" (p. 161) and 30% endorsed: "I've patted my tummy affectionately" (p. 161).

Because of the centrality of relationships and attachment in women's lives, and the strong desire to preserve relationships, if one's mother or partner urges abortion (or if there is pressure from others), this may cause tremendous stress for a woman who has attached to the pregnancy, but also strongly desires to preserve other relationships in her life, leading to ambivalence or decisional distress. Coercion and pressure by male partners also places a woman at risk for negative outcomes as discussed further below and in Chapter 2.

Ambivalence

Ambivalence is well known to be a risk factor for mental health problems after abortion (Adler, 1975; American Psychological Association, 2008; Baker et al., 1999, citing Dagg, 1991, Payne et al., 1976, and Adler, 1975; Baker & Beresford, 2009; Hern, 1990; Major & Cozzarelli, 1992; Needle & Walker, 2008;

Remennick & Segal, 2001; Reardon, 2003; Rue et al., 2004; Zimmerman, 1977). Coleman (2014) identified 29 studies in which ambivalence was identified as a risk factor.

The 2015 Merriam Webster dictionary definition of ambivalence is "simultaneous and contradictory attitudes or feelings (as attraction and repulsion) toward an object, person, or action." A woman experiencing ambivalence may have attached to the child, and at the same time may have fears about being a mother, or difficult circumstances that cause her to consider abortion, thus experiencing difficulty or distress in making her decision. When ambivalence exists, when the woman desires to continue the pregnancy even while also considering abortion, the conflict may be occurring because of her attachment to the unborn child. Her circumstances may cause her to lean toward abortion, yet because of her attachment to the fetus she agonizes over her decision, experiencing distress and delays. One woman stated, "I wanted to have that baby, but I was afraid" (Burke & Reardon, 2002, p. 225), an indication that attachment to the child was a factor in her experience of ambivalence.

There could be other reasons for ambivalence: for example, religious beliefs or personal values against abortion. Coleman (2014) identified 18 studies that confirmed a cluster of risk factors related to religious beliefs or personal values. Second or third trimester abortions may indicate ambivalence; if the woman had wholeheartedly desired abortion, she might have sought one much sooner. A late abortion may be a marker for decisional difficulty and having a late abortion is itself a risk factor (American Psychological Association, 2008; Baker & Beresford, 2009; Coleman, 2014; Reardon, 2003).

Perceived Coercion

Another risk factor that may be related to attachment is perceived coercion (Baker & Beresford, 2009, p. 57; Baker et al., 1999, p. 29, citing Bracken, Klerman & Bracken, 1978; Reardon, 2003), or alternatively "perceived pressure from others to terminate a pregnancy" (American Psychological Association, 2008, p. 11), or "pressure or coercion" (Coleman, 2014, p. 151). This is expressed by Needle and Walker (2008) as: "Feeling pressured into having an abortion for someone else's benefit (usually male partner or parent)" (p. 143).

Crucial is the word "perceived." The woman's experience is of primary importance. If she feels she is being pressured or coerced, she is at risk, even if someone else might look at her situation and think, "I don't know why she thinks that is pressure." For that woman, given her own unique personality and her own coping skills, her own relationships she values, if she feels the decision is not her own, or that she is not able to make her own free choice, then she is at risk for more negative psychological outcomes (Bracken, et al., 1978; Kimport, Foster, & Weitz, 2011; Pope, Adler, & Tschann, 2001).

Coercion and pressure are further discussed in Chapter 2.

Prior Mental Health as Risk Factor

Prior mental illness is a risk factor for having mental health problems after abortion (American Psychological Association, 2008; Baker, 1995; Baker et al., 1999; Baker & Beresford, 2009; Coleman, 2014; Needle & Walker, 2008; Reardon, 2003). The American Psychological Association (2008) stated, "Across studies, prior mental health emerged as the strongest predictor of postabortion mental health" (p. 4). Coleman identified 35 peer reviewed studies confirming that pre-abortion psychiatric illness is a risk factor for post-abortion problems. However, there is more than one perspective on this risk factor.

It is to be expected that many women with past psychiatric illness will also have future illness. Many psychiatric illnesses have frequent recurrences, or are chronic conditions. Women with past psychiatric illness are likely to have future psychiatric problems regardless of any pregnancy or its outcome. Thus, it seems logical for Needle and Walker to state, "this woman would be having problems even if she had not had an abortion" (2008, p. 146).

An alternative viewpoint is that women with psychiatric illness are known to be more vulnerable to a new episode or an exacerbation. Thus, if a woman with a past history of psychiatric illness experienced attachment to her child, experienced ambivalence, and then was pressured or forced by a parent or husband to terminate a desired pregnancy, she would be even more at risk of having an episode of illness, or an additional diagnosis.

Published research shows a worsening of psychiatric illness may occur after abortion. Remennick and Segal (2001) reported approximately one-fourth of Israeli women and one-third of Russian women experienced symptoms of depression after abortion including insomnia, fatigue, poor concentration and sadness. Some women reported having had these symptoms previously but "after abortion things got worse" (p. 58). One woman reported pregnancy-related dreams at night and distress when seeing babies in public places, indicating part of her distress related to the loss of the pregnancy. Qualitative studies of women with prior mental illness to understand the additional consequences of abortion may be useful for further research.

The situation may be similar for women with a history of prior sexual abuse or other trauma. They have a pre-existing problem and are at increased risk of having psychiatric problems later. However, for women who may have attached to the unborn child and perhaps have a coerced abortion, the distress may add to the trauma already experienced to produce more severe effects. More research is needed to clarify the effect of abortion in these circumstances, but it is well established that women with a past history of abuse or trauma are at increased risk for mental health problems after abortion (Baker et al., 1999; Baker & Beresford, 2009; Coleman, 2014; Hamama, Rauch, Sperlich, Defever , Seng, 2010; Needle & Walker, 2008; Reardon, 2003; Rue et al., 2004.) A meta-analysis including articles from 22 countries (Pereda, 2009) showed that 20% of women had experienced childhood sexual abuse, and a study from the Centers for Disease Control (2014) shows that 25% of American women have experienced childhood sexual abuse. Thus, this is a pre-existing risk factor for many women who may consider abortion.

Do Risk Factors Cause Increased Risk?

The American Psychological Association (2008) cautions that one cannot assume every risk factor causes psychological problems after abortion. A risk factor may be "associated with causes without themselves being a part of the causal mechanisms in play" (p. 20). Consider a hypothetical study in which women carrying cigarette lighters in their purse were found to be at increased risk for lung cancer, though further research might reveal cigarettes, not lighters, as the cause of the increased cancer risk. The lighters are a co-occurring risk factor that was not causal. The report states that the best way to resolve questions of causation would be randomized clinical trials, but it would be unethical "to randomly assign women who have unwanted pregnancies to an abortion versus delivery versus adoption group" (p. 8).

While it is true that a randomized clinical trial would be theoretically ideal and completely unethical, we are not helpless to study the problems in other ways. A case can be made that some risk factors may be a cause of psychological problems some women experience after abortion - or that abortion is a cause of psychological problems in women who experience a particular risk factor. Consider, in light of the well-known Bradford Hill Criteria, or Hill's Criteria for Causation, a woman with the risk factor of attachment or meaningful pregnancy who has an abortion.

Mufel et al. (2002) demonstrated that attachment was highly significant as a predictor of PTSD. With a p value of 0.01, the association is unlikely to be due to chance. But Hill (1965) said to demonstrate causation, not only should there be an association, but also consistency should be demonstrated by multiple investigators in multiple locations, giving similar results. As we have considered, many other studies have similarly identified attachment and meaningful pregnancy as risk factors (American Psychiatric Association, 2008; Baker & Beresford, 2009; Coleman, 2014; Reardon, 2003; Remennick & Segal, Rue et al, 2004), and this has been demonstrated with women on at least three continents.

Hill (1965) also stated, "I would myself put a good deal of weight upon similar results reached in quite different ways, e.g.

prospectively and retrospectively" which we also see in risk factor literature; for example, a retrospective study by Rue et al. (2004) and a prospective one by Stalhandske et al. (2012) using both quantitative and qualitative methods.

Hill (1965) additionally recommends that biological plausibility be demonstrated, though he says he would not insist on this because "what is biologically plausible depends on the biological knowledge of the day." Considering the attachment literature and our limited knowledge about the biology of maternal-fetal attachment and reactions some women have reported (dreams about babies and cognitions preoccupied with the child), it may be possible to view this as plausible. However, the mechanisms for attachment and the neurochemistry of psychiatric illness are not yet fully understood.

Perinatal Loss

It is widely accepted that women may experience grief or distress after a miscarriage or stillbirth. If a woman reported she experienced distress because of miscarriage, few people would dispute that perception. But in the case of induced abortion, the woman is not *believed* when she reports on her experience. Instead, counselors familiar with Needle and Walker (2008) may believe the woman is denying or ignoring the roots of the real problem, which must be something other than abortion.

However, perinatal care specialists are now recognizing similarities among various types of perinatal loss, including induced abortion. Therapist Kate Kripke, founder of the nonprofit organization Perinatal Progress, includes abortion in discussing these   losses:

> Losing a baby though miscarriage, elective termination, stillbirth, childbirth, after a NICU stay, SIDS, or any other time is, without a doubt, one of the most difficult experiences that a parent will ever endure. There are no words to explain the depth of despair that a parent goes through when attempting to

understand the shift that occurs when all hopes and expectations suddenly drop out from underneath anything stable. (Kripke, 2013)

The Wisconsin Association for Perinatal Care (2002) also includes both elective abortion and abortion for medical reasons as losses that may require intervention. This makes sense when one considers the comments of women themselves who loved and then lost a child to abortion (Dykes et al., 2010; Mufel et al., 2002; Stalhandske et al., 2012).

Conclusion

Hill (1965) concluded that whether or not there is statistical certainty about causes (in general, not specifically about abortion), in "real life" it is important to take practical steps to protect health when possible. The Royal College of Psychiatrists in Great Britain did just that when they updated their 1994 position statement on abortion to state:

> Healthcare professionals who assess or refer women who are requesting an abortion should assess for mental disorder and for risk factors that may be associated with its subsequent development. If a mental disorder or risk factors are identified, there should be a clearly identified care pathway whereby the mental health needs of the woman and her significant others may be met.
>
> The Royal College of Psychiatrists recognises that good practice in relation to abortion will include informed consent. Consent cannot be informed without the provision of adequate and appropriate information regarding the possible risks and benefits to physical and mental health. (Royal College, 2008)

Thus, the Royal College recommends women undergoing abortion should be screened for risk factors, and if any are present, mental health needs or potential needs should be addressed in treatment planning. In addition, the Royal College states informed consent must include information on risks vs. benefits of abortion. Their recommendations are similar to those of the National Abortion Federation (NAF), whose 2009 textbook (Baker & Beresford, 2009) recommends screening for risk factors and treatment planning that addresses identified risks.

In actual practice, it is not known to what extent screening is taking place. I was invited to give a presentation on risk factors at the 2013 triennial meeting of Medical Women's International Association (MWIA), and prepared slides based on the risk factors identified by Baker and Beresford (2009) and by American Psychological Association (2008). However, on arrival in South Korea, I learned that the presentation was canceled by MWIA leadership due to the perception that a discussion of risk factors would be a threat to women's reproductive rights.

When an international body of this stature is afraid to discuss known risk factors from a textbook of the National Abortion Federation, it raises questions as to whether women physicians are knowledgeable about these risk factors and whether they screen for them and incorporate findings into treatment plans. It also raises questions about the quality of informed consent, as physicians unaware of these risk factors would be unable to discuss them in an individualized risk versus benefit discussion with women prior to abortion. Thus, more education among physicians on this topic is clearly needed.

References

Adler, N. (1975). Emotional responses of women following therapeutic abortion. *American Journal Orthopsychiatry, 45,* 446-454.

Allanson, S. & Astbury, J. (1996). The abortion decision: fantasy process. *Journal of Psychosomatic Obstetrics & Gynaecology 17,* 158-167.

American Psychological Association. (2008). *Report of the Task Force on Mental Health and Abortion.* Washington, DC: Author. Retrieved from www.apa/org/pi/wpo/mental-health-abortion-report.pdf

Baker, A. (1995). *Abortion and options counseling: A comprehensive reference, revised, and expanded edition.* Granite City: Hope Clinic for Women.

Baker, A., Beresford, T., Halvorson-Boyd, G., & Garrity, J. M. (1999). Chapter 3, Informed consent, counseling, and patient preparation. In M. Paul, E. S. Lichtenberg E. S. Borgatta, D. A. Grimes, & P. G. Stubblefield, (Eds.). *A clinician's guide to medical and surgical abortion.* Philadelphia, PA: Churchill Livingstone.

Baker, A, & Beresford, T. (2009). Chapter 5, Informed consent, patient education and counseling. In M. Paul, E. S. Lichtenberg, L. Borgatta, D. A. Grimes, G. Stubblefield, & M. D. Creinin, (Eds.). *Management of unintended and abnormal pregnancy: Comprehensive abortion care.* Chichester, UK: Wiley-Blackwell.

Baluk, U. & O'Neill, P. (1980). Health professionals' perceptions of the psychological consequences of abortion. *American Journal of Community Psychology, 8,* 67-75.

Burke, T. & Reardon, D. C. (2002). *Forbidden grief: The unspoken pain of abortion.* Springfield: Acorn Books.

Bracken, M. B., Klerman, L., Bracken, M. (1978). Coping with pregnancy resolution among never married women. *American Journal of Orthopsychiatry, 48,* 320-324.

Centers for Disease Control and Prevention. (2014, May 13). Injury prevention and control: Division of violence prevention, Data and Statistics. Retrieved from http://www.cdc.gov/violenceprevention/acestudy/prevalence.html

Coleman, P. K. (2014). Women at risk for post-abortion mental health problems and abortion associated relationship challenges. In Pontifical Academy for Life, *Post-abortion trauma: Possible psychological and existential aftermaths* (pp. 147-210). Rome: Pontifical Academy for Life. Retrieved from http://www.academiavita.org/_pdf/documents/pav/post_abortion_trauma.pdf

Condon, J. T., Corkindale, C. (1997). The correlates of antenatal attachment in pregnant women. *British Journal of Medical Psychology, 70,* 359-372.

Conklin, M. P., & O'Connor, B. P. (1995). Beliefs about the fetus as a moderator of post-abortion psychological well-being. *Journal of Social and Clinical Psychology, 14*(1), 76- 95. doi: 10.1521/jscp.1995.14.1.76

Cranley, M. (1981). Development of a tool for the measurement of maternal attachment during pregnancy. *Nursing Research 30,* 281-284.

Dykes, K., Slade, P., Haywood, A. (2010). Long term follow-up of emotional experiences after termination of pregnancy: women's views at menopause. *Journal of Reproductive and Infant Psychology,29*(1), 1-20. doi:10.1080/02646838.2010.513046 .

Feldman, R., Weller, A., Zagoory-Sharon, O., & Levine, A. (2007). Evidence for a neuroendocrinological foundation of human affiliation: Plasma oxytocin levels across pregnancy and the postpartum period predict mother-infant bonding. *Psychological Science, 18,* 965-970.

Galbally, M., Lewis, J. A., van IJzendoorn, M., & Permezel, M. (2011). The role of oxytocin in mother-infant relations: A systematic review of human studies. *Harvard Review of Psychiatry, 19*(1), 1-14.

Hamama, L., Rauch, S. A., Sperlich, M., Defever, E., Seng, J. S. (2010). Previous experience of spontaneous or elective abortion and risk for posttraumatic stress and depression during subsequent pregnancy. *Depression and Anxiety, 27*(8), 699-707. doi: 10.1002/da.20714/abstract

Hern, W. (1990). *Abortion practice.* Philadelphia: Lippincott.

Hill, A. B. (1965). The environment and disease: Association or causation? *Proceedings of the Royal Society of Medicine, 58,* 295-300. Retrieved from http://www.edwardtufte.com/tufte/hill

Kimport, K., Foster, K., & Weitz, T. A. (2011). Social sources of women's emotional difficulty after abortion: lessons from women's abortion narratives. *Perspectives on Sexual and Reproductive Health, 43*(2), 103-109.

Kjelsvik, M., & Gjengedal, E. (2011). First-time pregnant women's experience of the decision-making process related to completing or terminating pregnancy: A phenomenological study. *Scandinavian Journal of Caring Sciences, 25*(1), 169-175.

Kripke, K. (2013, May 16). Thirteen things you should know about grief after miscarriage or baby loss. *Postpartum Progress.* Retrieved from http://www.postpartumprogress.com/13-things-you-should-know-about-grief-after-miscarriage-or-baby-loss

Levine, A., Zagoory-Sharon, O., Feldman, R., & Weller, A. (2007). Oxytocin during pregnancy and the early postpartum: Individual patterns and maternal-fetal attachment. *Peptides, 28,* 1162-1169.

Lydon, J., Dunkel-Schetter, C., Cohan, C.L., & Pierce, T. (1996). Pregnancy decision-making as a significant life event: A commitment approach. *Journal of Personality and Social Psychology 71*(1), 141-151.

Major, B., Mueller, P, Hildebrandt, K. (1985). Attributions, expectations and coping with abortion. *Journal of Personality and Social Psychology, 48*(3), 585-599.

Major, B. & Cozzarelli, C. (1992). Psychosocial predictors of adjustment to abortion. *Journal of Social Issues, 48*(3), 121-142.

Mueller, P. & Major, B. (1989). Self-blame, self-efficacy, and adjustment to abortion. *Journal of Personality and Social Psychology 57*(6), 1059-1068.

Mufel, N., Speckhard, A. & Sivuha, S. (2002) Predictors of posttraumatic stress disorder following abortion in a former Soviet Union country. *Journal of Prenatal & Perinatal Psych & Health, 17,* 41-61.

Needle, R. B. & Walker, L. E. A. (2008). *Abortion counseling: A clinician's guide to psychology, legislation, politics, and competency.* New York: Springer Publishing Company.

Pereda, N., Guilera, G., Forns, M., Gomez-Benito, J. (2009). The prevalence of child sexual abuse in community and student samples: A meta-analysis. *Clinical Psychology Review, 29*(4), 328-338.

Pope, L. M., Adler N. E., Tschann, J. M. (2001). Postabortion psychological adjustment: are minors at increased risk? *Journal of Adolescent Health, 29*(1), 2-11.

Reardon, D. C. (2003). Abortion decisions and the duty to screen: Clinical, ethical, and legal implications of predictive risk factors of postabortion maladjustment. *Journal of Contemporary Health Law & Policy, 20*(1), 33-114. Retrieved from http://scholarship.law.edu/cgi/viewcontent.cgi?article=1172&context=jchlp

Remennick, L. I., & Segal, R. (2001). Sociocultural context and women's experiences of abortion: Israeli women and Russian immigrants compared. *Culture, Health, And Sexuality, 3,* 49-66. Retrieved from http://www.jstor.org/stable/3986607?seq=1#page_scan_tab_contents

Royal College of Psychiatrists (2008, March 14). Position statement on women's mental health in relation to induced abortion. London: Author. Retrieved from
http://www.patheos.com/blogs/warrenthrockmorton/2008/08/20/royal-college-of-psychiatrists-statement-on-abortion-and-mental-health/

Rue, V. M., Coleman, P. K., Rue, J. J. & Reardon, D. C. (2004). Induced abortion and traumatic stress: a preliminary comparison of American and Russian women. *Medical Science Monitor, 10*(10), SR5-16.

Stalhandske, M. L., Makenzius, M., Tyden, T., & Larsson, M. (2012) Existential experiences and needs related to induced abortion in a group of Swedish women: A quantitative investigation. *Journal of Psychosomatic Obstetrics & Gynaecology 33*(2), 53-61. doi: 10.3109/0167482X.2012.677877

Wilmoth, G. H. (1992). Abortion, public health policy, and informed consent legislation. *Journal of Social Issues, 48,* 1-17.

Wisconsin Association for Perinatal Care (2002). Position statement: Childbearing loss and grief. Retrieved from http://www.perinatalweb.org/assets/cms/ uploads/files/childbearin_loss_and_grief_statement.pdf

Zimmerman, M. K. (1977). *Passage through abortion:* The personal and social reality of women's experiences. New York: Praeger Publishers.

Chapter 8

Abortion Recovery Counseling: Pro-choice, Pro-life, and Pro-voice Common Ground

by Martha Shuping

Everyone Agrees: Counseling Should be Available

The Beijing Declaration and Platform for Action (United Nations, 1995), produced with consensus of 189 nations, was hailed by feminists worldwide as "the most progressive blueprint ever for advancing women's rights" (UN Women, 2015). This document, while not mandating legalization of abortion, states that where abortion is available, women must have prompt access to post-abortion counseling (United Nations, 1995).

Recognition by the U.N. of this need for access to post-abortion counseling is consistent with research. In 1992, the *Journal of Social Issues* dedicated an entire issue to research concerning the psychological effects of abortion. The editor stated, "There is now virtually no disagreement among researchers that some women experience negative psychological reactions postabortion" (Wilmoth, 1992, p. 5). While it is not possible to definitively state the numbers of women affected, there is no question some women experience psychological problems after abortion, and the availability of counseling or psychotherapy is a necessity.

Despite this consensus, there are divergent viewpoints regarding the time period during which counseling may be needed, the nature of the problems, and the issues to be addressed. As a result, there are very different viewpoints regarding the type of counseling that should be provided. Availability of counseling from diverse perspectives, and choice among multiple methodologies, allows the varied recovery needs to be met.

The *2015 Clinical Policy Guidelines* of the National Abortion Federation (NAF) list five references for abortion-related counseling. The book by Needle and Walker (2008) and the book by

Anne Baker (1995) are considered classics by many in regard to a pro-choice approach for post-abortion counseling. A chapter by Baker and Beresford (2009) in a textbook of the NAF, and a recent book by Alissa Perrucci (2012) are also on that list. We will rely on these resources as representative of pro-choice counseling perspectives and practices. Although in some ways clearly different from the pro-life perspective, there are several broad areas of "common ground" regarding the issues typically addressed by pro-choice and pro-life counselors.

A pro-choice counseling protocol suggests therapists address several key issues, including a need to "forgive herself if she is blaming herself in any way," to address "spiritual and religious issues," and to develop "a supportive network" (Needle & Walker, 2008, p. 149-150). Pro-life abortion recovery programs also address the need to forgive self, resolve spiritual issues, and receive support from others (Cochrane, 2015; Harper, 2008; United States Conference, 2009), with these issues thus representing "common ground" addressed by both pro-choice and pro-life counselors. In addition, the opportunity to express emotions related to the abortion, including loss or grief, is considered important by pro-choice (Needle & Walker, 2008; Baker, 1995; Perrucci, 2012), pro-voice (Aspen Baker, 2015), and pro-life authors (Cochrane, 2015; Harper, 2008; United States Conference, 2009), and by others who cannot be placed in one of the categories (Fredenberg, 2008; Wisconsin Association for Perinatal Care, 2002; Williams, 2000).

Pro-voice Post-abortion Support

Exhale is a "pro-voice" support service, founded by Aspen Baker as "a safe, confidential outlet" where women (and men also) "could express their intimate thoughts and feelings about their abortions" to "promote their health and emotional wellbeing" (Baker, 2015, p. 66). Baker states that "thousands of Internet searches for 'after-abortion' and 'abortion emotions' are made each month," and that the number of people phoning Exhale's "talkline" exceeds capacity, demonstrating the extensive need for post-abortion services (Baker, 2015, p. 53). Although Baker expresses skepticism regarding reports of psychological disorders associated with abortion, she acknowledges that many women seek out support groups through churches and pregnancy centers, or attend weekend retreats, an indication of the "need for support and connection" that "should not be ignored" (Baker, 2015, p. 51)

The core elements of the pro-voice perspective are "Listening" ("to truly understand where a person is coming from"), "Storytelling" (to "support people as they tell their own stories, in their own words, and in their own time"), and "Embrace gray areas" ("to accept the ambiguities of human experiences") (Baker, 2015, p. 25). Baker recognizes women may have various different emotions about an abortion, and points out that women who don't have a psychological disorder may still desire support or just a listening ear. Some women who have had abortions may not want to take sides as "pro-life" or "pro-choice" but want to be heard. The pro-voice Exhale is there to listen.

Baker says that women's emotions have become "the new battleground" (Baker, 2015, p. 50) with the pro-life side claiming that abortion causes severe emotional stress, while "the pro-choice movement was extremely uncomfortable with admitting any negative emotional repercussions after abortion" (Baker, 2015, p. 51). Since starting Exhale, Baker has received various complaints such as:

> "Exhale shouldn't talk about 'after-abortion' or 'postabortion' support."
> "Doesn't offering women support imply that women need it?"
> "I'm worried that your language will be co-opted or used against abortion."
> (Baker, 2015, p. 52).

Baker points out that sometimes women's stories do not match up with the preferred pro-choice or pro-life narrative, and there can be a desire to censor the stories for that reason. However, the pro-voice perspective is to allow women to tell their stories in their words and to receive support (Baker, 2015).

Fredenberg (2008) founded an organization, Abortion Changes You, that is non-religious, and focused, like Exhale, on telling one's story. Her book tells her own story, provides space for journaling, and includes chapters on building support and exploring emotions including grief and loss. Baker (2015) recognizes Fredenberg's outreach, including a website (Abortion Changes You, 2009), as similar to her own in many respects, though categorizing Fredenberg as pro-life.

Short Term vs. Long Term, Over Years or a Lifetime

There is lack of agreement regarding the time frame during which women desire counseling for abortion issues. Needle and Walker (2008) state that although "some women may have some temporary negative or ambivalent feelings" after abortion (p. xxxii) "very few women develop any emotional reaction that lasts beyond a few days post-abortion" (p. 176). "Most abortion centers find that grief reactions among women who have had abortions clear up within 6 months post-abortion even without professional intervention" (p. 113).

In contrast, Curley and Johnston (2013), in a study involving university women on three campuses in Canada and the U.S., reported that all women with an abortion in their past "reported symptoms of post-traumatic stress disorder (PTSD) and grief lasting on average 3 years," and more than half the post-abortive women desired treatment for abortion-related symptoms.

A Norwegian study, comparing post-abortive women to women who miscarried, followed the women from 10 days until 5 years after the pregnancy ended (Broen, Moum, Bødtker, & Ekeberg, 2005). At five years, the post-abortive women had significantly higher scores for guilt, shame and avoidance compared to those who miscarried, and significantly increased anxiety compared to the general public.

Kersting et al. (2005) anticipated women 2-7 years after abortion would show a significantly lower degree of traumatic experience and grief compared to women 14 days after abortion. In fact, the degree of trauma symptoms was the same for both groups. The degree of grief differed on only one subscale.

This a special case, because the abortions were due to fetal malformation, which is associated with increased risk of adverse psychological reactions (American Psychological Association, 2008; Baker & Beresford, 2009). However, these results show that for some post-abortive women, grief and trauma symptoms can persist for many years.

In a qualitative study of women at the age of menopause looking back at their abortions, "participants described the long-term emotional impact of their TOP(s) as predominantly negative" (Dykes, Slade and Haywood, 2010, p. 15). Thus, "Accessibility of post-termination counselling throughout life is recommended" (p. 1) emphasizing that counseling may be needed "not necessarily just in the immediate aftermath, but at different points after the procedure" (p. 18).

Anne Baker agrees some women may desire counseling later in life when facing "life and death issues," though she states that "most women don't need additional counseling after an abortion" (Baker, 1995, p. 186). However, Baker admits abortion clinics have little data on how most of their patients fare after the abortion. "Most abortion providers do not call patients back to find out how they are feeling, simply because of patient confidentiality. Many patients live with people whom they have not told and don't want them to find out" (Baker, 1995, p. 186). Although patients are informed they may return for counseling if desired, the "majority go on with their lives and never call back" (Baker, 1995, p. 186). She adds, "Most abortion clinics report the same experience"; most women do not return to the clinics for individual or group counseling. Needle and Walker (2008, p. xxxi) state, "Rarely do abortion centers provide counseling for women because when they did offer groups, few women came to them." That few women return to seek counseling at the abortion clinic leads to the assumption abortion patients have no need or desire for counseling.

The only routine follow up of psychological outcomes is through patient evaluation forms given to patients the day of abortion before they leave the clinic, from which, "Normally we get an 8% rate of return" (Baker, 1995, p. 186). Of the 8% who complete the form, reassuringly, the vast majority endorses their belief they made the "best decision," and they "have someone to talk to" (p. 186). However, there is no data on the 92% who did not complete the forms, and who may have had a different experience.

Thus, abortion clinics lack data on the outcomes of the majority of their patients in the short term and the long term and lack definitive information on their needs or desires regarding counseling. Since relatively little post-abortion counseling takes place at abortion clinics, clinics have limited ability to give input into what counseling methods and practices have been most helpful to those desiring counseling.

Regardless of whether the timeline is expected to be very short term or longer term, there is clear agreement that post-abortion counseling should be available when desired throughout the lifespan, and clear evidence that some women have psychological symptoms associated with their abortion which persist well beyond the immediate post-abortion period.

Common Ground: "The Forgiveness Triad"

Forgiveness therapy has been utilized, studied, and found useful in many populations, from incest survivors (Freedman & Enright, 1996) to cardiac patients (Waltman, Russell, Coyle, Enright, Holter, & Swoboda, 2008). The term "forgiveness triad" has been used to refer to three aspects of forgiveness: forgiving self, receiving forgiveness and forgiving others (Enright & Human Development, 1996, p. 107).

Most faith-based post-abortion programs include specific content to facilitate women receiving forgiveness from God, forgiving themselves, and extending forgiveness to others who may have hurt them as part of their abortion experience (Cochrane, 2015; Harper, 2008; United States Conference, 2009). In one study of faith-based abortion recovery programs with both Catholic and Protestant participation, "a prominent theme throughout the qualitative data was the women's reported facilitation of forgiveness and reconciliation . . . in relationship to others involved in the abortion decision, toward themselves personally, and with God." (Layer, Roberts, Wild & Walters, 2004). Forgiveness in these three aspects is discussed by both pro-choice and pro-life authors.

Self-Forgiveness

Counselors from all perspectives agree self-forgiveness is an issue that often must be addressed. Needle and Walker (2008, p. 150) state that pro-choice therapy should help the woman to "forgive herself if she is blaming herself in any way." This is also addressed in faith-based pro-life abortion recovery counseling. In the leader's manual for Project Rachel (the official Catholic outreach to post-abortive women), there is an entire section headed, "Self-Forgiveness" (United States Conference, 2009, pp. 19-21), which explicitly states, "she must let go of self-shame and recrimination," and that it is God's will for her to forgive herself.

Pro-choice Anne Baker gives an example of using cognitive therapy to facilitate self-forgiveness. "What is she saying to herself when she is feeling guilty? Self-forgiveness depends on the self-talk she engages in and what she does for herself" (Baker, 1995, p. 80). Rather than saying, "I don't deserve forgiveness," Baker suggests encouraging the woman to say, "I'm human and I sometimes make mistakes, just like everyone else. I forgive myself and I move on."

The Christian support group workbook *SaveOne* also addresses self-forgiveness, citing *Healing for Damaged Emotions,* by David Seamonds, who cites the Bible on forgiving others, then asks: "What if you are the brother or sister who needs to be forgiven, and you need to forgive yourself" (Harper, 2008, p. 39).

Although *SaveOne* is designed to be used for self-help or for peer-led support groups, and was not written as a tool for therapists, a cognitive approach is used in regard to forgiveness, specifically using Biblical statements and concepts to replace shame-based statements women may use in their self-talk. The workbook asks women to identify whether they are making statements such as "I'm worthless," "I've made too many mistakes," or "I don't deserve to be forgiven," (Harper, 2008, p. 54). Women are asked to consider changing their thought processes, in light of Romans 12:2 (Harper,

2008, p. 53) which urges them to be "transformed by the renewing of your mind" (New International Version). Other suggested verses include Isaiah 54:4: "the shame of your youth . . . will be remembered no more" (New Living Translation). Negative self-talk is replaced by positive self-talk based on Scripture.

Faith-based programs can be particularly effective for women of faith. Baker (1995) points out, "Self-talk and affirmations must be believed to be effective." While some women may believe their own positive self-talk after an intervention by a therapist, for many women of faith it is much more powerful to use the words of the Bible which may have a higher level of believability.

Receiving Forgiveness

Needle and Walker (2008, p. 149) identify issues related to forgiveness by God as appropriate to consider within pro-choice therapy, suggesting that the woman "explore her relationship with G-d," and that she "explore ways in which people find forgiveness in her religion." Baker (1995, p. 86) suggests that the Biblical story of the "Prodigal Son may help restore her faith in a loving, forgiving God." Harper (2008) writes of God's forgiveness using Scripture verses paired with her own explanations. "God . . . created us, and . . . has an unending supply of grace and favor with your name on it" (p. 81). *Forgiven and Set Free* (Cochrane, 2015, p. 123), the first widely used post-abortion support group workbook, originally published in 1986, encourages women to replace negative self-talk with the thought, "you are forgiven and deeply loved by our Lord." The Catholic *Project Rachel Manual* (United States Conference, 2009, p. 20), says it is God's will "that she accept . . . forgiveness and forgive herself," linking God's forgiveness with self-forgiveness and release of shame.

It is a matter of choice for the woman whether she prefers to seek help within pro-choice therapy or through her own faith community. However, abortion is often very isolating and social support is important to women's ability to cope with stress (Azar, 2010). It would seem preferable when possible for women to seek help within their own faith communities with the support of others who share their beliefs, rather than continuing in isolation.

Although pro-choice counselors sometimes fear that faith-based programs create more feelings of guilt, the materials and training process within the major faith-based programs are designed to facilitate healing and forgiveness. Most Christian post-abortion programs include women who have had abortions in leadership or peer-support roles. Women who attend faith-based programs do not experience being judged, because many of the women providing the programs have personally experienced abortion.

The need for resolution of abortion within one's own religious framework may be universal. In Thailand, which is no more than 1% Christian (thus, essentially no Christian teaching as a source of guilt), thousands of women seek resolution of guilt and shame after abortion through Buddhist ceremonies (Yongcharoenchai, 2015). Similar Buddhist and Shinto rituals are also frequently sought by women and men in Japan after abortion (Chamberlain, 1994, WuDun, 1996).

Forgiveness of Others

Pro-choice author Alissa Perrucci (2012) recognizes some women are coerced into abortions they have not freely chosen. She gives examples of a husband coercing a wife, a parent forcing a daughter (citing a study by Henshaw and Kost, 1992, in which teens reported being forced), as we cover in more detail in Chapter 2. Women involved in intimate partner violence may be forced by a partner to have an abortion, as we cover in more detail in Chapter 1. Women in these circumstances may have anger toward those who pressured them or who failed to give the support they desired. Men also may experience anger in cases in which the woman chose abortion when the man desired to continue the pregnancy.

Anne Baker (1995) gives an example of a woman who experienced reproductive coercion, whose partner used condoms but later admitted to having put holes in the condoms, intending to cause pregnancy. She suggests that a woman in this situation write a letter to express her anger, imagining her partner hearing her anger, possibly reading the letter aloud to a friend to "have a good laugh over it" (p. 89).

In fact, in the Rachel's Vineyard retreat protocol, a substantial amount of time is set aside for women to write such a letter, to partners or parents, but when letters are read within the group, there is no laughter. The strong emotions are validated by peers. Then women may be ready to release anger through a cognitive restructuring exercise, or other activities.

I have conducted more than fifty Rachel's Vineyard retreats. During the instructions for the "anger letters" women are encouraged to write a letter (not to be sent) to anyone toward whom the woman feels angry or "unfinished." Women are not instructed to whom the letter should be directed, and the abortion clinic or abortion providers are not suggested as possible candidates. Nor is there any content within the retreat that specifically addresses issues related to the clinic or providers, unless a woman spontaneously discloses emotions of her clinic experience. Nonetheless, it is not infrequent that women direct their expression of anger toward the clinic, the counselor or the provider, if they feel that they received poor counseling or were not protected from coercion. Nonetheless, the exercise is directed toward expression of anger, so the women is free to release it and be at peace, not to continue harboring anger counter-productive to her recovery.

The Project Rachel Manual also includes sections on expression of anger and forgiveness of others, recommending women write a letter to express anger, possibly sharing the letter with a priest, and then choosing to symbolically release the anger by burning or burying the letter (United States Conference, 2009). Most faith-based abortion recovery workbooks and support groups for men and women facilitate forgiveness of others (Cochrane, 2015; Harper, 2008).

It is important to note there is no specific protocol for any post-abortion treatment that has been established as "empirically validated treatment" for treatment of issues related to abortion (Needle & Walker, 2008). However, there has been a meta-analysis conducted on nine different published studies of forgiveness therapy protocols, with a conclusion that "process-based group interventions showed significant effects, and the process-based individual interventions showed large effects. Consequently, effectiveness has been shown for use of forgiveness in clinical and other settings" (Baskin & Enright, 2004). In discussing the specific criteria for a treatment to be declared as "empirically-supported treatment" (Chambless & Hollon, 1998), Baskin & Enright note that across the body of research, all requirements have been met, such as a written manual, and comparison with a psychological placebo or against an existing treatment. However, all requirements have not been met by the same protocol meeting all requirements and then being replicated by a second research team. Thus, Baskin and Enright suggest that forgiveness therapy protocols should be considered in an older categorization of "Probably Efficacious Treatments," though additional properly designed research may establish some as "empirically supported therapies" in future.

Forgiveness Intervention Program for Post-Abortion Men

One of the few studies designed to scientifically test a post-abortion healing program involved men whose partners elected to have an abortion (Coyle & Enright, 1997). The intervention was based on a psychological process model of forgiveness. The model includes twenty steps or units divided into four phases: (a) Uncovering phase, (b) Decision phase, (c) Work phase, and (d) Outcome phase. The model is not intended to be linear with fixed steps to occur in a rigid order. Rather, as individuals work toward forgiveness, they may work on some of the steps more than once or may skip some steps. Each individual's forgiveness journey is unique but follows a somewhat similar process. The model may be applied to forgiving another, forgiving self and receiving forgiveness (Enright & the Human Development Study Group, 1996).

Ten men who self-identified as having been hurt by a partner's abortion participated in the Coyle and Enright (1997) study. The age ranged from 21 to 43 years and their partners' abortions occurred from six months to 22 years prior to their participation. Six were Christian, one Muslim, and three agnostic.

Five were opposed to their partner's abortion, one was supportive, and one was not informed of it until months after it occurred. The remaining three were ambivalent.

Participants were randomly assigned to either the treatment or the wait-list control group. Those in the control group received the treatment after a 12-week waiting period. All were administered pre- and post-tests to evaluate the effectiveness of the intervention. This was provided on an individual basis by a nurse therapist once per week for 12 weeks. Following treatment, participants demonstrated significant gain in forgiveness and reductions in anger, anxiety, and grief as compared with controls. Similar significant findings were evident among control participants after they participated in the treatment program.

Considering the forgiveness process model has proven effective with many populations and different types of injuries (Baskin & Enright, 2004), it is likely the same process could be used successfully with post-abortive women also. Use of this protocol would involve a longer process with a different structure compared to the currently available faith-based group programs or retreats, and it is also a more structured approach to forgiveness than in the suggested pro-choice counseling. However, this may be useful for any women who continue to have unresolved issues after completion of pro-life or pro-choice counseling or recovery programs. Its design may make it particularly appropriate for those who prefer a program that is not faith-based; there is nothing about the protocol that should link it specifically to a pro-choice or pro-life viewpoint.

Common Ground: Developing a Support System

Lack of emotional support has been identified as a risk factor predisposing to mental health problems after abortion (American Psychological Association, 2008; Baker & Beresford, 2009; Baker et al., 1999), so it makes sense that Needle and Walker (2008) view establishing support as a key piece in abortion recovery. The supportive group format of their suggested post-abortion counseling protocol provides built-in support from other women, and encourages women to draw on their own support system of family or friends, or to build a new support network if needed. Women are encouraged to go out for coffee with others, or join a bicycle club.

Pro-life abortion recovery programs also frequently use weekly support group formats for a period of 6 to 12 weeks, or a weekend retreat program which allows for interaction and mutual support by participants. Some faith-based programs (for example, Rachel's Vineyard and Save-One) allow husbands and wives to participate together if desired, or participants may bring a family member or close friend as a support person. This helps broaden the woman's support network, since the person who accompanies her will learn more about the woman's experience and be better prepared to be a support to her later. In addition, the Rachel's Vineyard weekend has a religious service to give closure on the final day of the weekend retreat, and each person is able to invite family members or friends if desired, again broadening their support network; there is also time built in on the last day to discuss follow-up plans for continuing to receive any needed support when they return home.

Aspen Baker says about 15% of Exhale's talkline callers are friends, immediate family or partners of the post-abortive woman, though she doesn't say whether these callers are seeking support for themselves because of their feelings or because they want to learn how to support the woman. Both Rachel's Vineyard and SaveOne have the policy of allowing anyone affected by an abortion to come and receive support for themselves, so a family member or husband could participate on their own if they wish, to deal with their own emotions.

Abortion can be a very isolating experience. In many cases, women had the abortion to keep their pregnancy secret. Yet a high degree of secrecy is also a risk factor for mental health problems (American Psychological Association, 2008; Baker & Beresford, 2009). In a study of participants in faith-based support programs, about half reported two or fewer people knew about their abortion, so they had few people they could talk to outside the group (Layer, 2005). McAll and Wilson (1987) pointed out that often the few who know about the abortion sometimes prefer not to talk about it (for example, a parent or partner who desired the abortion to keep the pregnancy secret). A group program provides social support that is vitally needed for many women.

The post-abortion treatment protocol outlined by Needle and Walker (2008) suggests group or individual therapy. However, they acknowledge it is rare for an abortion center to provide counseling because in the past, few women have sought counseling or support at abortion clinics. On the other hand, Aspen Baker (2015, p. 51) notes the existence of "hundreds if not thousands of post-abortion service providers" located in churches, pregnancy centers and retreat venues, and the fact that women actively seek help through these programs. Stacy Massey (personal communication, November 3, 2015) states that 55,000 people seek referrals for abortion recovery counseling through the online Care Directory of Abortion Recovery International, which lists thousands of providers. Rachel's Vineyard (2016) reports providing nearly 1,000 retreats annually, in 48 states and 57 countries.

Common Ground: Grief

The counseling protocol suggested by Needle and Walker (2008, p. 149) suggests exploration of the woman's emotions, whether positive or negative, including grief: "If a woman needs to cry or grieve, allow her to do so." Perrucci (2012, p. 41), in discussing pre-abortion counseling, gives an example of a patient who says, "I will miss the baby after it's gone," indicating that loss of the child may be a source of grief for some women. Anne Baker has a chapter titled "Exploring the Client's Feelings about the Abortion," that includes a section on "Sadness and Loss" (1995, p. 80-81). Baker states there may be a number of causes for sadness, but identifies that some women experience grief in regard to the loss of the baby. Baker suggests asking the woman how she has coped with losses in the past, to help her to utilize similar coping mechanisms. Baker states that "not all women feel sad about an abortion," and some "feel no loss" (p. 81). But it is acknowledged by pro-choice (Baker, 1995; Perrucci, 2012), pro-life (Burke, 1994; Burke & Reardon, 2002; Cochrane, 2015; Harper, 2008; Layer et al., 2004; McAll & Wilson, 1987; United States Conference, 2009), pro-voice (Baker, 2015) and apparently neutral authors (Fredenberg, 2008; Fredenberg, et al., 2011; Wisconsin Association for Perinatal Care, 2002; Williams, 2000) that some women do experience grief associated with the loss of the child, and that helping women resolve grief issues is within the scope of abortion counseling. Although there are complex differences regarding how this grief is conceptualized and addressed by authors of varied perspectives, recognition that grief counseling may be needed by some women represents an area of common ground.

A small study of 83 women revealed mild grief an average of 11 years after elective abortion (Williams, 2000). Some women reported this was the first opportunity they had to discuss their abortion, and that participating in the study provided validation of their feelings. Williams suggests that due to the controversy surrounding abortion, some women may feel unable to express their grief (also a theme of Burke and Reardon, 2002, in their book *Forbidden Grief,* and recognized as disenfranchised grief by Speckhard and Rue, 1993). Williams (2000) recommends that counseling should be offered to all women after abortion, since there is currently no way to predict which women may be at higher risk for developing grief of longer duration or greater intensity, and that intervention immediately after termination may prevent development of complicated grief. Williams also states that much more research is needed to better understand grief after abortion.

The Wisconsin Association for Perinatal Care issued a position statement on "Childbearing Loss and Grief" (2002, p. 6) recognizing grief associated with sixteen types of reproductive loss, including elective abortion and abortion induced for medical reasons. Suggested interventions after abortion include "mementos" or "ritual" appropriate to the woman's beliefs (p. 6). Perrucci also suggests that "maintaining a connection through a ritual or a memento" may be helpful for some women (2012, p. 42).

Ritual may be as simple as the lighting of a candle by a Swedish woman (Stalhandske, Makenzius, Tyden, & Larsson, 2012) or as complex as the mizuko kuyō ritual performed in Japan and at Buddhist centers in the U.S. (Wilson, 2009). McAll and Wilson (1987) reported on a series of cases in which ritual mourning (a

Memorial service that included Christian Communion) was observed to be helpful to psychiatric patients and their families in resolving grief and improving psychiatric symptoms. Tentoni, in a paper presented at the American Psychological Association convention in 1993, reported on his experience in having women return to the abortion clinic, and sit outside for a few minutes to talk to the fetus; if they wished, "they could leave something behind as an offering" (p. 4).

A 2004 study used a pretest-posttest design to evaluate a faith-based group intervention with participants drawn from Catholic and nondenominational Christian agencies (Layer et al., 2004; Layer, 2005). Data analysis revealed statistically significant reductions in shame, avoidance, and hyperarousal. In a qualitative portion of the research, the majority of women identified grieving rituals as being among the most beneficial elements of the intervention, including writing letters to the child and to God, and more than 80% reported their religious beliefs were important in resolving their grief. The model studied by Layer, et al. (2004) is similar to many faith-based interventions currently in use (Cochrane, 2015; Harper, 2008; United States Conference 2009).

Nancy Buckles, while Acting Director of Counseling and Psychological Services at Indiana University, developed a secular approach, utilizing gestalt therapy over a period of several weeks, to facilitate resolution of grief. "Women who need to say goodbye to a fetus need to let go of the affect still attached to it. Yet the existence of that fetus and its impact on their lives is something these women clearly do not want to forget. The second part of the process, then, becomes the establishing of positive remembrance of the significant meaning of its existence to the woman" (Buckles, 1992, p. 181). In this process, women first express "appreciations, resentments, and regrets" (p. 181), then create a memorial such as a sculpture, or a garden, or something meaningful to the woman.

Mementos or "memorials" are frequently used in processing grief after any pregnancy loss, including abortion. The *Project Rachel Manual* suggests examples such as a statue of an angel with a child, a locket, or a tree planted in the yard (United States Conference, 2009). Harper (2008) gives an example of a single candle placed with family photos, or something creative to be completed over time such as painting a mural or planting a garden. Creation of gardens has become a very popular means of processing grief of any reproductive loss; many websites and blogs, associated with individuals or with pregnancy loss organizations (without focusing specifically on abortion) provide advice for designing memorial gardens (Czukas, 2015).

The Rachel's Vineyard model incorporates many elements similar to those used in other interventions, including grieving rituals such as lighting a candle, naming the child, and receiving mementos that are provided at a Memorial service. A review article (Zeanah, 1989) states that current practices in caring for families after perinatal loss include encouraging the parents "to name the child and to plan a memorial service congruent with their religious beliefs" (p. 467).

An outcome survey on the Rachel's Vineyard program (Shuping, 2004) was distributed to 263 participants of weekend retreats in 22 states, with 242 responding. Participants were asked to rate their experience using a negative number if harmful, a zero if neither helpful nor harmful, or positive numbers 1 - 5 if helpful, with 5 being the most helpful. There were no negative ratings and no ratings of zero; the average rating was 4.75, indicating a high degree of reported benefit. Those surveyed were primarily in two clusters: one cluster had attended the retreat within an average of 4.8 months previously, and the other had attended a retreat on average 3 years previously. This was intended as a pilot study, using a convenience sample, and additional research is needed. However, it appears that many participants experience the Rachel's Vineyard as helpful, and that results may be of enduring benefit.

Although the possibility of grief after abortion and the potential need to address this in a counseling or support process is acknowledged by authors from all perspectives (pro-choice, pro-life, pro-voice, and others), there are differences from one intervention to another, making each unique in some ways. Additional research is needed to identify which protocols and which specific elements are most beneficial, though because of the diversity of women and men seeking help, availability of multiple types of interventions may be useful.

Conclusion

Even though we have identified some issues of common ground that exist between pro-life and pro-choice counseling and support programs, and a need for much more research on efficacy of different programs, there may be some important differences between therapy from pro-choice or pro-life perspectives. Examining differences in perspective or theoretical approach, and differences in practices between the two types of providers, may help us understand why some women experience a preference for one type of support over another.

References

Abortion Changes You. (2009). Retrieved from
    http://www.abortionchangesyou.com

American Psychological Association Task Force on Mental Health and Abortion. (2008). *Report of the task force on mental health and abortion.* Washington, DC: Author. Retrieved from www.apa/org/pi/wpo/mental-health-abortion-report.pdf

Azar, B. (2000). A new stress paradigm for women. *Monitor on Psychology, 31*(7), 42. Retrieved from
    http://www.apa.org/monitor/julaug00/stress.aspx

Baker, A. (2015). *Pro voice: How to keep listening when the world wants a fight.* Oakland: Berrett-Koehler Publishers, Inc.

Baker, A. (1995). *Abortion and options counseling: A comprehensive reference,* revised and expanded edition. Granite City: Hope Clinic for Women.

Baker, A., Beresford, T., Halvorson-Boyd, G., & Garrity, J. M. (1999). Chapter 3, Informed consent, counseling, and patient preparation. In M. Paul, E. S. Lichtenberg, L. Borgatta, D.A. Grimes, & P. G. Stubblefield (Eds.). *A clinician's guide to medical and surgical abortion.* Philadelphia, PA: Churchill Livingstone.

Baker, A., & Beresford, T. (2009). Chapter 5, Informed consent, patient education and counseling. In M. Paul, E. S. Lichtenberg, L. Borgatta, L., D. A. Grimes, P. G. Stubblefield & M. D. Creinin (Eds.). *Management of unintended and abnormal pregnancy: Comprehensive abortion care.* Chichester, UK: Wiley-Blackwell.

Baskin, T. W. & Enright, R. D. (2004). Intervention studies on forgiveness: A meta-analysis. *Journal of Counseling and Development, 82,* 79-90.

Broen, A. N., Moum, T., Bødtker, A. S., & Ekeberg, Ø. (2005). The course of mental health after miscarriage and induced abortion: a longitudinal, five-year follow-up study. *BMC Medicine, 3,*18. doi: 10.1186/1741-7015-3-18

Buckles N. B. (1982). Abortion: A technique for working through grief. *Journal of the American College Health Association, 30,* 181-182. doi: 10.1080/01644300.1981.10393070

Burke, T., & Reardon, D. C. (2002). *Forbidden grief: The unspoken pain of abortion.* Springfield: Acorn Books.

Burke, T. K. (1994). *Rachel's Vineyard: A psychological and spiritual journey of post-abortion healing: A model for groups.* Staten Island: Alba House.

Chambless, D. L., & Hollon, S. D. (1998). Defining empirically supported therapies. *Journal of Consulting and Clinical Psychology, 66*(1), 7-18.

Chamberlain, G. L. (1994, Sept. 17). Learning from the Japanese (pro-life rituals in Buddhism and Shinto). *America, 171*(7), 14-16. Retrieved from http://ccbs.ntu.edu.tw/FULLTEXT/JR-EPT/gary.htm

Cochrane, L. (2015). *Forgiven and set free: A post-abortion Bible study for women, revised and updated edition.* Grand Rapids: Baker Books.

Coyle, C. T. & Enright, R. D. (1997). Forgiveness intervention with postabortion men. *Journal of Counseling and Clinical Psychology, 65*(6), 1042-1046.

Curley, M., & Johnston, C. (2013). The characteristics and severity of psychological distress after abortion among university students. *The Journal of Behavioral Health Services & Research, 40*(3). doi: 10.1007/s11414-013-9328-0

Czukas, E. (2015). Planning a memorial garden after a pregnancy loss. Retrieved from http://miscarriage.about.com/ od/rememberingyourbaby/a/Planning-A-Memorial-Garden-After-A-Pregnancy-Loss.htm

Dykes, K., Slade, P., Haywood, A. (2010). Long term follow-up of emotional experiences after termination of pregnancy: women's views at menopause. *Journal of Reproductive and Infant Psychology,* 1-20. doi:10.1080/02646838.2010.513046

Enright, R. D. & the Human Development Study Group. (1996). Counseling within the forgiveness triad: On forgiving, receiving forgiveness, and self-forgiveness. *Counseling and Values, 40,* 107-126.

Fredenburg, M. (2008). *Changed: Making sense of your own or a loved one's abortion experience.* San Diego: Perspectives.

Fredenburg, M., Gaul, M., Stewart, L., and Strauss, G. (2011). *Grief and abortion: Creating a safe place to heal.* San Diego: Perspectives.

Freedman, S. R., and Enright, R. D. (1996). Forgiveness as an intervention goal with incest survivors. *Journal of Consulting Clinical Psychology, 64*(5), 983-92.

Harper, S. (2008). *SaveOne: A guide to emotional healing after abortion.* Garden City, NY: Morgan James Publishing.

Henshaw, S. & Kost, K. (1992). Parental involvement in minors' abortion decisions. *Family Planning Perspectives, 25*(4), 196-204.

Kersting, A., Dorsch, M., Kreulich, C., Reutemann, M., Ohrmann, P., Baez, E., & Arolt, V. (2005). Trauma and grief 2–7 years after termination of pregnancy because of fetal anomalies – a pilot study. *Journal of Psychosomatic Obstetrics & Gynecology, 26*(1), 9-14. Retrieved from http://www.ncbi.nlm.nih.gov/pubmed/15962717

Layer, S. D, Roberts, C., Wild, K., and Walters, J. (2004). Postabortion grief: evaluating the possible efficacy of a spiritual group intervention. *Research on Social Work Practice, 14*(5), 344-350.

Layer, S. D. (2005). New research shows benefits of post-abortion grief groups. *Center of Tomorrow, 1*(4), 1162-1169.

McAll, K., & Wilson, W. P. (1987). Ritual mourning for unresolved grief after abortion.   *Southern Medical Journal, 80*(7), 817-821

National Abortion Federation (2015). *2015 Clinical Policy Guidelines.* Washington, DC: National Abortion Federation. Retrieved from http://prochoice.org/wp-content/uploads/2015_NAF_CPGs.pdf

Needle, R., and Walker, L. (2008). *Abortion counseling: A clinician's guide to psychology, legislation, politics, and competency.* New York: Springer Publishing Company.

Perrucci, A. C. (2012). *Decision, assessment and counseling in abortion care: Philosophy and practice.* Lanham, MD: Rowman & Littlefield.

Rachel's Vineyard (2016). Retreat schedules. Retrieved from http://www.rachelsvineyard.org/weekend/retreat-schedule-index.aspx

Shuping, M. W. (2004). Rachel's Vineyard outcome survey. Paper presented at Rachel's Vineyard Leader's Conference, Greensboro, NC.

Speckhard, A., & Rue, V. (1993). Complicated mourning: Dynamics of impacted post abortion grief. *Pre-and Peri-natal Psychology Journal, 8*(1), 5-32.

Stalhandske, M. L., Makenzius, M., Tyden, T., & Larsson, M. (2012) Existential experiences and needs related to induced abortion in a group of Swedish women: a quantitative investigation. *Journal of Psychosomatic Obstetrics and Gynecology, 33*(2), 53-61. doi: 10.3109/0167482X.2012.677877

Tentoni, S. C. (1993). Post-abortion counseling: Helping to heal the grief. Paper presented at the 101st meeting of the American Psychological Association, Toronto, Ontario, Canada.

United States Conference of Catholic Bishops (2009). *Project Rachel ministry: A post-abortion resource manual for priests and Project Rachel leaders.* Washington, DC: Author. Retrieved from http://hope afterabortion.com/wp-content/uploads/PDFs/ProjectRachelmanual-ENG

United Nations. (1995). *Beijing Declaration and platform for action.* New York: Author, Retrieved from http://www.un.org/esa/gopher-data/conf/fwcw/off/a--20.en

UN Women. (2015). The Beijing Platform for Action: Inspiration then and now. Retrieved from http://beijing20.unwomen.org/en/about

Waltman, M.A., Russell, D.C., Coyle, C.T., Enright, R.D., Holter, A.C., Swoboda, C.M. (2008). The effects of a forgiveness intervention on patients with coronary artery disease. *Psychology and Health.* doi: 10.1080/08870440801975127

Williams, G. B. (2000). Grief after elective abortion: Exploring nursing interventions for another kind of perinatal loss. *AWHONN Lifelines, 4*(2), 37-40.

Wilmoth, G. H. (1992). Abortion, public health policy, and informed consent legislation. *Journal of Social Issues, 48,* 1-17.

Wilson, J. (2009). *Mourning the unborn dead: A Buddhist ritual comes to America.* New York: Oxford University Press.

Wisconsin Association for Perinatal Care (2002). Position statement: Childbearing loss and grief. Retrieved from http://www.perinatalweb.org/assets/cms/uploads/files/childbearin_loss_and_grief_statement.pdf

WuDunn, S. (1996, January 25). In Japan, a ritual of mourning for abortions. *New York Times.* Retrieved from http://www.nytimes.com/1996/01/25/world/in-japan-a-ritual-of-mourning-for-abortions.html?pagewanted=all

Yongcharoenchai, C. (2015). Haunted by the ghosts of abortion. *Bangkok Post,* June 14. Retrieved from http://www.bangkokpost.com/news/special-reports/591353/haunted-by-the-ghosts-of-abortion

Zeanah, C. H. (1989). Adaptation following perinatal loss: A critical review. *Journal of the American Academy of Child & Adolescent Psychiatry, 28*(4), 467-631.

Chapter 9

The Case that Abortion is Not a Threat to Women's Mental Health

A Summary of the
Report of the American Psychological Association
Task Force on Mental Health and Abortion
Composed by Rachel M. MacNair

The political position of the American Psychological Association (APA) on abortion is to favor its availability as a matter of women's rights. APA has appointed two task forces. The first one had a report published in 1989, and a follow-up task force began in 2006. Both were composed of people who agreed with APA's political position. Their charge was to consider the empirical evidence about the aftermath of abortion on those women who have them. The final version of the recent task force's report is in the *American Psychologist* (Major, et al., 2009). A 105-page earlier version of the report is on the web (American Psychological Association Task Force, 2008). This report is at the time of this writing the most comprehensive perspective on the data from the abortion-as-option perspective. The wording "not a threat to women's health" comes from the press release announcing the report on August 12, 2008. Below we detail ideas for that report that anyone interested in this area should be familiar with. We save any critique for Chapter 10.

Summarizer Rachel M. MacNair served as one of 20 reviewers of the original draft of the report

Task Force members
(in the same order as authors are listed in the report):
Left, Brenda Major
Right: Mark Appelbaum

Left: Linda Beckman
Right: Mary Ann Dutton

Left: Nancy Felipe Russo
Right: Carolyn M. West.

Framing the Question

The first consideration is how the research question is framed. This will be crucial to how research is designed and what conclusions are drawn.

We start with the common question of the political discourse: "Does abortion cause harm to women's mental health?" (Major et al., 2009, p. 864). Scientifically, the best way to determine causation would be to have random clinical trials with a control group. Yet randomly assigning some women to become pregnant with unwanted pregnancies and then randomly assigning some of them to have abortions and others not to would have obvious ethical problems even if the huge practical problems could be overcome – that is to say, it is out of the question.

It is possible to posit causality with prospective longitudinal studies. "Prospective" means the sample is started before the time of abortion or non-aborted pregnancy occurs, in contrast to

~ 139 ~

"retrospective" designs in which the data rely on people's memories of what occurred in the past. With retrospective studies, the selection process of who is in the sample could be biased by such memories or other factors. "Longitudinal" means a long-term study in which data are taken from the same people at different times, as opposed to the "cross-sectional" study such as surveys that simply take the data at one point in time. Prospective longitudinal studies are therefore much more expensive and time-consuming and involve keeping track of people over time.

Such studies can help establish causality as long as the abortion occurred before the mental health outcome variable and there is covariation with it. Additionally, other variables must be controlled for, variables that might have to do with both abortion and the mental health outcome, so that alternative explanations are ruled out.

For example, a woman may be more likely to get an abortion after having been subjected to intimate partner violence, but is later distress due to the abortion only, the domestic violence only, or both? Even with controlling for other variables, it is not certain that all possible alternative explanations have been considered. Women have reasons for their abortions, after all, and those reasons are often associated with stressors.

Another way of framing the question is: "What is the prevalence of clinically significant mental disorders among women who have had an abortion?" (Major et al., 2009, p. 865). This first requires having a clearly defined representative sample of women with similar characteristics, and knowing what the prevalence of clinical disorders is among those who have never had abortions. Then, any observed differences in the incidence of those disorders between women who have and who have not undergone abortion may inform us about the prevalence among women who have had abortions.

A problem with this, however, is that women who have not had abortions because they have never been pregnant do not provide relevant information concerning the best policy for women who are in fact pregnant and do not wish to be. Avoiding a medical procedure by having no need of such a procedure can be expected to be better for mental health than having a problem and then a procedure. No one would argue that putting casts on broken legs is inadvisable simply because the casting experience was stressful. While never having a broken leg is not stressful, once the leg is broken, having it treated is better than not having it treated.

Therefore, a third way of framing the question is: "What is the relative risk of mental health problems associated with abortion compared with the risk associated with other courses of action that might be taken by a pregnant woman in similar circumstances (i.e., facing an unwanted pregnancy)?" (Major et al., 2009, p. 865). If women have never been pregnant, or if they planned a pregnancy and are delighted, then they do not constitute a proper comparison group. A more appropriate comparison group would be women who gave a child up for adoption or initially felt unable to care for a child they gave birth to – thereby controlling for the initial "wantedness" of the pregnancy.

Furthermore, this question still ignores an important point, which is that women experience abortion quite differently. They have different personalities, social contexts, reasons, and so on. So a final question is: "What predicts individual variation in women's psychological experiences following abortion?"

Conceptual Frameworks

There are four conceptual frameworks which have framed the research designs:

Traumatic Experience

This is the view from the abortion-as-violence perspective and will be covered in more detail in Chapter 10.

Stress and Coping

Any medical procedure carries some stress. In addition, the condition that led to the procedure is an additional stressor, and it can be difficult to disentangle the two forms of stress in terms of understanding the cause of any problems experienced after the procedure. Again, we are dealing with women who are already pregnant and therefore whose options are now narrowed down to terminating or giving birth:

> Research derived from a stress-and-coping perspective has identified several factors that are associated with more negative psychological reaction . . . . The most important of these is a history of mental health problems prior to the pregnancy. Other factors . . . include terminating a pregnancy that is wanted or meaningful, perceived pressure from others to terminate a pregnancy, a lack of perceived social support for mothers, and certain personality traits that increase vulnerability to stressors (e.g., low self-esteem, a pessimistic outlook, low perceived control) . . . the same factors for adverse reactions to abortion can also be factors for adverse reactions to its alternatives. (Major et al. 2009, p. 867)

The Sociocultural Context

The psychological experience will be strongly influenced by the larger social context in which women find themselves. Most particularly:

> Societal stigma is particularly pernicious when it leads to "internalized stigma" – the acceptance by some members of a marginalized group of the negative societal beliefs and stereotypes about themselves. Women who come to internalize stigma associated with abortion (e.g., who see themselves as tainted, flawed, or morally deficient) are likely to be particularly vulnerable to later psychological distress. A sociocultural context that encourages women to believe that they "should" or "will" feel a particular way after an abortion can create a self-fulfilling prophecy. (Major et al. 2009, p. 867)

Social messages that cause negative appraisals can be expected to cause greater distress than social messages that involve positive or benign ways of appraising the experience.

Co-occurring Risk Factors

Risk factors such as poverty, a history of emotional problems, or suffering from violent incidents including intimate partner violence will underlie both unwanted pregnancy and make a subsequent abortion more likely. Therefore, studies which simply show greater problems for women who have abortions tell us nothing. Such women would still have problems in the absence of abortion.

It is also common that problematic behaviors co-occur in the same individuals – including smoking, substance abuse, unprotected sexual intercourse – so that selecting women with abortions means selecting a disproportionate number of such individuals. The absence of abortion might make little or no difference, or may make matters worse.

Personality factors can also make unplanned pregnancy and abortion more likely. High impulsivity, and an avoidance style of coping with negative emotions, for example, are risk factors for delinquent behavior, doing poorly in school, substance abuse, and risky sexual behavior. The same characteristics that put women at risk for both problem behavior and unplanned pregnancy also put them at risk for poor mental health outcomes, no matter what the outcome of the pregnancy is.

The Review

The papers reviewed involved:

- Studies published in peer-reviewed journals
- Published in English
- From 1989 to 2008 (that is, not including studies from the previous task force's report)
- Measured an outcome of mental health subsequent to induced abortion
- Included a proper comparison group of women
- Mental health problems refers to clinically significant disorders

This came to 58 papers, primarily U.S. studies but some international samples as well.

Common methodological concerns included:

- **Inappropriate comparison groups**
Women without pregnancies or with planned-for pregnancies give no information of the impact concerning those women with unplanned pregnancies.

- **Inadequate control for co-occurring risk factors**

We must distinguish between sequelae of the abortion itself and associated outcomes that would still have occurred in the absence of abortion.

- **Sampling bias**

Women willing to participate in studies will be different from women who are not willing to, and this is especially so in the context where a country's laws are fairly restrictive. This threatens the generalizability of the findings.

- **Problems of under-reporting**

When the method of finding out if a woman has had an abortion is to ask her, this "retrospective recall" technique ordinarily suffers from the vagaries that go with people's memories. However, it has been noted to be especially problematic with abortion. Some women may honestly not remember the occurrence because they do not wish to, and many will remember but not feel comfortable in disclosing such a detail to a survey-taking stranger. Surveys commonly show a lower portion of women indicating they have had an abortion than would be expected from provider data. Particular groups may also be more likely to under-report – the unmarried, those of religions that oppose abortion, etc. – and this introduces a systematic bias into the sample.

In addition, there's a problem common to all studies with retrospective recall: those people who have disorders may be more likely to remember incidents and more likely to attribute current problems to them than people who have no such disorder.

- **Under-specification**

Details such as gestational age, type of procedure, or reason for the abortion are not included in the data, and any of these may have an impact on the emotional repercussions.

- **Attrition**

For any longitudinal study, there is a problem that some people who offered data at one time point may no longer be responsive at another point. The percentage of those who do not respond is the *attrition rate*. Experience has shown this to be especially high in studies of women who have had abortions. Those who dropped out may do so because they are more troubled and therefore do not wish to focus on the issues that the study requires of them. Alternatively, they may be less troubled and therefore less interested in further processing of a long-past minor experience. They also may not be particularly different from those that do respond, since making one's self available to researchers is often an activity the ordinary person does not prioritize. There is no way to know; they did not respond.

- **Poor outcome measurement**

Some studies actually have only one item to measure a mental health outcome, or otherwise have measurements which are inadequate. Still other studies only focused on negative outcomes, not taking benefits into account.

- **Statistical problems**

Doing too many tests for statistical significance means results of one test can be due to chance. The way "significance" is usually measured is to find a significance value of .05 or less, meaning a .05 (or less) probability of one test's result being due to chance. This upper limit is the same as five out of 100, or one in 20, of a probability of being due to chance. Run 20 tests, and one of them can easily come up with that .05 significance figure – but only due to chance. Even with only five tests, the researcher is more likely to come up with a significant finding which is actually due to chance rather than to the variable under study. There are several ways of handling this (pay attention in statistics class!), but may be a big problem if not done correctly.

- **Interpretation problems**

    Correlation is not causation, as discussed previously in the sub-section on co-occurring risk factors.

Most of the studies have one or more of these problems. One cannot learn about post-abortion aftermath by simply considering the number of studies that conclude one thing as opposed to the number of studies that draw a different conclusion. The quality of the studies must be taken into account.

Review of Studies

Secondary Studies Based on Already-Existing Medical Records and Large Surveys

A recent trend involves more studies based on large medical data bases already collected and large longitudinal studies already completed for other purposes. Each of these types of studies has large data sets that are useful for exploring the relationship between abortion and mental health. In the case of medical records, a major advantage is avoiding the problem of recall bias, in that the abortions are in the data base. For large data sets of either medical records or of surveys such as the National Longitudinal Survey of Youth, advantages include the fact that the prospective and longitudinal data are already collected, that the samples are already designed to be representative of the general population, and that attrition does not pose the same problems as for direct research on women known to have had abortions.

Still, problems as outlined above showed up in some of these studies and included not controlling for variables, not taking pre-abortion variables and characteristics of the abortion itself into account, and a lack of proper comparison groups. Context of abortions is also not included, only the fact that they happened.

Most studies were on U.S. data bases, but there were also studies done in Finland, Australia, New Zealand, and Norway. These all have different cultural contexts that may impact the findings.

~ 147 ~

Primary Data

Twenty papers were derived from research for which the data were collected by the researchers. The major ones were from the U.S., Norway, and Great Britain. Many of these studies suffered from the limitations outlined above.

Fetal Abnormality

This area suffers especially from low response rates and high attrition rates, many with inordinately small sample sizes. Not surprisingly, studies show that women who have a second-trimester abortion of what had previously been a wanted pregnancy for reasons of abnormality in the fetus suffered negative psychological aftermath. Nevertheless, this was not different from women who suffered a miscarriage at this point in the pregnancy; perinatal loss of wanted pregnancies is distressing.

Abortion-Only Studies

Though lack of any comparison group at all does not fit the inclusion criteria, these studies are still useful for identifying the points of variation in women's abortion experiences. The retrospective studies are too problematic to use, but some prospective studies are useful.

The women at higher risk two years after the abortion were those who had:

- a prior history of mental health problems
- younger age at the time of the abortion
- low social support, perceived or anticipated
- greater personal conflict about abortion
- low sense of their ability to cope with the abortion

Two studies considered specifically the effect of anti-abortion picketing of the clinic at the time the women seeking abortions came to the clinic. Cozzarelli and Major (1994) found that the more upset the women were, and the more aggressive the picketers were (as coded by observers), the greater the depression reported afterward. This was mitigated when pro-choice escorts were available, changing the context. A two-year follow-up found that the short-term impact had not become long-term, so negative psychological effects had dissipated (Cozzarelli, Major, Karrasch, & Fuegen, 2000).

Perceived stigma is found, with Major and Gramzow (1999) reporting that 45% in their sample felt a need to keep their abortion a secret from family and friends. (This adds to the observation that asking women in surveys if they have had an abortion is not the most effective or accurate way of finding out).

> Perceived need for secrecy, in turn, was associated with less disclosure of feelings to family and friends, increased thought suppression and intrusion, and increased psychological distress two years post-abortion (controlling for initial distress). Thus, feelings of stigmatization led women to engage in coping strategies that were associated with poorer adjustment over time. (Major et al. 2009, p. 882).

Conversely, women with more resilient personalities and/or social support coped better.

Other studies have found no difference in psychological aftermath based on what type of abortion procedure was used (surgical versus chemical) when the woman had a choice between procedures.

Conclusions

First

"The relative risk of mental health problems among adult women who have a single, legal, first-trimester abortion of an unwanted pregnancy for nontherapeutic reasons is no greater than the risk of women who deliver an unwanted pregnancy" (Major, et al. 2009, p. 885). This conclusion is similar to the previous task force of the American Psychological Association (Adler et al., 1990) and another review (Charles, Polis, Sridhara, & Blum, 2008).

Second

The relative risk is also no greater for women who abort an initially wanted pregnancy due to fetal abnormality as compared to women who miscarry or suffer a still birth.

Third

The relative risk after abortion does appear to be greater among young women in New Zealand, Australia, and Norway, though limitations make this unclear.

Fourth

The claim that the observed negative aftermath of abortion is due to the abortion itself rather than by co-occurring factors is not supported by the evidence.

Fifth

"The majority of women who terminate a pregnancy do not experience mental health problems" (Major et al., 2009, p. 885). Prevalence of those who do is low. Most women report being satisfied.

Sixth

Some women do have negative after-effects: "It is important that all women's experiences be recognized as valid and that women feel free to express their thoughts and feelings about abortion regardless of whether those feelings are positive or negative" (Major et al., 2009, p. 885).

The Interventionist Fallacy

Finally, since abortion is currently such a contested issue, it is important to be cautious of the *interventionist fallacy*. If abortion is associated with negative outcome, it does not follow that an intervention that makes abortions less accessible will thereby prevent those negative outcomes. Indeed, characteristic of women more likely to get abortions – poverty, problem behaviors, or exposure to violence – might then become more characteristic of women who deliver the pregnancies, and we could then find the findings reversed. The intervention might accordingly increase mental health problems as the stresses of giving birth to an unwanted child are carried by women with these characteristics.

References

For an extensive set of references, see the 105-page report at http://www.apa.org/pi/wpo/mental-health-abortion-report.pdf or the later published report (Major, et al. 2009).

Adler, N. E., David, H. P., Major, B. N., Roth, S. H., Russo, N. F., & Wyatt, G. E. (1990). Psychological responses after abortion. *Science, 248,* 41-44.

American Psychological Association, Task Force on Mental Health and Abortion. (2008). *Report of the Task Force on Mental Health and Abortion.* Washington, DC: Author. Retrieved from http://www.apa.org/pi/wpo/mental-health-abortion-report.pdf

Charles, V. E., Polis, C. B., Sridhara, S. K., & Blum, R. W. (2008). Abortion and long-term mental health outcomes: a systematic review of the evidence. *Contraception, 78*(6), 436-450. doi: 10.1016/j.contraception.2008.07.005

Cozzarelli, C., & Major, B. (1994). The effects of antiabortion demonstrators and pro-choice escorts on women's psychological responses to abortion. *Journal of Social and Clinical Psychology, 13*, 404-427.

Cozzarelli, C., Major, B., Karrasch, A., & Fuegen, K. (2000). Women's experiences of and reactions to antiabortion picketing. *Basic and Applied Social Psychology, 22*, 265-275.

Major, B., Appelbaum, M. Beckman, L., Dutton, M. A., Russo, N. F., & West., C. (2009). Abortion and mental health: Evaluating the evidence. *American Psychologist, 64*(9), 863-890.

Major, B., & Gramzow, R. H. (1999). Abortion as stigma: Cognitive and emotional implications of concealment. *Journal of Personality and Social Psychology, 77*, 735-745.

Chapter 10

Counterpoint:
Long-Lasting Distress after Abortion

by Martha Shuping

Some women report no distress after abortion, but some do report distress. This chapter is about those who do.

In 1973, as a university undergraduate, I served as a volunteer abortion counselor in a clinic for low-income women, helping women to access abortions. In my training, I was told that abortion was risk-free. Since I had no contact with the women after their procedures, I did not learn about abortion-related distress until many years later. As a psychiatry resident in 1985, I was assigned a patient who had been hospitalized for severe depression after an abortion. She was married, financially secure and had been pregnant with a child she wanted - but her husband did not want another child, and her pastor advised her to submit to her husband's wishes. She told me that before the abortion, she had been well, but afterward, she experienced severe depression and guilt. Thus, I learned that not everyone who obtains an abortion actually wants one, and that the accompanying distress can be severe. In this case, there was no doubt in the mind of my patient that her symptoms were related to the abortion itself. At that time, it didn't occur to me to evaluate her for posttraumatic stress disorder (PTSD), and no one made that diagnosis, but today I would ask more questions.

A textbook of the National Abortion Federation (Baker, Beresford, Halvorson-Boyd, & Garrity, 1999) has identified many "negative reactions" (p. 28-29) that some women have after abortion; some are trauma symptoms: nightmares about babies, insomnia, negative emotions of guilt, anger, worthlessness, and shame, "blocking out the experience," avoiding things that trigger memories about the abortion, "engaging in self-punishing behaviors such as substance abuse . . . and relationships with abusive partners," suicidal thoughts, "relentless thoughts of being a bad person," and various self-destructive behaviors (pp. 28-29).

Although most researchers agree these reactions can occur, there are unresolved questions regarding the scope of the problem which may be much larger than many clinicians have realized. The distress for some can be very long-lasting. In my clinical experience, I have worked with women ranging in age from teens to more than eighty who continued to have distress they attributed many years later to the abortion.

In this chapter, we consider the conceptual framework of "Abortion as Traumatic Experience," identified in the APA Task Force report covered in Chapter 9. Many authors have identified abortion as an event that can be traumatic for some women. Here, we will examine the evidence that many women suffer long-lasting distress specifically because of their abortion.

Diagnostic Criteria for PTSD

In 2013, the American Psychiatric Association published the 5th edition of its diagnostic manual, DSM-5, the most recent criteria for Posttraumatic Stress Disorder (PTSD). Many pertinent studies of PTSD used previous diagnostic criteria, but symptoms are similar. Many in the trauma field are removing the word "disorder" and refer only to post-traumatic stress (PTS). We will use the DSM-5 criteria as a way to organize the symptoms.

To diagnose PTSD, several specific symptoms must be associated with a specific trauma, beginning after the trauma occurred. A "subclinical" or "subthreshold" case occurs when symptoms are insufficient for a full diagnosis. Patients with only some symptoms may have substantial distress.

The National Vietnam Veteran's Readjustment Study (NVVRS) was a large, nationally representative study mandated by Congress to identify the prevalence of PTSD in American veterans of the war in Vietnam. Approximately 26% of male and female veterans in combat zones had PTSD symptoms at the time of the study, with 15% of men having full PTSD and 11% "partial PTSD" (Kulka et al.,1988; Price, 2015). Those with partial PTSD had impaired functioning. Large studies using community (non-military) samples have documented disability and increased risk of suicide with subthreshold PTSD (Marshall et al., 2001; Stein, Walker, Hazen, Forde, 1997).

A 2015 systematic review article on PTS and PTSD associated with reproductive loss (elective abortion, miscarriage and other losses) reported the prevalence rate varied depending on how respondents were recruited. Some demographic groups are at higher risk than others. The authors state it is currently not possible to determine a definite prevalence for specific PTSD symptoms following the various types of reproductive losses (Daugirdaitė, van den Akker, & Purewal, 2015).

In the section below, the diagnostic criteria are listed with examples of how these criteria may be met, using quotations from women and comments from published studies

Death Event

Current diagnostic criteria for PTSD begin with "exposure to actual or threatened death, serious injury, or sexual violence in one (or more)" of several specified ways (American Psychiatric Association, 2013, p. 143). This can be through "directly experiencing the traumatic event," or "witnessing in person the event(s) as it occurred to others" (p. 143).

Women sometimes see the fetus during the course of an abortion (Slade, Heke, Fletcher, & Stewart, 1998; Speckhard, 1997; Urquhart & Templeton, 1991), which may allow the woman to view the abortion as a human death event, even in the absence of prior attachment (Speckhard, 1997). Seeing the fetus was associated with increased PTSD symptoms (Slade, et al., 1998).

Whether or not the woman has seen or felt something that enhances her perception of the death of a human being, her subjective experience is paramount. If she perceives the fetus as human, its loss may be experienced as the death of her own child, as it was for "M. K." (Speckhard & Rue, 1992, p. 107): "I don't know how it's possible, but I know I felt when my baby died. I could feel when its life was sucked out. It was awful. I have never felt so empty."

The experience of fetal death is not the only source of trauma. Bleeding or pain may be perceived by the woman as traumatic (Burke & Reardon, 2002; Suliman et al., 2007; Speckhard, 1997; Speckhard & Rue, 2012).

Intrusion Symptoms

The diagnosis of PTSD must include at least one intrusion symptom, including:
1. Recurrent, involuntary, and intrusive distressing memories of traumatic event(s).
2. Recurrent distressing dreams in which the content and/or the affect of the dream are related to the traumatic event(s).
3. Dissociative reactions (e.g. flashbacks) in which the individual feels or acts as if the traumatic events were recurring.
4. Intense or prolonged psychological distress at exposure to internal or external cues that symbolize or resemble an aspect of the traumatic event(s)(American Psychiatric Association, 2013, p. 144).

Intrusion symptoms reported after abortion include nightmares, flashbacks and, and, memories that "seemed to intrude despite trying to forget" (Dykes, Slade, & Haywood, 2010, p. 11; Speckhard & Mufel, 2003). In a study comparing 331 Russian and 217 American women, 48% of the Russians and 65% of the

Americans reported one or more intrusion symptoms specifically related to a past abortion (Rue, Coleman, Rue, & Reardon, 2004). Slade et al. (1998) reported in a sample of 275 women having first trimester abortions that seeing the fetus was associated with nightmares, flashbacks and intrusive thoughts of the abortion.

Nightmares. A textbook of the National Abortion Federation (Baker et al., 1999) identified nightmares about babies as a possible negative reaction after abortion. In Rue et al. (2004), 30% of the American women reported nightmares associated with their abortion. A woman in Belarus reported vivid nightmares of her child in a pool of blood with arms and legs broken (Speckhard & Mufel, 2003); in the Belarusian sample, 32% had nightmares.

An American woman reported, "Three years after my second abortion I started having nightmares in which I saw myself in a baby parts cemetery and holding a dead baby in my arms and crying for the ones I lost. I was . . . holding a dead baby and trying to bring him back to life" (Burke & Reardon, 2002, p. 124). Another reported recurring nightmares about being in labor, "eager to see the baby," but the baby "comes out dead" and "it takes me hours to calm down" (Burke & Reardon, 2002, p. 124). Some report crying for hours after they awaken, and becoming afraid to sleep at night. Some engage in substance abuse to be able to sleep.

Flashbacks. In a flashback, the traumatic event is re-experienced; the memory is intense as if it were happening now, not the past. In Rue et al. (2004), 46% of the sample of American women reported flashbacks related to a past abortion, while Speckhard and Mufel (2003) reported 76% of a Belarusian sample reported flashbacks.

A woman reported a flashback to her abortion when she required emergency treatment for an ectopic pregnancy: "Having my feet up in stirrups, the smell of the hospital, the violation of instruments entering my body and taking a life from me . . . these things all came back to me, and I felt exactly like I was having an abortion. I cried and cried. I guess I was hysterical. The doctor had to give me a sedative" (Burke & Reardon, 2002, p. 122).

Women have described flashbacks with routine gynecology exams, sometimes with anxiety symptoms such as shortness of breath and palpitations (Burke & Reardon, 2002). Although flashbacks may be brief, the fear of one can contribute to women avoiding places and activities reminding them of the abortion.

Avoidance Symptoms

"Avoidance of or efforts to avoid distressing memories, thoughts, or feelings about or closely associated with the traumatic events" or avoidance of external reminders such as people or places "that arouse distressing memories, thoughts or feelings associated with the traumatic events" (American Psychiatric Association, 2013, p. 144-145). A danger is women may not seek counseling to help to resolve persistent abortion-related symptoms.

Rue et al. (2004) reported 19% of the Russian women and 50% of the Americans avoided thinking or talking about the abortion; 36% of the Americans reported three or more avoidance symptoms. In a Norwegian study comparing women who had miscarriages with women who had induced abortions, the latter scored significantly higher on the avoidance subscale of the Impact of Event Scale (IES) at 2 years and 5 years after the abortion (Broen, Moum, Bødtker, & Ekeberg, 2005). All the women interviewed by Dykes et al. (2010) avoided thinking about the abortion, and "all participants spontaneously used the term 'blocking it out' as a universally adopted strategy" (p. 11), though as one woman stated "blocking them out . . . doesn't work always" (p. 11). A National Abortion Federation textbook (Baker et al. 1999) reports "blocking out the experience; and avoiding anything that triggers memories of the event" as an adverse reaction. Bagarozzi (1994) and Mufel, Speckhard, and Sivhua (2002) reported avoidance.

Women in Belarus were interviewed in part to learn whether negative psychosocial reactions were the similar across divergent cultures (Speckhard & Mufel, 2003). In this non-random sample, 50% were clinically assessed as having PTSD. Many more had some symptoms. However, very few had sought professional treatment, which may have been related to their high degree of avoidance symptoms.

Avoidance symptoms can be disruptive to lives and relationships. One woman reported quitting her job to avoid being around a pregnant co-worker: "When I found out my co-worker was pregnant, I was overcome with anxiety and fear. I didn't want to even look at her. I knew I couldn't take watching her belly growing each day with a baby . . . I had to leave that job because of her pregnancy" (Burke & Reardon, 2002, p. 70). She reported physical symptoms such as a "knot in my stomach" and her heart pounding when around her pregnant colleague. Women in Belarus also reported avoiding pregnant women (Speckhard & Mufel, 2003).

"Suzanne" avoided routine gynecological exams for eight years until an infection forced her to seek treatment. She had a flashback on the exam table and left without being examined (Burke & Reardon, 2002).Women in Belarus stated they avoided the clinic where the abortion took place and avoided returning for gynecological exams (Speckhard & Mufel, 2003).

Rue et al. (2004) reported 25% of the American women in that sample had "difficulty being near babies" (p. SR11). For any woman who originally hoped to have children at a better time, this would be a particularly unfortunate symptom. A woman in Belarus stated: "I can't meet with babies. It's too painful. I broke the relationship with my girlfriend who asked me to baby-sit for a few hours with her daughter. I was rude to her" (Speckhard, & Mufel, 2003, p. 8).

Symptoms Related to Negative Changes in Thoughts and Moods

There are seven symptoms of this type, which must be (a) associated with the trauma, (b) persistent, and (c) either begin or worsen after the traumatic incident. Symptoms include a "persistent negative emotional state (e.g. fear, horror, anger, guilt, or shame) . . . markedly diminished interest in significant activities . . . detachment or estrangement from others" and "inability to experience positive emotions" (American Psychiatric Association, 2013, p. 145).

Persistent Negative Emotional State. Guilt and shame were expressed by the women interviewed by Dykes et al. (2010). In a Belarusian sample, 80% reported guilt, though most were not churchgoers, atheism had been enforced by the Soviets for 70 years there, and there were no protesters to engender guilt (Speckhard & Rue, 2003). In another cross-cultural study, 49% of Russian women, and 78% of American women reported guilt (Rue et al., 2004). In a Norwegian sample, post-abortive women had significantly higher scores for guilt and shame compared to those who miscarried, and significantly increased anxiety compared to general public (Broen et al., 2005). Grief, anger and guilt are also discussed in Chapter 8.

Detachment or Estrangement from Others. Symptoms include decreased interest in activities, "detachment or estrangement from others" and "inability to experience positive emotions" (American Psychiatric Association, 2013, p. 145). This may contribute to relationship problems. Studies find reports of increased communication problems (Coyle, Coleman & Rue, 2010; Freeman, Rickels, & Huggins, 1980; Rue et al., 2004), increased sexual dysfunction (Bagarozzi, 1993, 1994; Bianchi-Demicelli, et al., 2002; Bradshaw & Slade, 2003; Coleman, Rue & Spence, 2006; Coyle et al., 2010; Fok, Siu, & Lau, 2006; Miller, 1992; Rue et al., 2004; Speckhard & Mufel, 2003; Tornboen, Ingelhammar, Lilja, Moller & Svanberg, 1994) and increased separation and divorce (Barnett, Freudenberg, Wille, 1992; Bracken & Kasi, 1975; Coleman, Rue & Spence, 2006; Freeman et al.,1980; Lauzon, Roger-Achim, Achim, & Boyer, 2000; Rue et al., 2004).

Feelings of detachment may contribute to problems bonding with subsequent children (Coleman, Reardon, & Cougle, 2002; Coleman, 2009), or may contribute to increased child abuse and neglect, as detailed in Chapter 13.

Hyperarousal Symptoms

This group of symptoms has "marked alterations in arousal and reactivity" that began or worsened after the traumatic incident, including insomnia, "irritable behavior and angry outbursts . . .

reckless or self-destructive behavior . . . problems with concentration" (American Psychiatric Association, 2013, p. 145).

Insomnia. A large study examined 56,824 medical records comparing women who aborted to those who delivered (Reardon & Coleman, 2006). Those who had abortions were nearly twice as likely to be treated for sleep disorders during the first 180 days after the end of pregnancy compared to those who delivered, even though women who delivered may be expected to have sleep disturbance due to caring for a newborn. Women who aborted continued to be more likely to be treated for sleep disturbance than women who delivered for up to four years. Women with a history of sleep disorder were excluded from the study.

Reckless or self-destructive behavior. "Francine" described self-destructive behavior: "I cracked up my car three times, driving recklessly at extreme speeds. In one wreck, I broke four ribs and punctured my lung. My life became a series of calamities, accidents, and self-destructive benders" (Burke & Reardon, 2002, p. 140). Although "Francine" survived, her report is consistent with a study of Canadian government health care services showing women with an abortion history were more likely to receive treatment for accident-related injuries (Badgley, Caron, & Powell, 1977). Data from the Virginia Department of Medical Assistance Services showed women who had abortions had increased claims for treatment of accidental injuries compared to a case-matched sample of Medicaid recipients without abortions (Reardon, Strahan, Thorp, Jr., & Shuping, 2004). Records-based studies in the U.S. and Finland show post-abortive women approximately two to four times more likely to die from accidents (Gissler, Kauppila, Merilainen, Toukomaa, & Hemminki, 1997; Reardon, Ney, Scheuren, Cougle, Coleman, Strahan, 2002; Reardon, et al., 2004). Increased accidental deaths persisted over eight years (Reardon et al., 2002; Reardon et al., 2004). Possible reasons: (a) increased risk taking or self-destructive behavior; (b) suicides not classified correctly; and (c) substance abuse (Burke & Reardon, 2002; Reardon et al., 2004).

Other Trauma Symptoms

Substance abuse. Substance abuse is strongly associated with PTSD, though not listed as a symptom in DSM-5. The onset of PTSD often precedes onset of substance abuse, suggesting causality (Chilcoat & Breslau, 1998, Saxon et al., 2001). Patients sometimes self-medicate to reduce flashbacks and hyperarousal; there is neurobiological evidence (Armony & LeDoux, 1997; Coleman, 2005; Jacobsen, Southwick & Kosten, 2001; Kreek & Koob, 1998).

Many studies show a strong association between alcohol or drug abuse after abortion (Coleman, 2005). Reardon and Ney (2000) considered only women with no prior history of substance abuse, finding those who aborted were subsequently 4.5 times more likely to engage in substance abuse compared to those who delivered.

A study using data in the National Longitudinal Survey of Youth compared women who aborted (n = 213), women who delivered an unintended pregnancy (n = 535) and women with no pregnancies (n = 1,144), controlling for multiple variables (Reardon, Coleman & Cougle, 2004). Four years later, women who aborted experienced significantly higher risk for frequent marijuana and alcohol use.

Another study examined data from the Christchurch Health and Development Study, a 25-year study of a birth cohort of 1,265 New Zealand children (Fergusson, Horwood, & Ridder, 2006). About 500 female participants ages 15-25 years were compared in three groups: (a) never pregnant; (b) pregnant no abortion; (c) abortion. There was no significant difference between the never pregnant and the pregnant no abortion group, but the abortion group demonstrated significantly higher rates of illicit drug dependence, and also higher rates for other severe adverse mental health problems, after controlling for numerous potential confounders.

An Australian study (n = 1,223), controlling for pre-existing substance abuse, behavior problems, and other variables, found young women with a past abortion had almost three times the risk of lifetime illicit (non-marijuana) substance use disorder, and twice the risk for an alcohol use disorder, compared to those with no previous abortion (Dingle, Alati, Clavarino, Najman, & Williams, 2008).

Suicide. Suicidal thoughts and behaviors are not listed in DSM-5, but are the ultimate self-destructive behavior. Sheila Harper (2008), author of a workbook used in abortion recovery support groups, reported attempting suicide due to persistent abortion-related distress (Harper, 2009). She described having the gun in her hand when her roommate unexpectedly came home early and interrupted the attempt.

There are reports of attempted or completed suicides coinciding with the anniversary date of the abortion or expected due date of the aborted child (Tishler, 1981). British artist Emma Beck, who committed suicide after an abortion in 2007, wrote: "I told everyone I didn't want to do it, even at the hospital . . . now it is too late . . . I want to be with my babies" ("Artist hanged herself," 2008).

A record-based study in Finland linking medical records and death certificates showed women who aborted had a 650% higher risk of death from suicide compared to women who carried to term (Gissler, Hemminiki, & Lonnqvist, 1996).

A study of more than 173,000 California Medicaid records, controlling for age and prior psychiatric illness, revealed women who aborted were 3.1 times more likely to die from suicide compared to women who delivered. The increased risk persisted over 8 years (Reardon et al., 2002). The risk was highest for younger women.

A records-based U.K. study compared suicide attempts before and after pregnancy events (Morgan, Evans, Peter, & Currie, 1997). Women who aborted had a significantly increased rate of suicide attempts after the abortion compared to previously and compared to those who gave birth. The authors concluded: "The increased risk of suicide after an induced abortion may therefore be a consequence of the procedure itself" (p. 902).

Fergusson et al. (2006) reported that young women who aborted had significantly higher risk of suicidal behaviors compared to those who were pregnant, and compared to those who were pregnant but did not abort.

Delayed Onset of PTSD

Under DSM-5 criteria, to diagnose PTSD, the symptoms must be present for at least one month. There is also a category "with delayed expression" if the full criteria are not met until at least 6 months have passed (American Psychiatric Association, 2013, p. 145-146). Thus, PTSD is a longer-term *chronic* condition compared to "acute stress disorder" in which symptoms begin immediately and persist for three days to one month.

Engelhard, van den Hout, and Arntz, (2001) reported some women after an involuntary pregnancy loss experienced late onset PTSD during their next pregnancy. A delayed reaction after abortion has been reported in Belarusian women and in Western samples (Speckhard & Mufel, 2003; Mufel et al., 2002; Speckhard, 1997; Speckhard & Rue, 2012). Circumstances such as gynecological problems, infertility, illness or accidents with subsequent children can trigger symptoms. Some women report distress did not occur until seeing the ultrasound of their first intended pregnancy, or holding their child after first completed pregnancy, which altered their view of the aborted fetus (Speckhard, 1997; Mufel et al., 2002).

This is consistent with observations in U.S. government data on PSTD from the NVVRS. The majority of the veterans with full PTSD had delayed onset after more than 6 months, with 40% first meeting diagnostic criteria for PTSD 2-5 years after being in Vietnam, and another late-onset cluster being diagnosed 6-22 years after being in Vietnam (Schnurr, Lunney, Sengupta, & Waelde, 2003).

Considering this, studies examining PTSD in the first three months after abortion may find a smaller number of cases compared to what would emerge with longer follow up.

Long-lasting Effects of Trauma

According to the National Comorbidity Survey, the effects of trauma are often very long-lasting. Over one third of people with PTSD fail to recover even after many years (Kessler, Sonnega,

Bromet, Hughes, & Nelson, 1995). Of American veterans of the war in Vietnam with full or partial PTSD, 78% continued to experience symptoms when interviewed 20-25 years after the war (Schnurr, et al., 2003).

Several studies show symptoms of PTSD occurring 3 to 5 years after an abortion (Barnard, 1990, 1991; Broen et al, 2005; Curley & Johnston, 2013). Others have diagnosed PTSD still present 9 to 11 years after the abortion (Anderson, Hanley, Larson & Sider, 1995; Rue et al., 2004), or longer (Dykes et al., 2010). (See also Chapter 8).

Clarifying the Conclusions of the APA Task Force

Majority of Women Excluded

The Task Force on Mental Health and Abortion of the American Psychological Association concluded that "The relative risk of mental health problems among adult women who have a single, legal, first-trimester abortion of an unwanted pregnancy for nontherapeutic reasons is no greater than the risk of women who deliver an unwanted pregnancy" (Major, et al. 2009, p. 885). This conclusion applies only to women in these subgroups:

• Adult women, age 21 and above (excludes 18% of U.S. abortion patients who are teens; Jones, Finer, and Singh, 2010).
• Single abortion - not repeats (excludes about half of U.S. abortions; Cohen, 2007).
• First-trimester abortion (excludes 11% of U.S. abortions, which are late-term; Guttmacher Institute, 2014).
• Unwanted pregnancy (excludes the pressured/coerced and ambivalent, prevalence unknown).
• Non-therapeutic reasons (excludes those terminating due to medical reasons).

Thus, the conclusion applies to only a minority of women having abortions. More than half of U.S. abortion patients are excluded. The exact number excluded cannot be determined due to overlap between categories, and lack of definitive prevalence data for some subgroups.

Studies Not Considered

Inclusion criteria required that studies have an appropriate comparison group, though the task force additionally considered some "abortion only" (no comparison group) studies from the U.S. (but not other countries) that were viewed as providing additional insight. Due to falling outside the criteria, several studies assessed as good quality in the review by Daugirdaitė et al. (2015) were not considered.

A prospective study from South Africa (Suliman et al., 2007) was conceived by a physician who provided anesthesia for abortions, with patients referred to the study at pre-abortion counseling. The study controlled for prior mental health, with psychological rating scales before and after the abortion on the same day, and at 1 and 3 months. The baseline *point prevalence* of PTSD was 11.3%, similar to U.S. community samples. (Point prevalence is the percentage having the disorder at the current point, not cumulative lifetime prevalence). Prevalence of PTSD at 3 month follow up was 18.2%, which the authors considered high; this was higher than the results of Rue et al. (2004) but lower than other studies such as Engelhard et al. (2001). Because PTSD symptoms at 3 months were partially explained by severity of pre-existing PTSD symptoms and disability, and also by post-termination dissociation, the authors recommended screening in advance to determine which women may be at risk for PTSD, to assure those affected receive appropriate follow-up treatment.

Prevalence

The fifth conclusion of the APA Task Force (Chapter 9), that the "majority" of women do not suffer symptoms, is not helpful in establishing whether or not abortion can be traumatic. It is widely accepted that PTSD occurs only in a percentage of those exposed to any trauma.

In the NVVRS, lifetime prevalence of PTSD – veterans who had ever suffered – was 30.9% for full PTSD and 22.5% for partial PTSD (Kulka et al., 1988; Price, 2015). Thus, the majority of combat veterans did not meet full criteria for PTSD, though slightly more than half, 53%, had at least some symptoms over their lifetimes. At the time of the study only 15.2% of male combat veterans had current full PTSD. Similarly, the National Women's Study showed 31% of women who were raped have PTSD symptoms at some time afterwards, with 11% still having it currently (Kilpatrick, 2000). Thus, a majority of combat veterans and a majority of rape survivors did not meet diagnostic criteria for full PTSD. Yet PTSD in these groups is still considered a substantial clinical problem meriting attention.

The Problem of Non-response

Recently, a 4-year nationally representative longitudinal study was conducted of U.S. abortion patients, compared to women who sought abortion but were unable to obtain one (Biggs, Rowland, McCulloch, & Foster, 2016). Authors reported only a 1% prevalence of PTSD symptoms attributable to the index pregnancy, but the methods used did not allow researchers to pinpoint whether symptoms were due to the pregnancy, the abortion, or other factors.

The Turnaway Study, which was the source of the data (Biggs et al., 2016), started with only a 38% participation rate. Women were offered $15 for informed consent by phone, and $50 for a telephone interview about a week after an abortion or after being turned away (Dobkin et al., 2014), but only 38% completed that first interview (Rocca, Kimport, Gould, & Foster, 2013). Of those, 65% continued through the 4 years. Thus, final results are based on only about 25% of the much larger group originally invited.

Some studies indicate that low participation rates or high drop-out rates may distort results. After a workplace disaster in Norway, 246 employees were required to participate in medical evaluations for PTSD (Weisaeth, 1989). At baseline pre-disaster, employees had a record of cooperation with the company medical officer. After the disaster, some were resistant and required repeated contacts; eventually participation reached 100%. The initial resistance was significantly associated with severity of PTSD at 7 months. The authors stated that if the initial refusals had been accepted, "the potential loss to the follow-up would have included 42% of the PTSD cases, and 64% of the severe PTSD cases would have fallen out, resulting in distorted prevalence rates of PTSD" (p. 131). Additionally, "The initial resistance in many who later developed PTSD was found to relate to the psychological defences such as avoidance which is seen both PTSD and acute post-traumatic stress syndrome."

Relief vs. Stress

Many expect relief after abortion, an outcome reported in the literature. The APA Task Force reported "Abortion can be a way of resolving stress associated with an unwanted pregnancy, and, hence, can lead to relief. However, abortion can also engender additional stress of its own" (American Psychological Association, 2008, p. 10). Several authors have stated that relief can be followed by or coexist with trauma symptoms (Curley & Johnston, 2013; Mufel et al., 2002; Speckhard & Mufel, 2003; Speckhard & Rue, 2012); the existence of short-term relief does not negate the reality of trauma symptoms in some of the very same women, or in other women. Additionally, some authors have reported dissociation around the time of the abortion, which may be mistaken for relief, but which is associated with risk of subsequent PTSD (Speckhard & Rue, 2012; Suliman, 2007).

Conclusions

It is certain that for some women, abortion is a traumatic stressor capable of causing PTSD symptoms. In my own clinical experience, women have reported nightmares *specifically related to the abortion,* not past sexual abuse. Flashbacks are triggered by reminders of the abortion, not previous trauma. When this is the case, the woman herself may be the best judge of what is distressing for her. For the women I have treated, most, if not all, would say that the most central aspect of their distress is the loss of the child. There are certainly women who do not think of the fetus as a child, but for those who experience distress, this is often a central issue. (See also Chapter 7, on attachment as a risk factor).

There are pre-existing psycho-social risk factors and neurobiological and genetic factors influencing who develops PTSD and who does not. This is reported in many studies, not only abortion samples (Price, 2015; Sherin & Nemeroff, 2011; Strahl, 2012). Nonetheless, for many women, abortion is a cause or a contributing cause of PTSD symptoms. For others, abortion may be an additional trauma exacerbating PTSD symptoms or adding symptoms.

Because of risk factors, some authors recommend pre-abortion screening to identify the most vulnerable (Curley & Johnston, 2013). Opportunities for women to consider their risks and possible alternatives to abortion may help prevent later distress. Screening and prevention are extremely important because distress after abortion can be very long-lasting and very disabling.

Cross-cultural research indicates that although not all women experience trauma symptoms, those who are distressed report similar types of symptoms across cultures, including avoidance, intrusion, hyperarousal symptoms, and negative emotions. Even after many decades of state-enforced atheism, low religiosity, and lack of protestors, many Belaursian and Russian women still experienced guilt.

Because PTSD symptoms can be delayed, it is important to provide follow up and availability of treatment options over time. However, for women to access appropriate treatment, clinicians must be aware that some women experience abortion as a stress and may be vulnerable to abortion-related mental health problems.

Many of my patients have reported that prior mental health treatment was not helpful, because therapists did not believe that the abortion was the cause of their distress, and therefore they did not address the patient's identified concerns. This has led women in growing numbers to seek help through alternative sources such as peer-led support groups. The Abortion Recovery InterNational Care

Directory reports that their website receives more than 50,000 contacts annually, seeking referrals to local support groups. Rachel's Vineyard conducts approximately one thousand weekend retreats annually worldwide, Sheila Harper's SaveOne has 145 chapters worldwide, and Project Rachel has 162 local branches throughout the U.S. There are too many groups to name or count them all. This shows that many women are identifying abortion as a source of distress and are seeking help. Yet they will likely not be discovered in research utilizing large databases since these support groups are usually free of charge, and are not reimbursable by health insurance, being peer-led.

An important point is that it was the women themselves who founded the very first national support group organization. It is the women who have had abortions who have written most of the widely used support group workbooks, who head many of the national and international abortion recovery organizations, and who lead almost every local group. Some organizations such as Project Rachel and Rachel's Vineyard make use of both peer support volunteers as well as professional counselors. When a dozen women get together for a support group, usually the leader or co-leader is personally post-abortive. Women who feel that they were helped through these programs are eager to "give back" by helping others with abortion recovery. Many women who were distressed by their abortion experience also gravitate toward pregnancy resource centers where they volunteer in order to give women the range of choices they wish they had been offered.

There is more to know about women's experiences than what is currently in the large data sets. To better understand the full picture and the range of experiences, more qualitative work would helpful in order to listen to women's stories and understand, rather than dismiss those who experienced trauma. Studies that evaluate the effectiveness of peer-led alternative support programs will also be useful.

References

American Psychiatric Association (2013). *Desk reference to the diagnostic criteria from DSM-5*. Washington, DC: Author.

American Psychological Association. (2008). Report of the Task Force on Mental Health and Abortion. Washington, DC: Author. Retrieved from http://www.apa.org/pi/wpo/mental-health-abortion-report.pdf

Anderson, R. L., Hanley, D. C., Larson, D. B., & Sider, R. C. (1995). *Methodological considerations in empirical research on abortion.* In P. Doherty (Ed.). *Post-abortion syndrome: Its wide ramifications* (pp. 103-115).Dublin: Four Courts Press.

Armony, J. L., & LeDoux, J. E. (1997). How the brain processes emotional information. In R. Yehuda & A. C. McFarlane (Eds.). *Psychobiology of posttraumatic stress disorder* (pp. 259-270). New York: Academy of Sciences.

Artist hanged herself. (2008, Feb 22). *The Telegraph.* Retrieved from http://www.telegraph.co.uk/

Badgley, R. F., Caron, D. F., Powell, M. G. (1977). *Report of the Committee on the Operation of the Abortion Law*. Ottawa: Ministry of Supply and Services, 313-321.

Bagarozzi, D. (1993). Posttraumatic stress disorders in women following abortion: Some considerations and implications for marital/couple therapy. *International Journal of Family and Marriage, 1,* 51–68.

Bagarozzi, D. (1994). Identification, assessment and treatment of women suffering from posttraumatic stress after abortion. *Journal of Family Psychotherapy, 5*(3), 25–54. doi:10.1300/j085V05N03_02

Baker, A, Beresford, T., Halvorson-Boyd, G., & Garrity, J. M. (1999). Chapter 3, Informed consent, counseling, and patient preparation. In M. Paul, E. S. Lichtenberg, L. Borgatta, D. A. Grimes, & P. G. Stubblefield, (Eds.), *A clinician's guide to medical and surgical abortion*. Philadelphia, PA: Churchill Livingstone.

Barnard, C. A. (1990). *The long-term psychosocial effects of abortion.* Portsmouth, NH: Institute for Pregnancy Loss.

Barnard, C. A. (1991). Stress reactions in women related to induced abortion. *Association for Interdisciplinary Research in Values and Social Change Newsletter 3*(4).

Barnett, W., Freudenberg, N., & Wille, R. (1992). Partnership after induced abortion: a prospective controlled study. *Archives of Sexual Behavior, 2,* 443-455.

Biggs, M. A., Rowland, B., McCulloch, C. E., Foster, D. G. (2016). Does abortion increase women's risk for post-traumatic stress? Findings from a prospective longitudinal cohort study. Retrieved from http://bmjopen.bmj.com/content/6/2/e009698.full?sid=b5362408-d3b6-4800-8857-f045635a1ff0

Bianchi-Demicelli, F., Perrin, E., Ludicke, F., Bianchi, P. G., Chatton, D., & Campana, A. (2002). Termination of pregnancy and women's sexuality. *Gynecologic and Obstetetric Investigation, 53,* 48-53. *BMJ Open 6,* e009698 doi:10.1136/bmjopen-2015-009698

Bracken, M. B., & Kasi, S. (1975). First and repeat abortions: a study of decision-making and delay. *Journal of Biosocial Science, 7,* 473-491.

Bradshaw, Z., & Slade, P. (2003). The effects of induced abortion on emotional experiences and relationships: A critical review of the literature. *Clinical Psychology Review, 23,* 929-958.

Broen, A. N., Moum, T., Bødtker, A. S., & Ekeberg, Ø. (2005). The course of mental health after miscarriage and induced abortion: a longitudinal, five-year follow-up study. *BMC Medicine, 3,*18. doi: 10.1186/1741-7015-3-18. Retrieved from http://www.biomedcentral.com/1741-7015/3/18

Burke, T., & Reardon, D. C. (2002). *Forbidden grief: The unspoken pain of abortion.* Springfield: Acorn Books.

Chilcoat, H. D., & Breslau, N. (1998). Posttraumatic stress disorder and drug disorder. *Archives of General Psychiatry, 55,* 913-917.

Cohen, S. A. (2007). Repeat abortion, repeat unintended pregnancy, repeated and misguided government policies. *Guttmacher Policy Review 10*(2). Retrieved from www.guttmacher.org/pubs/gpr/10/2/gpr100208.html

Coleman, P. K. (2005). Induced abortion and increased risk of substance abuse: A review of the evidence. *Current Women's Health Reviews, 1,* 21-34.

Coleman, P. K. (2009). The psychological pain of perinatal loss and subsequent parenting risks: Could induced abortion be more problematic than other forms of loss? *Current Women's Health Reviews, 5*, 88-99.

Coleman, P. K., Reardon, D. C., & Cougle, J. (2002). The quality of the caregiving environment and child developmental outcomes associated with maternal history of abortion using the NLSY data. *Journal of Child Psychology and Psychiatry and Allied Disciplines, 43*, 743-758.

Coleman, P. K., Rue, V. M., & Spence, M. (2006). Intrapersonal processes and post-abortion relationship challenges: A review and consolidation of relevant literature. *The Internet Journal of Mental Health 4*(2). Retrieved from http://ispub.com/IJMH/4/2/3804

Coyle, C. T., Coleman, P. K., Rue, V. M. (2010). Inadequate preabortion counseling and decision conflict as predictors of subsequent relationship difficulties and psychological stress in men and women. *Traumatology, XX*(X), 1-15. doi: 10.1177/1534765609347550

Curley, M, & Johnston, C. (2013). The characteristics and severity of psychological distress after abortion among university students. *The Journal of Behavioral Health Services & Research 40*(3), 279-293.

Daugirdaitė, V., van den Akker, O., & Purewal, S. (2015). Posttraumatic stress and posttraumatic stress disorder after termination of pregnancy and reproductive loss: A systematic review. *Journal of Pregnancy, 2015*(646345). doi: 10.1155/2015/646345.

Dingle, K., Alati, R., Clavarino, A., Najman, J. M., Williams, G. M. (2008). Pregnancy loss and psychiatric disorders in young women: An Australian birth cohort study. *The British Journal of Psychiatry, 193,* 455-460. doi: 10.1192/bjp.bp.108.055079

Dobkin, L. M., Gould, H., Barar, R. E., Ferrari, M., Weiss, E. I., Foster, D. G. (2014). Implementing a prospective study of women seeking abortion in the United States: Understanding and overcoming barriers to recruitment. *Women's Health Issues 24*(1), e115–e123. Retrieved from www.ansirh.org/sites/default/files/publications/files/dobkin-jan14-implementing_a_prospective_study_of_women_seeking_abortion.pdf

Dykes, K., Slade, P., & Haywood, A. (2010). Long term follow-up of emotional experiences after termination of pregnancy: women's views at menopause. *Journal of Reproductive and Infant Psychology, 29*(1), 1-20. doi:10.1080/02646838.2010.513046

Engelhard, I. M., van den Hout, M. A., Arntz, A. (2001) Posttraumatic stress disorder after pregnancy loss. *General Hospital Psychiatry, 23*, 62-66.

Fergusson, D. M., Horwood, L. J., & Ridder, E. M. (2006). Abortion in young women and subsequent mental health. *Journal of Child Psychology & Psychiatry 47*, 16-24.

Fok, W. Y., Siu, S. S. N., & Lau, T. K. (2006). Sexual dysfunction after a first trimester induced abortion in a Chinese population. *European Journal of Obstetrics & Gynecology, 126*, 255-258.

Freeman, E. W., Rickels, K., & Huggins, G. R. (1980). Emotional distress patterns among women having first or repeat abortions. *Obstetrics and Gynecology, 55*(5), 630–636.

Gissler, M., Hemminiki, E., & Lonnqvist, J. (1996). Suicides after pregnancy in Finland, 1987–94: register linkage study. *British Medical Journal, 313*, 1431. doi: 10.1136/bmj.313.7070.1431

Gissler, M., Kauppila, R., Merilainen, J., Toukomaa, H., & Hemminki, E. (1997). Pregnancy-associated deaths in Finland 1987-1994: Definition problems and benefits of record linkage. *Acta Obstetricia et Gynecologica Scandinavica, 76*(7), 651-657. doi: 10.3109/00016349709024605

Guttmacher Institute (2014). *Fact sheet: Induced abortion in the United States.* New York: Author.

Harper, S. (2008). *SaveOne: A guide to emotional healing after abortion.* Garden City, NY: Morgan James Publishing.

Harper, S. (2009). *Survivor.* Garden City, NY: Morgan James Publishing.

Jacobsen, L. K., Southwick, S. M. & Kosten, T. R. (2001). Substance use disorders in patients with posttraumatic stress disorder: A review of the literature. *American Journal of Psychiatry, 158*(8), 1184-1190.

Jones, R. K., Finer, L. B., & Singh, S. (2010). Characteristics of U.S. abortion patients, 2008. New York: Guttmacher Institute.

Kessler, R. C., Sonnega, A., Bromet, E., Hughes, M., Nelson, C. B. (1995). Posttraumatic stress disorder in the National Comorbidity Survey. *Archives General Psychiatry, 52*(12), 1048-60.

Kilpatrick, D. G. (2000). The mental health impact of rape. Retrieved from https://mainweb-v.musc.edu/vawprevention/research/mentalimpact.shtml

Kreek, M. J., & Koob, G. F. (1998). Drug dependence: Stress and dysregulation of brain reward pathways. *Drug and   Alcohol Dependence, 51,* 23-47.

Kulka, R. A., Schlenger, W. E., Fairbank, J. A., Hough, R. L., Jordan, B. K., Marmar, C. R., & Weiss, D. S. (1988). Contractual Report of Findings from the National Vietnam Veterans Readjustment Study, Volume I: Executive Summary, Description of Findings, and Technical Appendices. National Vietnam Veterans Readjustment Study. Retrieved from www.ptsd.va.gov/professional/articles/article-pdf/nvvrs_vol1.pdf

Lauzon, P., Roger-Achim, D., Achim, A., & Boyer, R. (2000). Emotional distress among couples involved in first trimester abortions. *Canadian Family Physician, 46,* 2033-2040.

Major, B., Appelbaum, M. Beckman, L., Dutton, M. A., Russo, N. F., & West., C. (2009). Abortion and mentalhealth: Evaluating the evidence. *American Psychologist, 64*(9), 863-890.

Marshall, R. D., Olfson, M., Hellman, F., Blanco, C., Guardino, M., Struening, E. (2001). Comorbidity, Impairment, and Suicidality in Subthreshold PTSD. *American Journal of Psychiatry, 158,* 1467-1473. doi: 10.1176/appi.ajp.158.9.1467

Miller, W. B. (1992). An empirical study of the psychological antecedents and consequences of induced abortion. *Journal of Social Issues, 48,* 67-93.

Morgan, C. M., Evans, M., Peter, J. R., & Currie, C. (1997). Suicides after pregnancy: mental health may deteriorate as a direct effect of induced abortion. *British Medical Journal, 314,* 902.

Mufel, N., Speckhard, A. & Sivuha, S. (2002). Predictors of posttraumatic stress disorder following abortion in a former Soviet Union country. *Journal of Prenatal & Perinatal Psych & Health,17,* 41-61.

Price, J. L. (2015) Findings from the National Vietnam Veterans' Readjustment Study. *U.S. Department of VeteranAffairs, PTSD: National Center for PTSD.* Retrieved from http://www.ptsd.va.gov/professional/research-bio/research/vietnam-vets-study.asp

Reardon, D. C., & Coleman, P. K. (2006). Relative treatment rates for sleep disorders and sleep disturbances following abortion and childbirth: A prospective record based study. *Sleep 29*(1), 105-106.

Reardon, D. C., Coleman, P. K., & Cougle, J. (2004) Substance use associated with prior history of abortion and unintended birth: A national cross sectional cohort study. *American Journal of Drug and Alcohol Abuse, 26,* 369-383.

Reardon, D. C., & Ney, P. (2000). Abortion and subsequent substance abuse. *American Journal of Drug and Alcohol Abuse, 26,* 61-75.

Reardon, D. C., Ney, P. G., Scheuren, F. J., Cougle, J. R., Coleman, P. K., Strahan, T. (2002). Deaths associated with pregnancy outcome: A record linkage study of low income women. *Southern Medical Journal, 95,* 834.

Reardon, D. C., Strahan, T. W., Thorp, Jr. J. M., & Shuping, M. W. (2004). Deaths associated with abortion compared to childbirth—a review of new and old data and the medical and legal implications. *Journal of Contemporary Health Law and Policy, 20*(2), 279-327.

Rocca, C. H., Kimport, K., Gould, H. & Foster, D. G. (2013). Women's emotions one week after receiving or being denied an abortion in the United States. *Perspectives on Sexual and Reproductive Health, 45*(3), 122–131, doi: 10.1363/4512213

Rue, V. M., Coleman, P. K., Rue, J. J. & Reardon, D. C. (2004). Induced abortion and traumatic stress: a preliminary comparison of American and Russian women. *Medical Science Monitor, 10*(10), SR5-16.

Saxon, A. J., Davis, T. M., Sloan, K. L., McKnight, K. M., McFall, M. E., & Kivlahan, D. R. (2001). Trauma, symptoms of posttraumatic stress disorder, and associated problems among incarcerated veterans. *Psychiatric Services, 52*(7), 959-964. doi: 10.1176/appi.ps.52.7.959

Schnurr, P. P., Lunney, C. A., Sengupta, A., & Waelde, L. C. (2003). A descriptive analysis of PTSD chronicity in Vietnam veterans. *Journal of Traumatic Stress, 16*(6), 545–553. doi: 10.1023/B:JOTS.0000004077.22408.cf

Sherin, J. E., & Nemeroff, C. B. (2011). Post-traumatic stress disorder: The neurobiological impact of psychological trauma. *Dialogues in Clinical Neuroscience, 13*(3), 263–278. Retrieved from http://www.ncbi.nlm.nih.gov/pmc/articles/PMC3182008/

Slade, P., Heke, S., Fletcher, J., & Stewart, P. (1998). A comparison of medical and surgical termination of pregnancy: choice, emotional impact and satisfaction with care. *British Journal of Obstetrics & Gynaecology, 105*(12), 1288-95. Retrieved from http://www.ncbi.nlm.nih.gov/pubmed/9883920

Speckhard, A. (1997). Traumatic death in pregnancy: The significance of meaning and attachment. In C. R. Figley, B. E. Bride, and N. Mazza (Eds.), *Death and trauma: The traumatology of grieving* (pp. 67-100). Washington, D.C.: Taylor & Francis.

Speckhard, A., & Mufel, N. (2003). Universal responses to abortion? Attachment, trauma, and grief responses in women following abortion. *Journal of Prenatal &Perinatal Psychology & Health Volume,18*(1), 3-37.

Speckhard, A. C., & Rue, V. M. (1992). Postabortion syndrome: An emerging public health concern. *Journal of Social Issues, 48*, 3, 95-119.

Speckhard, A. C., & Rue, V. M. (2012). In C. R. Figley (Ed.), *Encyclopedia of trauma: An interdisciplinary guide.* Thousand Oaks, CA: SAGE Publications. doi: http://dx.doi.org/10.4135/99781452218595

Strahl, N. R. (2012). Biological effects of physical and psychological trauma. In C.R. Figley (Ed.), *Encyclopedia of trauma: An interdisciplinary guide.* Thousand Oaks, CA: SAGE Publications. doi: 10.4135/99781452218595

Stein, M. B., Walker, J. R., Hazen, A. L., Forde, D. R. (1997). Full and partial posttraumatic stress disorder: findings from a community survey. *American Journal of Psychiatry, 154*(8), 1114-9.

Suliman, S., Ericksen, T., Labuschgne, T., de Wit R., Stein, D., Seedat, S. (2007). Comparison of pain, cortisol levels, and psychological distress in women undergoing surgical termination of pregnancy under local anaesthesia versus intravenous sedation. *BMC Psychiatry, 7*(24). doi:10.1186/1471-244X-7-24

Tishler, C. (1981). Adolescent suicide attempts following elective abortion. *Pediatrics, 68*(5), 670-671.

Tornboen, M., Ingelhammar, E., Lilja, H., Moller, A., Svanberg, B. (1994). Evaluation of stated motives for legal abortion. *Journal of Psychosomatic Obstetrics and Gynecology, 15*(1), 27-33.

Urquhart, D. R., & Templeton, A. A. (1991). Psychiatric morbidity and acceptability following medical and surgical methods of induced abortion. *Journal of Obstetrics and Gynaecology, 98*, 396-399.

Weisaeth, L. (1989). Importance of high response rates in traumatic stress research. *Acta psychiatrica Scandinavica Supplementum, 355*,131-137.

Chapter 11

Lost Fatherhood

by Catherine Coyle

From a feminist perspective, the perceived role of mothers as sole care-takers of children has given way to an expectation that both parents are equally responsible for child care. While much of child care involves the mundane, a precious closeness develops between men and their children as men share in the physical care of those children. Men are finding that participation in what used to be entirely women's work has many psychological rewards. Women benefit by having their workload shared. Co-parenting brings easily identified advantages to both mothers and fathers, but what about the decision to reject parenthood via abortion? Does elective abortion help or hinder the feminist ideal of gender equality? What impact does induced abortion have on women's male partners?

Men's rights related to abortion vary considerably. Rahman, Katzive and Henshaw (1998) published a global review of laws pertaining to induced abortion and reported that fourteen countries required spousal authorization for the obtainment of abortion. In the United States, the Supreme Court ruled that women seeking abortion did not need consent from partners or husbands (*Planned Parenthood v. Danforth*, 1976). Subsequently, the court decided that a woman was not obligated to even inform her partner or spouse of the abortion (*Planned Parenthood v. Casey*, 1992). All legal power was accorded to women regarding abortion decisions. Similarly, in both Britain (Cook & Dickens, 1999) and Canada (*Tremblay v. Daigle*, 1989), men were denied a legal right to prevent a partner's abortion.

While granting women the sole right to determine pregnancy outcome may seem fair since only women can gestate, it fails to take into account how such unilateral power may work against the rights of women and children. For example, some (Leib, 2005; National Center for Men, 2006) have argued that the abortion option offered to women removes from men the responsibility for child support. Furthermore, Brake (2005) contends that if a man takes preventive measures to avoid pregnancy and it occurs in spite of his efforts, he should not be held responsible for the financial support of the child conceived. So, while single and divorced mothers retain a legal right to child support, the ability to persuade men to provide such support has been undercut by the premise that the baby was born not due to his activity or desire, but due to his female partner's decision not to abort. Therefore, a logical argument could be made that the ready availability of abortion rewards men who do not wish to follow the feminist ideals of fatherhood by assuming responsibility for children they had a part in creating.

Conversely, men who do wish to be equally contributing and sensitive fathers are told they must disregard any attachment they feel toward their unborn children until their female partners decide not to abort. The consequences of this situation are potentially harmful to mothers, fathers, and the children they co-create.

Impact of Abortion on Men

Nada Stotland (2003), abortion defender and former president of the American Psychiatric Association, observed that "Psychotherapeutic issues of perceived helplessness, guilt and loss may come up in the treatment of men whose partners are contemplating or having abortions" (p. 147). Elective abortion surely involves some sense of loss for many of the men whose partners terminate pregnancy. Yet men's tendency to comply with society's expectations by repressing their emotions (a common expectation for the traditional male role) may effectively prevent others from appreciating their suffering.

The effects of other forms of pregnancy loss on men, as well as men's responses to impending fatherhood, have been investigated. For example, Puddifoot and Johnson (1999) report that after miscarriage men evidenced higher "difficulty coping" and "despair" scores on the Perinatal Grief Scale than did women. Others have documented hormonal changes in men that occur during pregnancy and soon after birth (Berg & Wynne-Edwards, 2001; Storey, Walsh, Quinton & Wynne-Edwards, 2000). In addition, pregnancy and fathering have been recognized and discussed as important periods of men's development (Bozett, 1985; Palkovitz, 2014; Zayas, 1987; Sonne, 2005).

About 50 empirical reports concerning men and abortion have been published in the last four decades. These reports include case studies, clinical observations, qualitative and quantitative studies, three intervention studies, and two literature reviews. While the studies are limited by their number and by small sample sizes, the findings from them are consistent and therefore suggest that induced abortion has the potential to harm men's mental health. This chapter offers an overview of common findings from those reports concerning the psychological impact of elective abortion on men.

General Effects

One of the largest and earliest studies was published as a book by Shostak and McLouth (1984). These authors surveyed 1,000 men in abortion clinic waiting rooms while the men's partners underwent induced abortion. The same survey was administered to 75 men who had experienced a partner's abortion "months, and often years earlier" (p. 104). The survey focused on men's attitudes and opinions more than on the effects of abortion. However, it did query men about abortion decision-making, quality of relationship with partner before and after abortion, thoughts about fatherhood and the fetus, and the value of counseling for men. When asked if men would or did have disturbing thoughts about abortion afterward, 47% of clinic men anticipated such thoughts, as compared to 63% of post-abortion men who actually experienced such thoughts. When asked if they thought men involved with abortion generally have an easy time of it, 68% of the clinic men and 75% of the post-abortion men disagreed.

In two previous studies (Shostak, 1979, 1983), that same question was asked and 72% of men in the former and 75% in the latter disagreed that abortion is easy for men. Similarly, only 9.3% of participants in another study stated that abortion did not affect them while the rest reported fear, anxiety, and tension (Schelotto & Arcuri, 1986). In a study from Vietnam, men with moral doubts about abortion and those who were ambivalent expressed feelings of unease, guilt, and worry (Johansson, Nga, Huy, Dat & Holmgren, 1998). Coyle, Coleman, and Rue (2010) queried men via an online survey and, using a 10-point Likert scale for a question about stress, found that 71.1% of them described their abortion experience as causing "high" to "overwhelming" stress. These studies suggest that elective abortion is not a benign experience for all men and that substantial numbers of men may not be receiving the attention they need following a partner's abortion.

Relief

A few studies have reported relief as a response to a partner's abortion. In a European study, Kero, Lalos & Wulff (2010) reported that most men, who remained with their partners during a home abortion, "considered their experiences during the expulsion had been 'easier than expected' and their dominant feeling was one of relief" (p. 264). Two studies of couples who received a diagnosis of fetal abnormality also observed relief among men; Jones et al. (1984) reported relief among 75% of male partners and White-van Mourik, Connor, and Ferguson-Smith (1992) reported that 32% of men experienced relief. A large number of men in these two studies also experienced depression (50% in Jones et al., 1984 and 47% in White-van Mourik et al., 1992).

Ambivalence

Ambivalence was found to be the predominant response in three studies. Kero et al. (1999) asked men to choose words to describe their abortion experience; 57% of men chose words indicative of both positive and negative emotions while 29% chose only negative words. In a similar study (Kero & Lalos, 2000), the most commonly chosen words were "responsibility," "maturity," and "grief" and most men experienced "conflicts of conscience." Still more ambivalent reactions were observed in a third study (Kero & Lalos, 2004) in which men were described as experiencing the abortion as a "responsible act" but also finding it to be "painful and ethically problematic" (p. 135).

Anger

A number of studies have identified anger as a male response to abortion (Coyle & Enright, 1997; Coyle & Rue, 2010; Coyle & Rue, 2015, Ferguson & Hogan, 2007; Naziri, 2007; White-van Mourik et al., 1992). Coyle et al. (2010) found that 79.8% of male partners reported abortion-related anger and that disagreement regarding the abortion decision was a predictor of men's anger. Similarly, Naziri (2007) observed that intense anger was especially apparent when partners disagreed about pregnancy termination. For some men, anger may serve the role of defense mechanism against more vulnerable emotions such as anxiety and helplessness (Coyle & Rue, 2010). Men may find anger to be less threatening than those other negative emotions. In addition, anger may be more consistent with "culturally prescribed 'masculine' ways" (Rue, 1996, p. 3) to express one's grief.

Anxiety

Many investigators have reported anxiety and/or helplessness among men whose partners elect abortion (Coyle & Enright, 1997; Coyle & Rue, 2010; Coyle & Rue, 2015; Dubois-Bonnefond & Galle-Tessonneau, 1982; Gordon & Kilpatrick, 1977;

Hallden & Christensson, 2010; Rothstein, 1991; Rue, 1985; Schelotto & Arcuri, 1986). For some men, anxiety or grief may lead to substance abuse (Ring-Cassidy & Gentles, 1998) or other behavioral problems (Dubois-Bonnefond & Galle-Tessonneau (1982). Anxiety may also contribute to and be exacerbated by intrusive thoughts about the fetus and/or sleep disturbances (Holmes, 2004; Shostak, 1983; Shostak & Mcouth, 1984). Some men identified anxiety as arising from the helplessness they felt upon being unable to protect the child they had co-created (Coyle & Rue, 2010).

PTSD

Some studies have observed trauma symptoms such as intrusive thoughts or sleep disturbances among men after a partner's abortion (Baker, Morrison & Coffey, 2011; Holmes, 2004; Poggenpoel & Myburgh, 2002; Shostak, 1983; Shostak & McLouth, 1984; Stern, 1999).

While men are typically not allowed to remain with their partners during the abortion procedure, Lauzon, Roger-Achim, Achim & Boyer (2000) reported that 21.3% of those men who did so thought it to be a traumatizing experience. A case study by Robson (2002) described a man who chose to support his wife by staying with her during a late-term, therapeutic abortion. Afterward, he suffered from re-experiencing the abortion which he had watched on a screen as it was being performed. In a case study (Baker et al. 2011) regarding a man whose wife elected to abort their third child twenty years prior, authors discuss the abortion as a traumatic event which led to the man being treated for PTSD. Coyle et al. (2010) found that inadequate pre-abortion counseling predicted symptoms of intrusion and avoidance and abortion decision disagreement predicted symptoms of intrusion, hyperarousal, and meeting diagnostic criteria for PTSD among men.

Grief

The most frequently reported reaction to abortion in the literature pertaining to men and abortion is grief. While many authors used the word "grief" in describing their findings, some referred to men's "sadness" or "loss."

A particularly striking finding in a number of studies is the intensity of men's grief long after the abortion occurred (Coyle et al., 2010; Coyle & Enright, 2007; Coyle & Rue, 2010, 2015; McAll & McAll, 1980). Mattinson (1985) noted that grief may be delayed after abortion and suggested that men may be especially vulnerable to abortion loss as they are often neglected by medical professionals and expected by society to repress their emotions. White-van Mourik et al. (1992) also raised the issue of unresolved grief, stating that 58% of male participants in their investigation were at risk.

Some studies referred to "depression" rather than "grief" and identified from 25.8% (Coleman & Nelson, 1998) to 47% (White-van Mourik et al. 1992) to 50% (Jones et al., 1984) to 82% (Blumberg, Golbus & Hanson, 1975) of male participants as depressed. Using the Ilfeld Psychiatric Symptom Index (IPSI) Lauzon et al. (2000) found that three weeks after abortion, "30.9% of men were still highly distressed" (p. 2033). Higher IPSI scores are associated with both depression and anxiety. Stern (1999) noted that "Post-abortion grief in men can result in a chronic depression during which sleep disturbances and nightmares are not uncommon" (p. 62).

Coyle and Rue (2015) observed that one of three salient themes among the male partners of women who aborted was "loss and grief." Similarly, in a mixed-methods study of men's experience of elective abortion, the primary meaning ascribed to abortion was "profound loss" (Coyle & Rue, 2010). Men experienced multiple losses, including loss of the partner relationship, loss of the child, loss of trust in themselves, and loss of hope for the future. The men's average total score on the Perinatal Grief Scale (PGS) was 101. Developers of the PGS explain:

> What does it mean to indicate that a score above 91 on the total PGS may be reason for concern? Simply that 97.5% of people studied so far have scores that are lower than that number. Practitioners may find it helpful to attend particularly to people who have this score or higher, as they may indeed be particularly vulnerable because of the loss. (Toedter, Lasker & Janssen, 2001, p. 220).

Therefore, some men may suffer from severe grief or even depression after abortion and require intervention. An additional challenge for men is society's lack of acknowledgment which disenfranchises their grief and increases the likelihood that men will suffer from complicated mourning or grief (Doka, 1989).

Responsibility, Guilt, and Regret

In a study by Major, Cozzarelli, Testa and Mueller (2006), researchers found that "men blamed the pregnancy more on their own character than did their partners" (p. 599). This concern with responsibility is apparent in other studies concerning men's reaction to abortion. Reich and Brindis (2006) reported that "notions of responsibility were central to men's accounts of the abortion experience and emerged in every interview. In some ways, the pregnancy itself marked a lack of responsible behavior" (p. 139) and "a majority of the men felt they were able to behave responsibly by helping to execute the decision to terminate" (p. 139). This is consistent with the observation by Kero and Lalos (2000) that, for some men, abortion is a way to exercise responsibility in a situation that came about due to their irresponsibility.

However, most studies did not describe male participants as seeing abortion as a responsible act. Rather, they observed guilt as a frequent aftermath of abortion (Coyle & Rue, 2010; Dubois-Bonnefond & Galle-Tessonneau, 1982; Gordon & Kilpatrick, 1977; Johansson et al., 1998; Jones et al., 1984; Poggenpoel & Myburgh, 2002; Rodrigues & Hoga, 2006; Speckhard & Rue, 1993; Stern, 1999; Rothstein, 1991; Rue, 1996; White-van Mourik et al., 1992).

Regret was also reported after abortion (Coleman & Nelson, 1998; Gordon & Kilpatrick, 1977; Stern, 1999). Of 26 men queried about a future unplanned pregnancy, only 7 stated they would choose abortion, 9 would choose birth, and 9 were unsure (Kero & Lalos, 2004). Similarly, in an online pilot study, Coyle (2006) found that 67% of men queried would not choose abortion again if they could go back to the time when the abortion decision was made. Only 13% would choose abortion if faced with another unplanned pregnancy in the future.

Helplessness and/or Victimization

Coyle & Rue (2015) recognized "helplessness and/or victimization" as a salient theme among men and stated that "Helplessness and victimization seemed to be two sides of the same coin with both arising from men's lack of power to determine the pregnancy outcome" (p.142). Helplessness appeared to be associated with sadness while victimization was associated with anger. In other studies, a feeling of "powerlessness" was evident among biological fathers (Myburgh, Gmeiner & van Wyk, 2001a) and helplessness was reported for Swedish men even among those who defended the abortion decision (Hallden & Christensson, 2010).

Perceived Role/Preferred Coping Style

Several investigators have noted men's attempts to be supportive and relieve their partners' pain (Hallden & Christensson, 2010; Robson, 2002; Rothstein, 1977b; Shostak & McLouth, 1984). Ferguson & Hogan (2007) determined that "the dominant pattern was for men to provide stoic support to the woman, they said, to help her deal with her distress and not to open up about their own wishes for the pregnancy or their feelings" (p. 15).

Robson (2002) also speaks of a man's need to fulfill his duty by suppressing his own feelings in an effort to support his partner. Robson adds that this tendency "should not be underestimated in terms of value for his own recovery in allowing his self-image and identity to remain intact" (p. 191).

Relationships and Sexuality

One study (Jones et al., 1984) reported improved relationships, with 70% of men stating they had increased closeness with partners after therapeutic abortion. Other studies reported negative effects on relationships (Coleman, Rue & Spence, 2006; Coyle, et al., 2010; Lauzon, et al. 2000; Myburgh, et al. 2001a; Rue, 1996; Shostak, 1979; Speckhard & Rue, 1993). Half of the male participants in an Italian study (Schelotto & Arcuri, 1986) indicated that their relationships with partners were negatively affected by abortion and, 15.6% blamed the abortion for ending those relationships. Similarly, in Shostak (1979), 20% of men believed that abortion contributed to relationship failure. Lauzon et al. (2000) found that "Fear of negative effects on the relationship is the variable most strongly associated with high distress for both men and women" (p. 2039).

Relationship problems have occurred subsequent to abortion even when couples agreed to abort (Naziri, 2007). In addition, abortion in a prior relationship has been found to be associated with negative outcomes in the current relationship (Coleman, Rue & Coyle 2009).

Abortion has also been associated with sexual problems. In one study, one-half of couples reported negative effects on sexual relationships after abortion (White-van Mourik et al., 1992) and impotence after abortion has also been reported (Rothstein, 1977a; White-van Mourik, 1992).

Adolescent Men

In a large longitudinal study (Buchanan & Robbins, 1990), 2,522 males were initially surveyed in middle school and then assessed for psychological distress in adulthood. Of the original sample, 15% experienced an unplanned pregnancy prior to the age of 21. This subgroup was divided into three categories based on pregnancy resolution: abortion (38.3%), parenthood without marriage or cohabitation (27.8%), and parenthood with marriage or cohabitation (33.9%). Psychological distress was assessed with a 22-

item measure of "dysphoric affect, psychophysiological correlates of anxiety or depression, and feelings of inability to cope with day-to-day life" (p. 418).

The mean psychological distress score was lowest for those men who never experienced adolescent pregnancy and highest for those men whose partners had abortions. Interestingly, "the effects of abortion or single parenthood are statistically significant, but those who had the child and married or lived together were not significantly more distressed than those who never experienced an adolescent pregnancy" (p. 420).

Healing after Abortion

Need and/or Desire for Counseling

Although pre- and post-abortion counseling are not routinely offered to men, a number of authors have recognized men's desire and/or need for counseling (Coyle et al., 2010; Coyle & Rue, 2015; Myburgh, et al. 2001b; Papworth, 2011; Rodrigues & Hoga, 2006). Rothstein (1977b) found that 20% of men expressed an interest in counseling while Lauzon et al. (2000) reported that 30.4% of men would have liked counseling. Mackenzius, Tyden, Darj & Larrson (2012) stated that men "should be considered as individuals with their own needs in the context of abortion" rather than simply treated as persons who happen to be accompanying female patients.

Speckhard & Rue (1993) point out that "Women and men who experience disenfranchised loss and whose grief and trauma reactions to abortion are impacted can hardly be expected to work through their loss with a professional community that is blind to their loss" (p. 29). Counseling can only be effective when counselors recognize men's needs and respect men's preferred methods of processing their grief. Along the same lines, Mester (1978) stated "It is suggested that the psychotherapist who is overly influenced by statistics and the sociopolitical climate and/or his own inner conflicts may unconsciously ignore or minimize the importance of an abortion experience for a specific patient in his [or her] care" (p. 98). Therefore, counselors must be aware of their own biases in order to successfully help men before or after abortion.

Treatment Programs

There have been only three formal studies to evaluate treatment programs for men who were struggling with a partner's abortion (Coyle & Enright, 1997; Gordon, 1978; Baker, et al. 2011).

Coyle and Enright (1997) developed and tested a 12-week forgiveness therapy program utilizing two groups to which participants were randomly assigned, a treatment group and a wait-list control group. Forgiveness therapy was associated with a significant increase in forgiveness and significant reductions in anxiety, anger, and grief.

Gordon (1978) tested the efficacy of a group crisis-counseling program for men who accompanied their partners to an abortion clinic. Counseling was associated with a significant decrease in state-anxiety.

The third investigation (Baker et al. 2011) was a case study involving the use of Prolonged Exposure (PE) for abortion-related PTSD in a 46 year old male being treated concurrently for alcohol dependence. Following 12 sessions of PE, the patient evidenced a decrease in symptoms of PTSD.

While each of these interventions proved to be successful, many of the counseling programs currently available to men are Christian in their worldview, facilitated by nonprofessionals, and have not been scientifically tested for efficacy. Frequently these programs have a commital aspect to them in which the men are able to commit the lost child to God in a formal, symbolic way. McAll & McAll (1980) described a case study involving a man whose depression and anorexia were resolved following a process of mourning for and commital of his aborted child. The notion of "spiritual healing" has been found to be a salient theme among men and, in every case where a man chose to comment on his healing experience, he did so in spiritual terms (Coyle & Rue, 2015). Furthermore, "Most (81%) of the men's statements concerning healing included some mention of forgiveness including receiving forgiveness, self-forgiveness, or both" (Coyle & Rue, 2015, p. 144) suggesting that these forms of forgiveness were critical aspects of their healing.

Future Research

Although the available evidence indicates that a partner's elective abortion may negatively impact some men's mental health, we do not know the magnitude of that impact because most studies have used small samples. Research involving large, representative samples is needed in order to better understand the effects of abortion on men and to accurately determine the number of men who may be negatively affected. Research is urgently needed to assess the level of risk posed by elective abortion for men, to inform the development of treatment programs for them, and to test such programs for efficacy. An aborting woman's born children and the parents of both partners may also be affected by abortion, but these family members have not been studied in the context of induced abortion. A single study by Ney, Sheils and Gajowy (2010) found distress among children who had previously occupied the same womb as the aborted fetus. There are as yet no published studies concerning potential grandparents.

The societal impact of elective abortion applies not only to the mental health of men, but also to the rights of women. We know that there has been an epidemic of men abandoning their children. When men refuse to pay child support, a minimal expectation, the feminization of poverty increases. There is a critical need for research on the direct psychological impact of abortion on male child-rearing practices (i.e. child support payments as well as more substantive participation). Specifically, studies should attempt to determine if the correlation of high abortion rates and high non-support rates is causal or only coincidental, and if causal, in which direction(s).

Conclusion

In contrast to the growing body of research concerning the psychological impact of abortion on women, relatively few studies have addressed the psychological impact of abortion on men. Society continues to view abortion as a women's issue. Both the media and politicians portray abortion as being of consequence to women only. Therefore, little thought or attention is given to men's reactions to elective abortion. Furthermore, the effect that this lack of attention to men has on their female partners remains unconsidered, as if women were isolated in pregnancy and pregnancy outcome situations. Neither men nor women benefit from this failure to acknowledge each of them in the context of abortion.

References

Baker, A., Morrison, J. A. & Coffey, S. F. (2011). Using prolonged exposure to treat abortion-related Posttraumatic Stress Disorder in alcohol dependent men: A case study. *Clinical Case Studies, 10*(6), 427-439.

Berg, S. J. & Wynne-Edwards, K. E. (2001). Changes in testosterone, cortisol, and estradiol in men becoming fathers. *Mayo Clinical Proceedings, 76*(6), 582-592.

Blumberg, B. D., Golbus, M. S. & Hanson, K. H. (1975). The psychological sequelae of abortion performed for a genetic indication. *American Journal of Obstetrics & Gynecology, 122*(7), 799-808.

Bozett, F. W. (1985). Male development and fathering throughout the life cycle. *American Behavioral Science, 29* (1), 41-54.

Brake, E. (2005). Fatherhood and child support: Do men have a right to choose? *Journal of Applied Philosophy, 22* (1), 55-73.

Buchanan, M. & Robbins, C. (1990). Early adult psychological consequences for males of adolescent pregnancy and its resolution. *Journal of Youth and Adolescence, 19* (4), 413-424.

Coleman, P. K. & Nelson, E. S. (1998). The quality of abortion decisions and college students' reports of post-abortion emotional sequelae and abortion attitudes. *Journal of Social and Clinical Psychology, 17* (4), 425-442.

Coleman, P. K., Rue, V. M. & Coyle, C. T. (2009). Induced abortion and intimate relationship quality in the Chicago Health and Social Life Survey. *Public Health, 123,* 331-338.

Coleman, P. K., Rue, V. M. & Spence, M. (2006). Intrapersonal processes and post-abortion relationship challenges: A review and consolidation of relevant literature. *The Internet Journal of Mental Health, 4* (2).

Cook, R. J., & Dickens, B. M. (1999). Human rights and abortion laws. *International Journal of Gynecology & Obstetrics, 65*(1), 81-87.

Coyle, C. T. (2006). An online pilot study to investigate the effects of abortion on men. *Association for Interdisciplinary Research in Values and Social Change Research Bulletin, 19* (1).

Coyle, C. T., Coleman, P.K. & Rue, V.M. (2010). Inadequate preabortion counseling and decision conflict as predictors of subsequent relationship difficulties and psychological stress in men and women. *Traumatology, 16* (1). 16-30. doi: 10.1177/15344765609347550

Coyle, C. T. & Enright, R. D. (1997). Forgiveness intervention with post-abortion men. *Journal of Consulting and Clinical Psychology, 65,* (6), 1042-1046.

Coyle, C. T. & Rue, V. M. (2010). Men's experience of elective abortion: A mixed-methods study of loss. *Journal of Pastoral Counseling, XLV,* 4-31.

Coyle, C. T. & Rue, V. M. (2015). Men's perceptions concerning disclosure of a partner's abortion: Implications for counseling. *The European Journal of Counselling Psychology, 3*(2), 159-173. doi: 10.1111/j.1471-6712.2012.01068.x

Coyle, C. T. & Rue, V. M. (2015). A thematic analysis of men's experience with a partner's elective abortion. *Journal of Counseling and Values,60,* 138-150.

Doka, K. J. (Ed.) (1989). *Disenfranchised grief: Recognizing hidden sorrow* (pp. 187-198). Lexington, MA: Lexington Books.

DuBois-Bonnefond, J. & Galle-Tessonneau, J. (1982). Psychopathological effects of voluntary termination of pregnancy on a father called up for military service. *Psychologie Medicale, 14* (8), 1187-1189.

Ferguson, H. & Hogan, F. (2007). Men, sexuality, and crisis pregnancy: A study of men's experiences. *Crisis Pregnancy Agency Report Number 18.* Dublin.

Gordon, R. A. (1978). Efficacy of a group crisis-counseling program for men accompanying women seeking abortions. *American Journal of Community Psychology, 6* (3), 239-246.

Gordon, R. A. & Kilpatrick, C. (1977). A program of group counseling for men who accompany women seeking legal abortions. *Community Mental Health Journal, 13* (4), 291-295.

Hallden, B. & Christensson, K. (2010). Swedish young men's lived experiences of a girlfriend's early induced abortion. *International Journal of Men's Health, 9* (2), 126-143.

Holmes, M. C. (2004). Reconsidering a "woman's issue:" Psychotherapy and one man's post abortion experiences. *American Journal of Psychotherapy, 58*(1), 103-115.

Johansson, A., Nga, N. T., Huy, T. Q., Dat, D. D. & Holmgren, K. (1998). Husbands' involvement in abortion in Vietnam. *Studies in Family Planning, 29*(4), 400-413.

Jones, O. W., Penn, N. E., Shuchter, S., Stafford, C. A., Richards, T., Kernahan, C.,...& Dixson, B. (1984). Parental response to mid-trimester therapeutic abortion following amniocentesis. *Prenatal Diagnosis, 4* (4), 249-256.

Kero, A. & Lalos, A. (2000). Ambivalence – a logical response to legal abortion: A prospective study among women and men. *Journal of Psychosomatic Obstetrics and Gynecology, 21* (2), 81-91.

Kero, A. & Lalos, A. (2004). Reactions and reflections in men, 4 and 12 months post-abortion. *Journal of Psychosomatic Obstetrics and Gynecology, 25*(2), 135-143.

Kero, A., Lalos, A. & Wulff, M. (2010). Home abortion – experiences of male involvement. *The European Journal of Contraception and Reproductive Health Care, 15,* 264-270.

Lauzon, P., Roger-Achim, D., Achim, A. & Boyer, R. (2000). Emotional distress among couples involved in first-trimester induced abortions. *Canadian Family Physician,* October (46), 2033-2040.

Leib, E. J. (2005). A man's right to choose: Men deserve voice in abortion decision *Legal Times, XXVIII* (14).

Major, B., Cozzarelli, C., Testa, M. & Mueller, P. (2006). Male partners' appraisals of undesired pregnancy and abortion: Implications for women's adjustment to abortion. *Journal of Applied Social Psychology, 22* (8), 599-614. doi: 10.1111/j.1559-1816.1992.tb00992.x

Mattinson, J. (1985). The effects of abortion on a marriage. Abortion: Medical Progress and   social implications, *Ciba Foundation Symposium, 115,* 165-177.

McAll, R. K. & McAll, F. M. (1980). Ritual mourning in anorexia nervosa. *Lancet, 2* (8190), 368.

Mester, R. (1978). Induced abortion and psychotherapy. *Psychotherapy and Psychosomatics, 30*(2), 98-104.

Myburgh, M., Gmeiner, A. & van Wyk, S. (2001a). Support for adult biological fathers during termination of their partners' pregnancies. *Health SA Gesondheid, 6* (1), 38-48.

Myburgh, M., Gmeiner, A. & van Wyk, S. (2001b). The experience of biological fathers of their partners' termination of pregnancy. *Health SA Gesondheid, 6* (1), 28-37.

National Center for Men (2006). Roe vs. Wade – for Men. Retrieved from: http://www.nationalcenterformen.org/page7.shtml

Naziri, D. (2007). Man's involvement in the experience of abortion and the dynamics of the couple's relationship: A clinical study. *The European Journal of Contraception and Reproductive Health Care, 12*(2), 168-174.

Ney, P. G., Shiels, C. K. & Gajowy, M. (2010). Post abortion survivor syndrome: Signs and symptoms. *Journal of Prenatal and Perinatal Psychology and Health, 25* (2)107-129.

Palkovitz, R. (2014). *Involved fathering and men's adult development: Provisional balances.* Psychology Press.

Papworth, V. (2011). Abortion services: The need to include men in care provision. *Nursing Standard, 25* (40), 35-37.

Planned Parenthood of Central Missouri v. Danforth, 428 U.S. 52 (1976)

Planned Parenthood of Southeastern Pennsylvania v. Casey, 505 U.S. 833 (1992)

Poggenpoel, M. & Myburgh, C. P. H. (2002). The developmental implications of a termination of pregnancy on adolescents with reference to the girl and her partner. *Education, 122*(4), 731-741.

Puddifoot, J. E. & Johnson, M. P. (1999). Active grief, despair, and difficulty coping: Some measured characteristics of male response following their partner's miscarriage. *Journal of Reproduction and Infant Psychology, 17*(1), 89-93.

Rahman, A., Katzive, L., & Henshaw, S. K. (1998). A global review of laws on induced abortion, 1985-1997. *International Family Planning Perspectives*, 56-64.

Reich, J. A. & Brindis, C. D. (2006). Conceiving risk and responsibility: A qualitative examination of men's experiences of unintended pregnancy and abortion. *International Journal of Men's Health, 5*(2), 133-152.

Ring-Cassidy, E. & Gentles, I. (1998). Abortion: Its effect on men. In E. Ring-Cassidy & I. Gentles (Eds.). *Women's Health after Abortion: The Medical and Psychological Evidence* (pp. 237-253). Toronto: de Veber Institute.

Robson, F. M. (2002). "Yes!-A chance to tell my side of the story": a case study of a male partner of a woman undergoing termination of pregnancy for foetal abnormality. *Journal of Health Psychology, 7*(2), 183-193.

Rodrigues, M. M. L. & Hoga, L. A. K. (2006). Spontaneous and induced abortion: Feelings experienced by men. *Revista Brasileira de Enfermagem, 59*(1), 14-19.

Rothstein, A. (1977a). Men's reactions to their partners' elective abortions. *American Journal of Obstetrics and Gynecology, 128*(8), 831-837.

Rothstein, A. (1977b). Abortion: A dyadic perspective. *The American Journal of Orthopsychiatry, 47*(1) 111-118.

Rothstein, A. (1991). Male experience of elective abortion: Psychoanalytic perspectives. In N. L. Stotland, editor. *Psychiatric aspects of abortion.* Washington, D.C.: American Psychiatric Association, p. 145-158.

Rue, V. M. (1985). Abortion in relationship context. *International Review of Natural Family Planning, 9*(2), 95 -121.

Rue, V. M. (1996). His abortion experience: The effects of abortion on men. *Ethics and Medics, 21*, 3-4.

Schelotto, G. & Arcuri, C. (1986). Supposing it hurt me too? Abortion: The anguish experienced by men. *Planned Parenthood in Europe Regional Information Bulletin, 15* (1), 25-34.

Shostak, A. & McLouth, G. (1984). *Men and abortion: Lessons, losses, and love.* New York: Praeger.

Shostak, A. (1983). Men and abortion: Three neglected ethical aspects. *Humanity and Society, 7*(1), 66-85.

Shostak, A. (1979). Abortion as fatherhood lost: Problems and reforms. *The Family Coordinator, 28*(4), 569-574.

Sonne, J. C. (2005). The varying behaviors of fathers in the prenatal experience of the unborn: Protecting, loving, and "Welcoming with Arms Open," vs. ignoring, unloving, competitive, abusive, abortion minded or aborting. *Journal of Prenatal and Perinatal Psychological Health, 19*(4), 319-140.

Speckhard, A. & Rue, V. (1993). Complicated mourning: Dynamics of impacted post abortion grief. *Journal of Prenatal and Perinatal Psychology, 8*(1), 5-32.

Stern, E. M. (1999). Men and post-abortion grief. *Journal of Couples Therapy, 8*(2), 61-71.

Storey, A. E., Walsh, C. J., Quinton, R. L. & Wynne-Edwards, K. E. (2000). Hormonal correlates of paternal responsiveness in new and expectant fathers. *Evolutionary Human Behavior 21*(2): 79-95.

Stotland, N. L. (2003). Abortion and psychiatric practice. *Journal of Psychiatric Practice, 9*(2), 139-149.

Toedter, J., Lasker, J. N. & Janssen, L. (2001). International comparison of studies using the perinatal grief scale: A decade of research on pregnancy loss. *Death Studies, 25*(3), 205-228.

Tremblay v. Daigle, 2 S.C.R. 530, 62 D.L.R. (4th) 634 (1989)

White-van Mourik, M. C., Connor, J. M., & Ferguson-Smith, M. A. (1992). The psychological sequelae of a second-trimester termination of pregnancy for fetal abnormality. *Prenatal Diagnosis, 12* (3), 189-204.

Zayas, L. H. (1987). Psychodynamic and developmental aspects of expectant and new fatherhood: Clinical derivatives from the literature. *Clinical Social Work, 15*(1), 8-21.

Chapter 12

Doctors and Staff

by Rachel M. MacNair

The Psychological Aspects of Providing Abortions

Noted in the literature and from my own personal communications with abortion staff, possibilities for psychological reactions include:

- Being pleased with doing good work for patients and community.

- Feeling stress because of the controversy.

- Feeling burnout, especially where clinics are set up on something of an assembly-line organization with minimal contact with the patients.

- Posttraumatic Stress Disorder (PTSD) symptoms would be expected from the theoretical abortion-as-violence perspective. A belief that abortion constitutes killing a human being, or even an organism with the status similar to that of animals, would necessitate this reaction in a portion of providers.

There is no controversy that stress and burnout are problems. There is of course controversy over whether PTSD is a problem; that is foundational to the dispute.

Being Pleased with Good Work

Studies specifically using job satisfaction surveys for abortion staff were not found in the literature; there have been two surveys, both quite old, that do not find satisfaction and are covered under PTSD below. Nevertheless, some doctors clearly have high satisfaction.

While satisfied people are normally not newsworthy and therefore no prevalence could be ascertained from media interviews, there is at least qualitative documentation of such sentiment. For example, these remarks come from an interview with Dr. Cheryl Chastine:

> I have no regrets about my path. This is even more important, and more rewarding, than I'd thought it could be. Every day I go to work, I can make it possible for someone to leave an abusive relationship, care for their children, continue their education, deal with an illness. Every day, my patients hug me and thank me and tell me I've helped them get their life back. (Grimes, 2015)

One book, a case study of an abortion clinic, offers a positive assessment (Lunnenborg, 1992). Several abortion doctors have written their autobiographies to put their work in a positive light: Donald Sloan (2002), Suzanne Poppema (1996), and Susan Wicklund (2007).

Stress Peculiar to this Field

In several countries, and especially in the United States, there are protesters who have picketed abortion clinics, doctor's other offices, or even their homes. The abortion-as-option perspective sees this as an unjustified imposition on people doing their jobs. Some of those of the abortion-as-violence perspective might see this as justified in the same way as picketing the offices of military contractors and polluters would be. The comparison is odious to those of the abortion-as-option perspective, but quite necessary to those of the abortion-as-violence perspective.

In the United States, extra stress is added on those occasions when the shooting of abortion staff is reported in the news, which commonly receives nation-wide coverage. Such vigilante shootings are of course regarded as intolerable by all perspectives within peace psychology – as well as practically everyone else but the few isolated vigilante-minded people. The militant-minded fringe has been a problem in many social movements, especially the anti-war movement of the 1960s.

Dr. Warren Hern, as director of the Boulder Abortion Clinic, did respond to the first shooting incident with an opinion in the *New York Times* that listed some other sources of stress:

> Increasingly, doctors have been made to feel irrelevant. Feminist abortion clinics treat doctors like technicians and are especially contemptuous of male physicians. Entrepreneurs who treat abortion strictly as a retail business also tend to treat doctors as technicians. Doctors who perform abortions have usually acquiesced in these roles, and their status has plummeted lower than that of physicians who do insurance company examinations.
>
> I know of clinics that don't allow doctors to speak to patients, and of others where medical policy is set and changed by administrators without consulting physicians. Pro-choice organizations often ignore, patronize and disparage the contributions of physicians who specialize in abortions, in contrast with their support for well-known physicians in conventional specialties who perform some abortions. (Hern, 1993).

Burnout

Burnout has three components (Maslach, 1982), with each one developing from what came before:

1. Emotional exhaustion
Feeling overwhelmed by emotional demands imposed by others.

2. Depersonalization
Developing a detached, callous, even dehumanized response.

3. Feeling of reduced personal accomplishment
This results in part from the uncaring actions that come with depersonalization.

Those who are most at risk of burnout deal with many people over an extended period of time, are on constant call, and expected to deal with problems in a caring manner. Social workers, child-care givers, teachers, and most definitely social activists are subject to burnout. It is a topic with which all peace psychologists and activists should be familiar – an occupational hazard of any form of activism. People get very involved and become overwhelmed.

The solutions are fairly straightforward: take breaks, vacations, downshifts (doing work but not the stressful kind), get appreciation, accentuate the positive, engage in small talk, use relaxation techniques, be in tune with inner feelings.

Posttraumatic Stress Disorder

PTSD is a set of symptoms that result from a trauma; for a full list for diagnosis purposes, see the DSM-5 (American Psychiatric Association, 2013) or the ICD-10 (World Health Organization, 1992); the ICD-11 is due out shortly. The international definition is more narrative, but the American version divides the symptoms into four clusters according to type: re-experiencing (including intrusive thoughts, flashbacks, and dreams); avoiding reminders of the trauma; negative thoughts and moods; and increased arousal (including outbursts of rage, hypervigilance, sleep disturbance, and reckless or self-destructive behavior). For diagnosis of a full disorder, a proper professional interview is required. However, having "sub-clinical" levels, meaning just a few symptoms not sufficient for a full disorder, can still be distressing to the individual. The "disorder" means that people are having trouble functioning, which is usually what motivates them to seek help and be diagnosed, but people can suffer from symptoms while still being fully functional. Combat veterans, for example, very commonly work full-time and vigorously despite the symptoms; indeed, workaholism may be one method of self-medicating. The DSM-5 in its discussion indicates that killing others can be one of the traumas that cause PTSD symptoms, which is of particular interest in this controversy.

Regarding research concerning abortion staff, if empirical studies are narrowed down to ones done by researchers who do not work in the abortion field themselves, and which include a large number of participants, there are at present only two. Neither has a control group, both are quite preliminary in nature, and both were done in the early days of U.S. legalization when the staff included people who had not volunteered for the duty. Both studies were done by researchers with a bias in favor of abortion availability. Yet in contrast to the varying results of the studies of post-abortion women, they both report the high prevalence of symptoms that fit under posttraumatic stress disorder.

The first involved surveys of 42 abortion doctors and nurses and was conducted by Marianne Such-Baer in 1974, before the term

Posttraumatic Stress Disorder (PTSD) was officially adopted. It noted that "obsessional thinking about abortion, depression, fatigue, anger, lowered self-esteem, and identity conflicts were prominent. The symptom complex was considered a 'transient reactive disorder,' similar to 'combat fatigue.' " (Such Baer, 1974, p. 439). Combat fatigue was a common colloquial term for PTSD at the time, when the official definition had not yet been formulated. Such-Baer further points out:

> Whether the professional had contact with the fetus significantly affected emotional reaction. Those staff members who had contact with the fetus reacted with much more discomfort to abortion work. Additionally, among the group of professionals who had fetus contact, there was very little variability in emotional response: All emotional reactions were unanimously extremely negative (Such-Baer, 1974, p. 439)

Roe (1989) directed the largest study, involving interviews with 130 abortion staff in San Francisco from 1974 until March 1975. It also did not mention PTSD nor any of its equivalent terms but did list symptoms consistent with PTSD:

> Ambivalent periods were characterized by a variety of otherwise uncharacteristic feelings and behavior including withdrawal from colleagues, resistance to going to work, lack of energy, impatience with clients and an overall sense of uneasiness. Nightmares, images that could not be shaken and preoccupation were commonly reported. Also common was the deep and lonely privacy within which practitioners had grappled with their ambivalence. (Roe, 1989, p. 1197)

They narrowed their interviews to those who expressed strong commitment to the work as a matter of supporting women's decisions; this reduced the sample to 105. Results: 77% bring up the theme of abortion as destroying a living thing. As for murder:

> This theme was unexpected among pro-choice practitioners yet 18% of the respondents talked about involvement with abortion this way at some point in the interview. This theme tended to emerge slowly in the interviews and was always presented with obvious discomfort. (Roe, 1989, p. 1194)

That being the case, it would come up much less often on written surveys and questionnaires.

There are also case studies by abortion staff studying or reporting on themselves which have been published in journals – no diagnosis, no prevalence, but enough illustration of symptoms to suggest that further research is warranted.

With burnout being an explanation for some experience, and symptoms such as hypervigilance being explained as due to the stresses of being protested, the best illustration of symptoms is dreams. These have the advantage of offering content, which allows for more confidence in the origin of the symptom. Dreams are so common that a mention of them can be expected in almost all presentations on the subject of abortion staff's emotional reactions.

This comes from an editorial discussing sessions in which abortion staff are talking about their feelings and was written by an author who supports the sessions as a way to help abortion staff continue doing the work:

> Their distress was typified by one nurse's dream. This involved an antique vase she had recently wished to purchase. In the dream she was stuffing a baby into the mouth of the vase. The baby was looking at her with a pleading expression. Around the vase was a white ring. She interpreted this as representing the other nurses looking upon her act with condemnation. One can clearly see the feelings of shame and guilt reflected in this dream.

> But more importantly, the dream shows that unconsciously the act of abortion was experienced as an act of murder. It should be noted that this nurse was strongly committed intellectually to the new abortion law. Her reaction was typical. Regardless of one's religious or philosophic orientation, the unconscious view of abortion remains the same. This was the most significant thing that was learned as a result of these sessions. (Kibel, 1972)

In another case, several doctors looked at the emotional impact on staff of late-term abortions, focusing on a particular technique called the D & E procedure. They published their report in the *American Journal of Obstetrics and Gynecology*:

> The two physicians who have done all the D & E procedures in our study support each other and rely on a strong sense of social conscience focused on the health and desires of the women. They feel technically competent but note strong emotional reactions during or following the procedures and occasional disquieting dreams. (Kaltreider, Goldsmith, & Margolis, 1979).

The *American Medical News* reported this from a National Abortion Federation conference: "They wonder if the fetus feels pain. They talk about the soul and where it goes. And about their dreams, in which aborted fetuses stare at them with ancient eyes and perfectly shaped hands and feet asking, 'Why? Why did you do this to me?'" (Gianelli, 1993)

A news item in the *ObGyn News* on emotional reactions to the late-term D & E procedures reports that one-fourth of the staff members reported an increase in abortion-related dreams and/or nightmares (Jancin, 1981).

Dr. Warren Hern recounts more dreams:

> Two respondents described dreams which they had related to the procedure. Both described dreams of vomiting fetuses along with a sense of horror. Other dreams revolved around a need to protect others from viewing fetal parts, dreaming that she herself was pregnant and needed an abortion or was having a baby. . . . In general, it appears that the more direct the physical and visual involvement (i.e. nurses, doctor), the more stress experienced. This is evident both in conscious stress and in unconscious manifestations such as dreams. At least, both individuals who reported several significant dreams were in these roles. (Hern & Corrigan, 1978)

The fate of the fetus is the most common theme, but Sallie Tisdale reports another effect.

> I have fetus dreams, we all do here: dreams of abortions one after the other; of buckets of blood splashed on the walls; trees full of crawling fetuses. I dreamed that two men grabbed me and began to drag me away. 'Let's do an abortion,' they said with a sickening leer, and I began to scream, plunged into a vision of sucking, scraping pain, of being spread and torn by impartial instruments that do only what they are bidden. I woke from this dream barely able to breathe and thought of kitchen tables and coat hangers, knitting needles striped with blood, and women all alone clutching a pillow in their teeth to keep the screams from piercing the apartment-house walls. Abortion is the narrowest edge between kindness and cruelty. Done as well as it can be, it is still violence – merciful violence, like putting a suffering animal to death. (Tisdale, 1987)

The image of the men grabbing her and forcing her through pain in private parts of her body suggests that in this dream, abortion is associated with rape.

Killing?

If all providers agreed abortion is nothing more than removing tissue, making a case for a psychological reaction to killing a human being would be difficult. However, contrary to the dichotomy throughout this book, there are instances where doctors who believe in abortion as option *also* understand it to be violence. Here we offer a sampling of quotations which are publically available.

An early example is abortion doctor Frank Behrend, M.D., who said this in tape-recorded speech November 7, 1977:

> Reference was made to my agreeing that abortion is taking a human life, which it is. However, let us remember that war is also legalized killing, that the pilot that dropped the atom bomb on Nagasaki and Hiroshima killed human life. He got medals for it. We bless our troops when they go into battle to kill human beings, so that the taking of human life, including the death penalty in certain states like Utah, where the man was shot, is not a strange behavior in a society.

Don Sloan, M.D. says in his book *Choice: a Doctor's Experience with the Abortion Dilemma:*

> Is abortion murder? All killing isn't murder. A cop shoots a teenager who "appeared to be going for a gun," and we call it justifiable homicide – a tragedy for all concerned, but not murder . . . And then there's war. In theory, soldiers shoot only at each other. But in practice, lots and lots of other folks get killed.

> We drop bombs where there are non-combatants – women and children and old people – and when they die we call it not murder but "collateral damage." Our soldiers get killed by "friendly fire" – often by people who aimed directly at them. Is that murder? All killing like that, to me, is morally wrong. But murder? (Sloan, 2002, p. 84)

An *American Medical News* article covered thoughts at a National Abortion Federation conference:

> A nurse who had worked in an abortion clinic for less than a year said her most troubling moments came not in the procedure room but afterwards. Many times, she said, women who had just had abortions would lie in the recovery room and cry, "I've just killed my baby. I've just killed my baby." "I don't know what to say to these women," the nurse told the group. "Part of me thinks, 'Maybe they're right'." Such self-doubt is not uncommon to the abortion field. (Gianelli, 1993).

Gender Issues

Throughout most of the decades of abortion legalization in the United States, it has been clear that the female portion of physicians providing abortions is considerably smaller than the female portion of physicians as a whole, and especially of those in the obstetrical-gynecological field where female representation has always been more predominant. This is no longer the case, as there has been a flood of young women into the abortion-provision field. Currently, about a third of U.S. physicians for whom abortion is a major part of their practice, as ascertained by their participation in clinics, are women. About a third of all physicians are women, and about one half are ob-gyns (Mitchell, 2012).

Why were women so under-represented in earlier decades, and what is the experience of women now? Abortion doctors

Susanna Poppema (1996) and Susan Wicklund (2007), in their respective books, indicated they had abortions themselves. Wicklund describes hers as a nightmarish experience. Part of her motivation was to help other women have a better experience than she did. She also indicates she re-experienced the incident: "time and again I flashed back to my own abortion. I carried those memories into every meeting" (p. 46) and "Every single day I worked, and with each patient I treated, I remembered that abortion" (p. 93). How prevalent this is – highly unusual or very near universal or somewhere in between – is simply not known. The difference in the psychology of women providers who have had their own abortions and those who have not may make an interesting psychological study in itself.

The question of sexual misconduct by some of the male providers comes up in discussions of abortion opponents. Several cases can be documented. They will not be discussed here, however, because of the absence of a control group: how many other doctors are also guilty? If male abortion providers have the same portion (or smaller portion) engaging in sexual misconduct with their patients as other male doctors, then documenting that some do leads to no useful conclusion other than that such behavior is not absent.

Some opponents argue that abortion is different because a large portion of women are trying to keep the pregnancy itself and therefore its termination a secret, unlike other medical procedures that may be private but would not motivate such strong efforts at concealment. This makes such women more vulnerable to abuse that the doctor believes the women will not report. There are, however, cases of non-abortion doctors who have gone through several cases of abuse before finally being reported, and there is no known registry that allows for comparison of groups even for those who do have legal proceedings – being sued or being charged with a criminal offense. At this point, the prevalence of the problem has not been ascertained, neither among male abortion doctors nor with a reasonable comparison group.

Conclusion: Research Needed

Though there have been hundreds of studies on the aftermath of abortion for the women who undergo them, and the area is hotly contested, the studies of abortion providers are much sparser and less contested. However, most researchers interested in the field have a political agenda. Many want to bolster a positive case for people becoming abortion providers or find ways of solving the problems to encourage more people to do so. Others want to make a negative case to discourage people from entering or remaining in the field. Either agenda detracts from a rigorous scientific approach.

The providers themselves may be inclined to view with suspicion any attempts by researchers other than those who agree with their point of view. Since one major strategy of abortion opponents is to discourage the supply, the suspicion is warranted.

There have been people involved in abortion provision who have joined the movement against abortion, which is fairly remarkable upon reflection of what they have to admit to having done if they join such a movement. Famous cases include Carol Everett (1992), Bernard Nathanson (1979) and Abby Johnson (2014). There are enough such people to make a valuable study as to the psychology of becoming active with the opposition. Again, however, researchers sympathetic to their point of view will encounter the most positive interaction. This could cause a slant in the study.

Having a team with both views represented might lend itself to an inter-subjective approach that would allow debates within the team to lead to more robust conclusions. Attempts at doing this have not yet been successful but could provide a fruitful avenue in the future.

References

American Psychiatric Association. (2013). *Diagnostic and statistical manual of mental disorders* (5th ed.). Washington, DC: Author.

Everett, C., Shaw, J. (1992). *Blood money.* Oregon: Multnomah Press Books.

Gianelli, D. M. (1993, July 12). Abortion providers share inner conflicts. *American Medical News.*

Grimes, A. (2015, November 24). An abortion provider speaks out: "I'll do whatever my conscience tells me I must". *Rolling Stone Magazine.* Retrieved from http://www.rollingstone.com/culture/news/an-abortion-provider-speaks-out-ill-do-whatever-my-conscience-tells-me-i-must-20151124?page=2

Hern, W. M., Corrigan, B. (1978, October 26). *What about us? Staff reactions to the D and E procedure.* Paper presented at the meeting of the Association of Planned Parenthood Physicians, San Diego. Retrieved from http://www.drhern.com/pdfs/staffrx.pdf

Hern, W. (1993, March 13). Hunted by the Right, forgotten by the Left. *New York Times.* Retrieved from http://www.drhern.com/huntedbytheright.htm

Jancin, B. (1981). Emotional turmoil of physicians, staff held biggest D and E problem. *Ob.Gyn. News, 16,* 15-31

Johnson, A. (2010). *Unplanned: The dramatic true story of a former Planned Parenthood leader's eye-opening journey across the life line.* San Francisco: Ignatius Press.

Kaltreider, N. B., Goldsmith, S., Margolis, A. J. (1979). The impact of mid-trimester abortion techniques on patients and staff. *American Journal of Obstetrics and Gynecology, 135,* 235-238.

Kibel, H. D. (1972). Editorial: Staff reactions to abortion. *Obstetrics and Gynecology, 39,* 1.

Lunnenborg, P. (1992). *Abortion, a positive decision.* New York: Bergin & Garvey.

Maslach, C. (1982). *Burnout: The cost of caring.* Englewood Cliffs, NJ: Prentice-Hall

Mitchell, J. (2012, December 4). Females now constitute one-third of nation's ranks of doctors and lawyers. *Wall Street Journal.* Retrieved from http://www.wsj.com/articles/SB1000142412788732371700457815943322 0839020

Nathanson, B. N. (1979). *Aborting America.* Toronto: Life Cycle Books.

Poppema, S. & Henderson, M. (1996). *Why I am an abortion doctor.* New York: Prometheus Books.

Roe, K. M. (1989). Private troubles and public issues: Providing abortion amid competing definitions. *Social Science and Medicine, 29,* 1191-1198.

Sloan, D. & Hartz, P. (2002). *Abortion: A doctor's perspective, a woman's dilemma.* New York: Donald I Fine.

Such-Baer, M. (1974). Professional staff reaction to abortion work. *Social Casework, 55,* 435-441.

Tisdale, S. (1987, October). We do abortions here. *Harper's,* 66-70.

Wicklund, S. & Kesselheim, A. (2007). *This common secret: My journey as an abortion doctor.* New York: Public Affairs.

World Health Organization. (1992). *International statistical classification of diseases and related health problems* (10th revision). Geneva, Switzerland: Author.

Chapter 13

Prevention of Child Abuse

Rachel M. MacNair

Abuse of children is among the most horrific forms of violence and is depressingly widespread world-wide. Therefore, it is important to know whether the impact of abortion on its prevalence is helpful, harmful or neutral.

The reasoning that abortion availability helps reduce such abuse includes:

- Abuse can be caused when children were born unwanted and are therefore resented. Having them not be born at all should accordingly result in a drop in the child abuse rate.

- There may be fewer births in those groups most likely to engage in child maltreatment.

The thesis that abortion availability is harmful includes these ideas:

- It removes a taboo on hurting children, and because it allows violence to children prenatally, violence will then be greater to postnatal children as well.

- It leads to children being treated as consumer products, rather than as human beings, thereby adding a requirement of "wantedness" by parents that children should not be required to meet.

The neutral position is the ordinary null hypothesis – abortion is not really under consideration when child abuse occurs.

Types of Abuse

First, we need to distinguish different types of child abuse:

1. Neglect

When children are not talked to nor read to, when basic needs such as food and clothing are not met, when children are ignored when they need attention, this is one form of abuse. That the children were never wanted – yet not placed for adoption – is one explanation for why they are neglected.

Other possible explanations include parents who are ignorant of what children need; who are too self-absorbed to notice their children's needs; were raised this way themselves and therefore understand this as the proper way to raise children; may lash out at the child as a scapegoat for frustrations from elsewhere; have an idealized view of having children without knowing what kind of work is involved; intended to have a baby but are not interested in the child that the baby turned into; and substance abuse or mental illness.

These reasons call for interventions that have nothing to do with the availability of abortion one way or the other. Still, when the cause is unwantedness of the child and adoption was for some reason not considered, the hypothesis is that abortion availability will have a helpful impact on lowering the rates of child abuse.

2. Physical abuse and emotional abuse

This occurs when abuse is aggressive, leading to physical injury or emotional scars. This could happen when the child was never wanted – but not placed for adoption – and therefore her or his presence is resented. It could also happen for the opposite reason: the child is *super*-wanted, but with unrealistic expectations about what can be achieved. The child is supposed to follow the father into the family business, for example, but shows no interest. The child is supposed to be brilliant in mathematics but is mathematically inept. The child is a real person who refuses to be perfect.

Additionally, some of the reasons for neglect can also apply here: the child is a scapegoat for other frustrations; the parents were raised this way and understand this is how it is done; substance abuse or mental illness; and so on. Nevertheless, if unwantedness is one of the reasons, then according to the abortion-as-option thesis, abortion availability should reduce abuse in at least those cases involving children who are undesired.

As a side note, the issue of non-injurious spanking as a form of discipline is regarded by some as abusive, and others consider the lack of it to be abusive on the grounds that children benefit from discipline. Peace psychologists tend to view spanking as an inadvisable form of discipline since it teaches violence as a problem-solver. Many peace psychologists work on developing and promoting a Positive Discipline approach instead (see http://www.positivediscipline.com). In any event, different philosophies of spanking are clearly a separate issue that is not likely to have anything to do with abortion availability.

3. Sexual abuse

In this case, it is quite clear that unwantedness cannot be the problem – the children are "wanted" for the wrong reason.

The Rise and Fall of Child Abuse Rates

Many countries have their child abuse rates statistics gathered by sampling technique with surveys, and others have no statistics at all. In the United States, all 50 states had child-abuse reporting laws by 1967, so the statistics come from all reports rather than sampling. Other developed countries have similar records; here we will focus on the U.S. as having the clearest pattern.

Child abuse rates skyrocketed after *Roe v Wade*, the decision legalizing abortion in all 50 states, was decided in 1973. The Bureau of the Census (1990) reports 452,800 reported (not substantiated, just reported) cases of abuse in 1973 to 2,959,100 in 1990. The rate per 1,000 population went from 2.16 in 1973 to 11.59 in 1990. Other sources report different rates due to different criteria, but all of them show a similar upsurge. This is consistent with the hypothesis that millions of abortions might act as other violence does, by serving as a model, and by desensitizing.

However, correlation is not causation, and those inclined to draw a conclusion only from the simple fact of upsurge need to use caution. A readily-available alternative explanation is that it was not that more child abuse was actually happening, but that people were more sensitive to it and more inclined to report it due to educational efforts and changing cultural mores about its acceptability. Additionally, different criteria have been used to determine and measure abuse. Therefore, figures and rates are not always comparable.

Then, around 1990, the child abuse rates in the United States started a downward trend (Finkelhor & Jones, L, 2006). Concurrently, so did the abortion rates (Henshaw & Kost, 2008).

The connection between the two may be coincidence, of course. The theory that abortion and child abuse are connected as two similar forms of violence would predict that lowering abortion would lower child abuse, but human behavior is not that simple.

Those of the abortion-as-option view have frequently proposed that greater contraception education and use grew over time and resulted in the abortion downturn. Effective campaigns against child abuse were growing at the same time, and becoming successful. Given the historical time period, with the rise of campaigns for human betterment, there were many additional positive social indicators at the same time.

When looking at outcomes for an entire society, innumerable variables could be explanations, and speculations as to why ranges broadly (on child abuse, see Finkelhor & Jones, 2006). We can never know whether the child abuse rates would not have been higher yet without abortion. Still, the evidence that abortion availability might have any kind of positive impact on child abuse rates requires more detailed study than merely the change in rates.

Empirical Evidence

The Case that Abortion Helps Prevent Abuse

In a sample of unmarried mothers receiving AFDC, child abuse and neglect are positively associated with unplanned childbearing and negatively associated with maternal age at first birth (Zuravin, 1987, 1988). Maternal age at birth is also negatively associated with the likelihood that a child is abused.

Marianne Bitler and Madeline Zavodny (2002, 2004) utilized the varying times at which abortion became legalized in different U.S. states before the 1973 court ruling that legalized it nation-wide. They then considered reports of child abuse by taking their age into account so as to have a measure of whether abortion would have been available at the time they were conceived. With this method, results suggest legalization lowered the reported cases. Legal restrictions on abortion, however, showed unclear results. Carlos Seiglie (2004) similarly found abortion access at the time of the pregnancy lowered reports of neglect.

A more targeted approach was taken by Sen & Wingate (2006), doing a longitudinal analysis of fatal injury to children in states that have passed regulations such as parental consent, informed consent, and waiting periods. With this approach, they found an association between such regulations and increased injury.

The Case that Abortion Helps Promote Abuse

If the abortion-as-violence hypothesis is correct, it suggests an even more targeted approach. Rather than a society-wide epidemiological investigation, the research question becomes more focused: "Are mothers who have abortions more likely to be abusive to their children?" This approach has been undertaken in several studies (Ney, Fung & Wickett, 1993; Coleman, Reardon, & Cougle, 2002; Coleman, Maxey, Rue, & Coyle, 2005; Coleman, Rue, Coyle, & Maxey, 2007). In these peer-reviewed studies, the answer is yes.

For example, Coleman et al. (2005) analyzed 518 women who had been identified by Baltimore Child Protective Services as having abused their children. Researchers compared women with no pregnancy loss, those whose loss was involuntary (miscarriage or stillbirth) and those with induced abortion. The women who had undergone at least one induced abortion were 114% more likely to be identified as having abused their children when compared to women with no loss. Those women who suffered involuntary loss were found to be no more likely to be identified as abusive than women with no pregnancy loss.

Additionally, there is the question of children who rather than being *unwanted* are instead *super-wanted*. Edward Lenoski (1980), Professor of Pediatrics and Emergency Medicine at the University of Southern California School of Medicine, conducted a study of 674 children who had suffered battering at the hands of one of their parents and compared them to 500 controls selected from the same emergency room. The comparison showed:

- 91% of the parents of abused children said they had wanted the pregnancy; 63% of the non-abused said so;
- 93% of the parents were married at the time of the birth of the abused child; 60% of the non-abused were;
- the mother of the abused children began wearing maternity clothes at an average of 114 days into the pregnancy, as compared to an average of 171 days for the mothers of the non-abused children;
- The child was named after a parent (usually, father's name with "Jr.") in 24% of the abused cases, but only 4% of the non-abused cases.

Since these are children for whom abortion was never contemplated, the role of abortion is not covered in this study. The role of "wantedness," however, is here reversed with the proposal that requiring wantedness of children may, in some cases, increase rather than reduce the risk of child abuse

In those cases where the child is super-wanted, the ready availability of abortion could make things worse by emphasizing the importance of the wantedness of children. Less abuse may accompany accepting children for who they are rather than for who their parents want them to be.

Sexual Abuse

Sexual abuse is in a different category from neglect or physical and emotional abuse, since the problem is clearly not that the child is unwanted, but is wanted for the wrong reason. Seiglie (2004), while reporting findings as mentioned above about abortion availability being associated with less neglect, also reported a positive association of abortion access with sexual abuse.

The pro-life movement is full of anecdotal cases of men who utilized the abortion clinic for the purpose of removing the evidence of their abuse (see, for example, from Feminists for Life, http://www.feministsforlife.org/incest-and-the-abortion-clinic/). These cases include both adult men who impregnate minors and incest abuse.

In actuality, the law in several countries upholds mandatory reporting to authorities when there are signs of possible sexual abuse of children under a certain age by adults. Pregnancy would certainly qualify as a possible sign of sexual abuse. If medical personnel follow the legal requirement of reporting suspected abuse, then abortion providers are in a unique position to prevent child sexual abuse and allow for its prosecution. If perpetrators knew this would occur, then it could have a powerful deterrent effect on sexual abuse.

Conversely, if medical personnel do not report, then they facilitate the abuse. Adult men who expect non-reporting may be more likely to engage in such abuse.

Scholarly investigation on this point is currently inadequate. It is urgently needed for the prevention of sexual violence toward children.

References

Bitler, M. P. & Zavodny, M. (2002). Child abuse and abortion availability. *The American Economic Review, 92*(2), 363-367. doi: 10.1257/000282802320191624

Bitler, M. P. and Zavodny, M. (2004). Child maltreatment, abortion availability, and economic condition. *Review of Economics of the Household 2*(2), 119-141.

Bureau of the Census. (1990). *Statistical abstract of the United States*. Washington, DC: United States Government Printing Office. Tables 296 & 297.

Coleman, P. K., Maxey, C. D., Rue, V. M., & Coyle, C. T. (2005). Associations between voluntary and involuntary forms of perinatal loss and child maltreatment among low-income mothers. *Acta Paediatrica, 94*, 1476 – 1483.

Coleman, P. K., Reardon, D.C., & Cougle J. (2002). The quality of the caregiving environment and child developmental outcomes associated with maternal history of abortion using the NLSY data. *Journal of Child Psychology and Psychiatry and Allied Disciplines, 43*, 743-758.

Coleman, P. K., Rue, V. M., Coyle, C. T., & Maxey, C. D. (2007) Induced abortion and child-directed aggression among mothers of maltreated children. *The Internet Journal of Pediatrics and Neonatology, 6*(2). Retrieved from http://ispub.com/IJPN/6/2/9364

Finkelhor, D. & Jones, L. (2006). Why have child maltreatment and child victimization declined? *Journal of Social Issues, 62*, 685-716.

Henshaw, S. K. & Kost, K. (2008). Trends in the characteristics of women obtaining abortions, 1974 to 2004. New York: Guttmacher Institute. Retrieved from http://www.guttmacher.org/pubs/2008/09/18/Report_Trends_Women_Obtaining_Abortions.pdf

Lenoski, E. (1980, Winter). A research study on child abuse. *Heartbeat*, 16-17.

Ney, P. G., Fung, T., & Wickett, A.R (1993). Relations between induced abortion and child abuse and neglect: Four studies. *Pre and Perinatal Psychology Journal 8*, 43-63.

Seiglie, C. (2004). Understanding child outcomes: An application to child abuse and neglect. *Review of Economics of the Household, 2*, 143-160. doi: 10.1023/B:REHO.0000031611.38185.d3

Sen, B., & Wingate, M. (2006, June 4). *Do abortion restrictions affect child fatal injury? A longitudinal analysis*. Paper presented at the meeting of the Economics of Population Health, Madison, WI. Retrieved from http://www.allacademic.com/meta/p91656_index.html

Zuravin, S. J. (1987). Unplanned pregnancies, family planning problems, and child mal-treatment. *Family Relations, 36*(2), 135-39.

Zuravin, S. J. (1988). Fertility patterns: Their relationship to child physical abuse and child neglect. *Journal of Marriage and the Family, 50*(4), 983-993.

Chapter 14

Differing Perspectives on Specific Populations

by Rachel M. MacNair

Some groups or communities need more focused attention because they have features particular to their group. We cover:

- People with disabilities
- Racial minorities
- People living in developing countries
- Sexual minorities (LBGT people)
- Conscientious Objectors

In all but the last case, there are three important features to consider:

1) Because abortion means a baby who likely would have been born is not born, abortions are viewed positively by people who hold that baby's community in contempt. As one US Supreme Court Justice put it when puzzled about restrictions on governmental funding, "Frankly I had thought that at the time *Roe* was decided, there was concern about population growth and particularly growth in populations that we don't want to have too many of" (Bazelon, 2009).

2) By virtue of having historically been targeted by bigotry, these groups have suffered from lack of choices and control over their own lives. Expressions of contempt have included assertions that they are not competent to make the best choices. This contempt is still keenly felt and resented.

3) These are all large communities. Accordingly, perspectives in each community vary widely, as with everybody else.

Pregnant Women with Disabilities

Most of us have minor disabilities, such as a need to wear glasses. Most will have temporary major disabilities at some time – a broken leg, recuperating from surgery, etc. People with disabilities that are both fairly severe and permanent are the focus here.

Abortion-as-Option Perspective

There is no monolithic view, of course, but in general there are two primary pro-choice perspectives:

- Women with disabilities especially need abortion as an option. They need more options in their lives in general. They live in a society that does not allow them as much self-determination and control over their own destinies as they ought to have.

- Women with disabilities are especially pressured to have abortion because of bigotry about what they can handle. As one pro-choice woman with spina bifida put it, "Aspects of this issue can be perplexing to people with disabilities because of the nature of the prejudice we experience. For example, the culture typically invalidates our bodies, denies our sexuality and our potential as parents" (Saxton, 1998).

Abortion-as-Violence Perspective

Perspectives include:

- Women with disabilities are already subjected to many forms of discrimination. Telling them they cannot handle a life event such as pregnancy can involve disdain and is also discriminatory.

- Abortion availability can be used as an excuse to avoid providing pregnant women with disabilities the extra services they need and deserve.

- Stigma associated with having disabilities is increased when it is used as a reason to avoid reproducing.

Alison Davis (pictured below) wrote in a classic article for the journal *Disability and Society*:

> Feminists, though accustomed to fighting for the emancipation of women, are failing to address this incongruous situation, and the double discrimination faced by women with disabilities. This is partly due to the fact that they regard abortion as an unequivocal "right."
>
> I will argue that far from being a right, abortion underlines women's oppression and is counter-productive to women in general, and to disabled women in particular. (Davis, 1987)

Alison Davis

Areas of Agreement

There are areas where people in the field of peace psychology are inclined to be in agreement, yet not necessarily in agreement with the whole of society. One basic point of agreement is that women with disabilities are entitled to have wanted pregnancies without facing prejudice. In her personal story on the web site of the American Psychological Association, psychologist Erin E. Andrews writes:

> When I found out I was pregnant, I was overjoyed, but also apprehensive. I am a congenital triple amputee who uses a power wheelchair for mobility. I was less concerned about the effects of my disability, and more concerned about the attitudes of others toward my pregnancy. As a rehabilitation psychologist, I am well aware that women with disabilities face barriers to reproductive health and that social biases exist which portray women with disabilities as asexual, infertile, and incapable as mothers. (Andrews, 2011)

Peace psychology has much to contribute in this area, with its knowledge of how prejudice works and how to counter it.

On another aspect, there is an argument over what would most block services needed by people with disabilities – in this case, pregnant women and mothers of minor children. One argument is that politicians who oppose abortion are also ones who block funding for services. The other is that abortion is promoted by politicians who find it to be a money-saver for taxpayers. In both cases, these are stereotypes, but stereotypes often have many people who fit them.

From the point of view of peace psychology, neither approach is acceptable. Abortion loses its character as an option if it is callously viewed as a way of saving tax money, and abortion opposition loses all credibility if it is not accompanied by advocacy for and provision of life-affirming services.

Fetuses with Disabilities

For a full book-length treatment of various perspectives in this debate, see Parens & Asch (2000).

Abortion-as-Option Perspective

The idea that fetuses with disabilities should necessarily be aborted comes from a eugenics perspective, which is outside the realm of perspectives within peace psychology. However, the view that women should have a choice while taking a prenatal diagnosis of disability into account is a common one. Jesudason & Epstein (2011) discuss in a *Contraception* journal editorial how there is a paradox here that must be addressed to be in harmony with the disability-rights community. Bertha Alvarez Manninen writes in *Disability Studies Quarterly*:

> Although I self-identify as pro-choice, I do believe certain instances of abortion can be classified as, in Judith Jarvis Thomson's words, indecent. . . . In particular, I am concerned with cases where fetuses that had been thus far welcomed and loved by their respective community are suddenly regarded as candidates for abortion simply because they may have been diagnosed with a disability. That is, I am worried about cases where disability is deemed sufficient grounds for dehumanizing a being who had been, up until that point, embraced. (Manninen, 2015).

Martha Saxton also writes from the disabilities-rights perspective:

> While today's feminists are not responsible for the eugenic biases of their fore-mothers, some of these prejudices have persisted or have gone unchallenged in the reproductive rights movement

today. Consequently many women with disabilities feel alienated from this movement. On the other hand some pro-choice feminists felt so deeply alienated from the disability community that they have been willing to claim, "The right wing wants to force us to have defective babies." Clearly there is work to be done. . .

The fact is, it is discriminatory attitudes and thoughtless behaviors, and the ostracization and lack of accommodation which follow, that make life difficult. The oppression, one way or another, is what's most disabling about disability. . .

But many parents of disabled children have spoken up to validate the joys and satisfactions of raising a disabled child. A vast literature of books and articles by these parents confirm the view that discriminatory attitudes make raising a disabled child much more difficult than the actual logistics of their unique care. . .

How is it possible to defend selective abortion on the basis of "a woman's right to choose" when this "choice" is so constrained by oppressive values and attitudes? . . . For those with "disability-positive" attitudes, the analogy with sex-selection is obvious. Oppressive assumptions, not inherent characteristics, have devalued who this fetus will grow into. (Saxton, 2004)

Abortion-as-Violence Perspective

It is one thing to abort a pregnancy because it is simply undesired; it is another to focus on the characteristics of the fetus. Deciding a previously-desired pregnancy is to be aborted because of features such as gender, disability, or any other fetus-focused reason is called "selective" abortion. Bigotry against the disabled is itself a form of violence.

Empirical evidence reveals a troubling impact of disability-selective abortions. In the United States, after the Americans with Disabilities Act (ADA) passed in 1990, this anti-discrimination and pro-accommodation legislation should have had a positive effect on perceptions of the disabled. For those well beyond infancy, it did. However, Fox & Griffin (2009) noted a dramatic decrease in the birth rate for Down Syndrome babies after its passage. With no reason to believe they were conceived at different rates before and after passage of ADA, and prenatal screening abilities being the same, authors attributed the decrease to demeaning media depictions that reinforced negative expectations. Fox and Griffen postulated that the decrease in birth rate of Down Syndrome babies was due at least in part to provisions of the ADA itself. Yet there is also the basic problem that assertions of pregnancy termination as a "right" and something over which a couple needs to make a choice can contribute.

A study focused on the media depictions from 1998 through 2006 in 148 full-text articles in the top 20 U.S. newspaper markets provided confirmation: disability was presented in negative terms (Mills & Erzikova, 2012). Though the ADA was popular and had bipartisan support, the negative framing came about because of positive portrayals of prenatal testing. A positive presentation of terminating the pregnancy when a disability diagnosis occurred was a common theme. Therefore, the ready availability of abortion and its positive portrayal sabotages the cause of disability rights.

Alison Davis (1987) originally took a pro-choice position, but upon learning of disability-selective abortions, decided she was against those; they targeted the kind of person she was. Upon noticing this was the converse of many people's views, and that legislation making exceptions for abortion prohibitions often included fetal disability as one such exception, she realized that if she was going to oppose selective abortions, she needed to not be selective herself and work to protect *all* unborn children.

Areas of Agreement

As is clear from the discussion above, one obvious area of agreement for those in the peace psychology field is that oppressive attitudes toward those with disabilities need to be changed. In the contexts of both prenatal testing and public education, at the very least, people need to be given *accurate* information about living with disabilities. If it is to be framed in either positive or negative terms, the positive framing is closer to reality, and is surely more likely to create and maintain supportive conditions for the disabled.

As Adrienne Asch put it in an oft-cited article:

> In order to make testing and selecting for or against disability consonant with improving life for those who will inevitably be born with or acquire disabilities, our clinical and policy establishments must communicate that it is as acceptable to live with a disability as it is to live without one and that society will support and appreciate everyone with the inevitable variety of traits. . . . If that professional message is conveyed, more prospective parents may envision that their lives can be rewarding, whatever the characteristics of the child they are raising. . . . If the child with a disability is not a problem for the world, and the world is not a problem for the child, perhaps we can diminish our desire for prenatal testing and selective abortion and can comfortably welcome and support children of all characteristics. (Asch, 1999, p. 1656)

Racial and Ethnic Minorities

We will focus on African-Americans because there is more relevant material available concerning them, but the same principles apply to ethnic minorities in general all over the world.

Abortion-as-Option Perspective

In the U.S., Trust Black Women is a coalition of groups that focuses particularly on "reproductive justice," which includes abortion but expands to other pressing matters affecting women and children (see www.trustblackwomen.org). From their web-site, this is an excerpt from a statement written by Marcia Gillespie and signed by many prominent African-American women:

> Choice is the essence of freedom. It's what we African-Americans have struggled for all these years. The right to choose where we would sit on a bus. The right to vote. The right for each of us to select our own paths, to dream and reach for our dreams. The right to choose how we would or would not live our lives.
>
> This freedom – to choose and to exercise our choices – is what we've fought and died for. Brought here in chains, worked like mules, bred like beasts, whipped one day, sold the next – for 244 years we were held in bondage. Somebody said that we were less than human and not fit for freedom. Somebody said we were like children and could not be trusted to think for ourselves.
>
> Somebody owned our flesh, and decided if and when and with whom and how our bodies were to be used. Somebody said that Black women could be raped, held in concubinage, forced to bear children year in and year out, but often not raise them. Oh yes, we have known how painful it is to be without choice in this land. . . .

Now once again somebody is trying to say that we can't handle the freedom of choice. Only this time they're saying African-American women can't think for themselves, and therefore, can't be allowed to make serious decisions. Somebody's saying that we should not have the freedom to take charge of our personal lives and protect our health, that we only have limited rights over our bodies. (Gillespie, 1989)

Abortion-as-Violence Perspective

This comes from social worker Erma Clardy Craven:

It takes little imagination to see that the unborn Black baby is the real object of many abortionists. Except for the privilege of aborting herself, the Black woman and her family must fight for every other social and economic privilege. This move toward the free application of a non-right (abortion) for those whose real need is equal human rights and opportunities is benumbing the social conscience of America into unquestioningly accepting the "smoke screen" of abortion. The quality of life for the poor, the Black and the oppressed will not be served by destroying their children. (Craven, 1972)

Edward Allred, one of the abortion doctors to whom Craven refers, stated:

When a sullen Black woman of 17 or 18 can decide to have a baby and get welfare and food stamps and become a burden to us all, it's time to stop. In parts of South Los Angeles, having babies for welfare is the only industry the people have. (*San Diego Union*, October 12, 1980)

Dr. Allred's aversion to government subsidies did not prevent him from accepting millions of dollars in California tax dollars for his abortion practice.

Life Dynamics has published a documentary called *Maafa 21* (available on the web at www.maafa21.com) whose thesis is to show the role of abortion in the American history of racism and in particular, how abortion has been used to eliminate African Americans:

> They were stolen from their homes, locked in chains, and taken across an ocean . . . But when slavery ended, their welcome was over. America's wealthy elite had decided it was time for them to disappear and they were not particular about how it might be done.

This lengthy documentary has been distributed to hundreds of thousands of people and is being enthusiastically shared. It is informative for anyone who wants to understand the relationship between abortion and racism.

People Living in Developing Countries

Abortion-as-Option Perspective

From the research arm of Planned Parenthood:

> Levels of unintended pregnancy vary across societies and over time; however, because no reversible method of birth control is perfect and few human beings use methods perfectly, women will always experience unintended pregnancies. Thus, there will always be a need for abortion, and for safe abortion services. Tragically, of the roughly 44 million abortions that take place globally each year, a rising proportion—now about half—are medically unsafe. Virtually all unsafe abortions occur in developing countries, taking a devastating toll on women's health and lives.

Reducing the incidence of unsafe abortion remains an urgent public health imperative. Beyond that, however, there is a growing recognition at the global level and within developing countries that access to comprehensive reproductive health services must include access to abortion—and that removing legal barriers to abortion not only protects women's health, but restores their dignity and vindicates their basic human rights. (Cohen, 2012)

Countries have widely varying laws that delineate what is allowed and who may be prosecuted in the context of induced abortion. There are horror stories of women who present to the hospital with bleeding and are incarcerated despite claims they suffered a natural miscarriage, because they had insufficient legal counsel to make their case.

However, even if laws allow for exceptions, if they prosecute only the doctor providing abortions rather than the women getting them, if they require substantial proof and have penalties involving licensure and not incarceration, those who regard abortion as a matter of women's rights will find all these prohibitions appalling.

Abortion-as-Violence Perspective

Richard Stith, a law professor with extensive contact in Latin America, gives this assessment:

We all know that many women are simply unable to effectively negotiate the terms and conditions of their sexual interactions and reproductive choices due to pervasive discrimination, coercion and violence against them. Unfortunately, legalization of abortion provides those coercers with another weapon that they can use against the women they dominate. In other words, abortion rights may truly be liberating for powerful women whose careers cannot easily accommodate children . . .

The developing world is much, much worse for most women. Except for a tiny elite segment of women (which unfortunately may be the only non-male presence at international conferences set up to propose new laws) abortion hurts women because it empowers husbands, sweatshop owners, and pimps to use them with impunity. The rule is very simple: Those who make real life choices for women are the real rights holders, regardless of who may have the formal legal right to make decisions. (Stith, 2015).

Nigerian Obianuju Ekeocha pictured below) is active with Culture of Life Africa; she is a biomedical scientist, and says:

I believe that to volunteer is heroic, to donate is generous, and to lament is pointless, but to sterilize the Africans and destroy the lives of their unborn children? That is dehumanizing cruelty and will not help Africa in the long or short run. . . .

So in this epic battle to lift Africa out of the pit of poverty, education becomes a most needed life-line. And for this reason it should become the epicentre of the on-going global discourse on poverty eradication. Indeed, the emphasis should be on the Africans having education rather than halving their population. (Ekeocha, 2012).

Lesbian, Gay, Bisexual and Transgendered (LGBT) People

Homosexual activity itself does not cause pregnancy. Inasmuch as bisexual people wish to engage in heterosexual contact and gays and lesbians may do so even if they find it unattractive, pregnancies may result, but would not be different in terms of abortion perspectives.

Abortion-as-Option Perspective

The U.S.'s National Gay and Lesbian Task Force officially has a pro-choice position, albeit one difficult to find on their web page. In this quotation from its executive director at the time, *Lawrence* refers to the U.S. Supreme Court case *Lawrence v. Texas* in 2003, which overturned sodomy laws; *Roe* refers to *Roe v. Wade* of 1973, legalizing abortion nationwide:

> This is about much more than access to abortion, as important as that is. It is about who controls our bodies and our sexualities. Reproductive freedom and gay rights are inextricably intertwined. Simply put, we would not have *Lawrence* but for *Roe*. (Foreman, 2007)

Abortion-as-Violence Perspective

This comes from an on-line LGBT pamphlet:

> Lesbian, gay, bisexual, transgendered, and intersex (LGBTI) people and the preborn have at least one thing in common: a good number of people try to deny them the most basic human rights, including the right to life. . . .
>
> America's abortion on demand policy is fueled by the philosophy which says that life is a privilege reserved for those who are wanted. While this attitude prevails, no LGBTI person -- nor, for

that matter, the disabled, the elderly, the terminally ill, or any other class of human beings who may be considered "unwanted" or "burdensome" -- are safe. (Pro-life Alliance of Gays and Lesbians, 2014)

Areas of Agreement

One concern has been that there may be a genetic test developed for sexual orientation. While this has been of less interest recently, it was a worry in the past that deserves some attention. Schuklenk, Stein, Kerin, & Byne (1997) regard the search for such a test as unethical because finding an "origin" is understood as homophobic, as if homosexuality were something requiring treatment. They express fear that a discovery would lead to prenatal screening and selective abortions. I know from personal communications there are other LGBT people who welcome the genetic research because it could show they are who they are as a basic matter of genetics. The actual science is one thing, independent of the moral conclusion to be drawn from what science finds.

Yet the point of agreement is clear: any potential for prenatal screening to selectively eliminate those with potential for homosexual orientation is a clear case of intense discrimination against LGBT people. If it were ever to come to pass, this would be a cause for alarm.

Conscientious Objectors

For centuries, when militaries drafted people, some refused on grounds of conscience. In the 20th century, several nations recognized a legal exemption for conscientious objection, generally allowing people to do other service instead. Now there are countries in which doctors, nurses, and midwives who refuse to participate in abortions are losing licenses or jobs.

Abortion-as-Option Perspective

Global Doctors for Choice funded a supplement issue of the *International Journal of Gynecology and Obstetrics* devoted to the issue of conscientious objection to abortion (Chavkin, 2013). It documents that the world-wide prevalence is extensive, documents harms they understand as arising from this, and argues for a balance between patients' rights and health workers' rights.

Fiala & Arthur (2014a) believe in no such balance, and published their paper explaining why conscientious objection status should not apply. We quote here from their popular-media summary:

> Reproductive health care is the only field in medicine where freedom of conscience is accepted as an argument to limit a patient's right to a legal medical treatment. It is the only example where the otherwise accepted standard of evidence-based medicine is overruled by faith-based actions. . . . the exercise of conscientious objection (CO) is a violation of medical ethics because it allows health-care professionals to abuse their position of trust and authority by imposing their personal beliefs on patients. Physicians have a monopoly on the practice of medicine, with patients completely reliant on them for essential health care. Moreover, doctors have chosen a profession that fulfills a public trust, making them duty-bound to provide care without discrimination. This makes CO an arrogant paternalism, with doctors exerting power over their dependent patients—a throwback to the obsolete era of "doctor knows best."
>
> Denial of care inevitably creates at least some degree of harm to patients, ranging from inconvenience, humiliation, and psychological stress to delays in care, unwanted pregnancy, increased medical risks, and death. Since reproductive health

care is largely delivered to women, CO rises to the level of discrimination, undermining women's self-determination and liberty. CO against providing abortions, in particular, is based on a denial of the overwhelming evidence and historical experience that have proven the harms of legal and other restrictions, a rejection of the human rights ethic that justifies the provision of safe and legal abortion to women, and a refusal to respect democratically decided laws. Allowing CO for abortion also ignores the global realities of poor access to services, pervasive stigma, and restrictive laws. It just restricts access even further, adding to the already serious abrogation of patients' rights. (Fiala & Arther, 2014b).

A similar argument is made by Ben Rich (2015).

Abortion-as-Violence Perspective

Since the abortion-as-violence perspective is that abortion kills a human being, the analogy to conscientious objection in the military is understood to be quite appropriate.

The Global Doctors for Choice special issue in its entirety only mentions once the actual motivation, and words it as a disagreement on when life begins (Chavkin, 2013). This is a very tepid and incomplete way of wording the problem.

Fiala & Arthur (2014a, 2014b) assert the motivation is to keep women in their traditional roles as wives and mothers and to produce children to be soldiers and citizens of the state. They cite no documentation of this point. Documentation would be difficult to come by. If found, it would likely be in people other than those risking licenses and losing jobs.

Here we have people considering the topic of conscientious objectors at length, yet they do not offer a forthright account of the CO's actual motivation. This is not what one would expect of people sincerely trying to understand the phenomenon.

Publicized conscientious objectors:
Top left: Sweden, Ellinor Grimark.
Top right: Croatia, Jaga Stojak
Middle: Scotland, Mary Doogan and Concepta Wood
Bottom: New York City, Catherina Cenzon-DeCarlo

References

Andrews, E. E. (2011, December). Pregnancy with a physical disability: One psychologist's journey. Spotlight on Disability Newsletter. Retrieved from http://www.apa.org/pi/disability/resources/publications/newsletter/2011/12/pregnancy-disability.aspx

Asch, A. (1999). Prenatal Diagnosis and Selective Abortion. *American Journal of Public Health, 89*(11), 1649-1657.

Bazelon, E. (2009, July 7). The place of women on the court. *The New York Times Magazine.* Retrieved from http://www.nytimes.com/2009/07/12/magazine/12ginsburg-t.html?_r=0

Chavkin, W. (Ed.). (2013). Supplemental issue: Conscientious Objection. *International Journal of Gynecology and Obstetrics, 123,* Supplement 3. Retrieved from http://www.ossyr.org.ar/pdf/bibliografia/314.pdf

Cohen, S. A. (2012). Access to safe abortion in the developing world: saving lives while advancing rights. *Guttmacher Policy Review, 15*(3). Retrieved from http://www.guttm acher.org/pubs/gpr/15/4/gpr150402.html#boxref1

Davis, A. (1987). Women with disabilities: Abortion and liberation. *Disability and Society, 2*(3), 275-284, doi: 10.1080/02674648766780331

Craven, E. C. (1972). In Hilgers, T. W. &, Dennis J. Horan, D. J. (Eds.) *Abortion and Social Justice.* New York: Sheed & Ward.

Davis, A. (1987). Women with disabilities: Abortion and liberation. *Disability and Society, 2*(3), 275-284.

Ekeoacha, O. (2012). *In defense of dignity: An African explains how to save Africa.* Retrieved from http://www.cultureoflifeafrica.org/Articles_2.html

Fiala, C. & Arthur, J. H. (2014a). "Dishonourable disobedience" – Why refusal to treat in reproductive healthcare is not conscientious objection. *Woman - Psychosomatic Gynaecology and Obstetrics, 1,* 12-23. doi: 10.1016/j.woman.2014.03.001

Fiala, C. & Arthur, J. H. (2014b). Why we need to ban "conscientious objection" in reproductive health care. *RH Reality Check.* Retrieved from http://rhrealitycheck.org/article/2014/05/14/why-we-need-to-ban-conscientious-objection-in-reproductive-health-care/

Foreman, M. (2007, May 11). Damn right we support a woman's right to choose. Letter to the Editor, *Washington Blade.* Retrieved from http://www.washingtonblade.com/2007/5-11/view/letters/10555.cfm

Fox, D. & Griffin, C. L. (2009). Disability-selective abortion and the Americans with Disabilities Act. *Utah Law Review*, 826-405. Retrieved from http://scholarship.law.wm.edu/cgi/viewcontent.cgi?article=2282&context=facpubs

Gillespie, M. (1989). *African American women are for reproductive freedom.* Retrieved from http://www.trustblackwomen.org/2011-05-10-03-28-12/publications-a-articles/african-americans-and-abortion-articles/36-african-american-women-are-for-reproductive-freedom

Jesudason, S. & Epstein, J. (2011). The paradox of disability in abortion debates: Bringing the pro-choice and disability rights communities together. *Contraception 84*, 541–543. Retrieved from http://www.arhp.org/publications-and-resources/contraception-journal/december-1

Manninen, B. A. (2015). The replaceable fetus: A reflection on abortion and disability. *Disabilities Studies Quarterly, 35*(1). Retrieved from http://dsq-sds.org/article/view/3239/3831

Mills, C. B., & Erzikova, E. (2012). Prenatal testing, disability, and termination: An examination of newspaper framing. *Disabilities Studies Quarterly, 32*(3). Retrieved from http://dsq-sds.org/article/view/1767/3096

Parens, E. & Asch, A. (Eds). (2000). *Prenatal testing and disability rights.* Washington, DC: Georgetown University Press.

Prolife Alliance of Gays and Lesbians. (2014). Gay rights and the right to life. Retrieved from http://www.plagal.org/brochures/gay-rights-and-the-right-to-life-2014.pdf

Rich, B. (2015). Your morality, my mortality: Conscientious objection and the standard of care. *Cambridge Quarterly of Healthcare Ethics, 24*(2), 214-230. doi: dx.doi.org/10.1017/S0963180114000528

Saxton, M. (2004). Disability rights and selective abortion. *Gender and Justice in the Gene Age.* Retrieved from http://www.gjga.org/conference.asp?action=item&source=documents&id=17

Schuklenk U., Stein E., Kerin J, Byne W. (1997). The ethics of genetic research on sexual orientation. *Hastings Center Report, 27*(4), 6-13.

Stith, R. (2015). An open letter to fellow human rights activists. Retrieved from http://consistent-life.org/blog/index.php/2015/08/03/fellow-human-rights-activists/.

Chapter 15

The Psychological and Social Impact of Legal Regulations

by Rachel M. MacNair

What is the empirical evidence for the consequences of various specific restrictions? Individual cases vary widely; women being pressured by men, parents, or employers may have different outcomes from women who are entirely comfortable with their own decision. The determined will likely have different reactions from the ambivalent.

Here we cover evidence on society as a whole. Much empirical evidence therefore comes from sociologists, economists, and political scientists.

While regulations vary quite a bit world-wide, some of which will be covered here, the bulk of studies come from the United States, and one from Mexico, due to differing laws in different states allowing for many "natural experiments." A natural experiment has a specific intervention and control group, yet not arranged by the experimenter. An early example comes from an 1854 London cholera outbreak with differing patterns of water sources, with a theory that cholera could be caused by contaminated water. Another example is the random lottery for the military draft for American men being sent to Vietnam, so those selected comprised an intervention group and those not selected were a comparison group.

Here, different states (U.S. and Mexican) had regulations in effect one year but not the previous year. Some impact one group more than another; for example, parental consent laws only matter to minors. Therefore, this could be analyzed as a natural experiment. Statistical methods of controlling for other associated variables are also a common feature of these studies.

Since it is abortion opponents who work to establish the restrictions, and they therefore have an interest in the success of their work from their point of view, we will cover here only empirical literature from those who either favor abortion availability or give no indication of an advocacy opinion, with one exception involving both sides of a specific dispute. Pro-life and pro-choice perspectives on the findings will be offered, usually using the more neutral, narrow, and descriptive labels of abortion-as-violence and abortion-as-option.

Women Who Ask and Are Turned Down

When abortions were primarily illegal and societal pressures for legalization were mounting, one method of easing restrictions allowed women to apply to a committee for permission to abort a pregnancy. A book reporting research from this condition is *Born Unwanted: Development Effects of Denied Abortion* (David, Dybrich, Matejcek, & Schuller, 1988). The largest study is the Prague Cohort Study, with smaller studies in Sweden and Finland. Women who applied, were denied, appealed, were denied a second time and gave birth were studied. Babies were pair-matched on social class, gender, exact time of birth, siblings, etc.

How would the children compare with the children from accepted pregnancies? The answer is complicated, but the author's summary includes:

> Inspection of the data reveals that the difference is not so much in UP [unwanted pregnancy] children failing more often, but rather in being substantially underrepresented among the students graded above average, very good, or outstanding . . . the UP children consistently appeared worse, primarily due to underrepresentation in the above-average categories. (David, et al. 1988, p. 88)

To re-iterate: "the UP subjects are not so much overrepresented on the extremely negative indicators as they are underrepresented on the positive ones" (p. 124).

If differences were due to selection bias because mothers were inarticulate or felt ambivalent enough to be unable to convince a committee, the authors believe this to be irrelevant. The effect is the same. They conclude abortion should be completely legal so no child goes through the disadvantages inherent in being born unwanted.

Those of the "abortion-as-violence" position, however, argue that if abortion is killing a human being, doing so to avoid being underrepresented among the above average seems rather draconian. (The headline covering the study in *Sisterlife*, then newsletter of Feminists for Life: *Prof Repulsed by Working Class; Recommends Elimination. Not Clear Who Will Repair His Mercedes.*)

An alternative hypothesis also fits the results: putting women through the exercise of twice requesting their children be aborted may explain why the children have a slight tendency not to do as well. The very exercise of making a judgment on whether to allow fetal life to continue may cast a shadow over subsequent events.

The children themselves do not seem to abide by the proposal they are better off dead. Only one suicide was found (David, et al., p. 43). Many mothers changed their minds, as over a third – 36% – denied they had made the abortion request, and 73% were satisfied with how the situation was resolved (p. 48). Only a few had placed the children for adoption.

Peace psychology has something to add, as one of the measures to ascertain children as problematic was the votes of classmates "as the greatest coward, braggart, loner, most audacious" (p. David, et al., 70). What kind of society has teachers encouraging children to vote on such labels, and records the vote for data? This is not consistent with the conflict-resolution or anti-bullying approach favored in peace education.

If similar findings were found for racial or ethnic or social class differences, peace advocates would respond with interventions to improve the outlook for such disadvantaged children. The differences observed are slight; such an approach appears quite workable.

Funding

In the United States, after the 1973 Supreme Court decision *Roe v. Wade* suddenly legalized abortion in all 50 states, the Medicaid program for funding medical services to low- income people included abortion. Then in 1976 a legislative provision, the Hyde Amendment, restricted Medicaid funding to only cases of rape, incest, and preventing the death of the pregnant woman. These being rare, in many states funding was immediately severed, while other states continued. This provided a natural experiment.

The research arm of Planned Parenthood, The Guttmacher Institute, reported that in states without funding, the abortion rate was 1.6 times higher for Medicaid-eligible women than for women of higher income. The fact that it is greater than one to one suggests poverty plays a role in abortion decisions. However, the rate in states with funding is 3.9 times higher for women on Medicaid (Boonstra, & Sonfield, 2000).

Yet childbirths in the states without funding either stayed the same or were also reduced (Levine, Trainor, & Zimmerman, 1995). The missing abortions were not entirely replaced by women continuing pregnancies, but by couples taking more care about becoming pregnant. Some assume pregnancies occur whether or not funding is available, so funding only determines whether those pregnancies continue. However, the impact does not appear to be entirely neutral.

Abortion does have a fairly unique feature. If I do not brush my teeth, I am the one who gets cavities. Even if cavity-filling is free of cost in money to me, I am motivated to avoid it because of the cost in time and unpleasantness. The same applies to a woman whose behavior can lead to pregnancy. *Yet it does not apply to the man who engages in the same behavior*. He will not go through surgery. If the government takes care of the bill, the activity is free to him.

This would be irrelevant if the woman entirely controls her sexual relationships, but becomes relevant when she does not. Even outside of male-dominated relationships, it becomes relevant to a couple's decision-making – when to have sex at all, or how much trouble to take to obtain a condom first.

Kane and Staiger (1996), writing in an economics journal (which helps to explain their language), found a similar drop in birthrates and abortions with funding and other restrictions. They regarded this as counter-intuitive, and explain it this way:

> women get information during the early months of pregnancy, and abort the pregnancy if the birth turns out to be unwanted based on this new information . . . the father's willingness to marry is an obvious example of such information. . . . Abortion (unlike contraception or abstinence) works as an insurance policy to limit the downside risk when that information is negative. Increasing the cost of abortion increases the cost of this insurance policy and discourages women from becoming pregnant. (Kane & Staiger, 1996, p. 468)

Henshaw and colleagues, (with the Guttmacher Institute) in doing a critique of the 1995 Levine et al. study as one of a set of 38 studies, said:

> the reduction in the birthrate is implausibly large. A simpler explanation is that the negative association between Medicaid funding restrictions and birthrates is spurious because of inadequate control for hard-to-measure factors, incorrect coding of Medicaid funding status and inadequate comparison states. (Henshaw et al, 2009, p. 13)

This may well be true, and as with all alternative explanations, should be taken seriously. However, we have just offered two theoretical reasons why the size of the reduction in the birthrate may not be implausible.

In their overview of 38 studies on the impact of the funding restrictions on various outcomes, Henshaw et al. (2009) conclude that studies on such outcomes as sexual behavior, prematurity, low birth weight, fatal injuries to children, lack of prenatal care, suicide, and number of abortion providers are inconclusive and suffer from methodological limitations. Some studies indicate funding restrictions may delay Medicaid-eligible women from having abortions by a few days in the first trimester, with the net impact on second-trimester abortions unclear.

Authors mention in their highlights that approximately one-fourth of pregnant women who would have had Medicaid-funded abortions instead give birth. The discussion in the article makes the figure less clear, as is common in the complicated real world. Being of the abortion-as-option position, authors point out the extra money spent on prenatal care, delivery, and governmental child payments is several times the cost of abortions. Those from the abortion-as-violence position regard this as irrelevant; people's well-being is what money, when considered properly, was invented to facilitate.

Distance of Facilities

An early study showed counties further away from the abortion clinics of Atlanta had lower abortion-to-live birth ratios than those nearer (Shelton, Brann, & Schulz, 1976). A more recent study in Texas using 1993 data found the probability of a pregnant woman choosing abortion appeared quite sensitive to availability variables; women in counties further away from clinics had a lower rate than those near (Brown, Jewell & Rous, 2001). Kane and Stagier (1996) also found that distance reduced pregnancies among adolescent women. The first two studies only considered women already pregnant, not the incidence of pregnancy itself.

Theodore Joyce (2011) found a natural experiment in Texas's Woman's Right to Know Act, in effect in January, 2004. It had a "demand-side" informed-consent requirement, and a "supply-side" element of requiring abortions above 16 weeks gestation to be performed in a hospital or ambulatory surgical center. Few Texas hospitals performed abortions, so the average distance to obtain an abortion past 16 weeks went from 33 miles in 2003 to 252 miles in

2004. Since both components went into effect at the exact same time and place, they could be compared.

The demand-side policies showed little impact in other gestational ages, but the drop in abortions past 16 weeks was dramatic – a 68% drop in numbers (taking into account that the outflow to other states quadrupled). New qualified centers for abortion provision after 16 weeks were then established in several Texas cities, but numbers remained below the 2003 level.

A more dramatic case of abortion availability in Texas occurred with a law establishing requirements many clinics could not meet, primarily that doctors have admitting privileges at local hospitals. There was a sudden closure of many clinics within a short time. In May 2013, there were 41 clinics; by November, only 22. A study comparing abortions from November 2012 -- April 2013 to November 2013 -- April 2014 (so the impact of time of year would be the same) found a 13% decrease in the abortion rate. Second-trimester abortions increased from 13.5% to 13.9% of all abortions (Grossman et al., 2014). This slight increase in proportion would be expected as a mathematical artifact of the lowered number of first-trimester abortions.

Price

The price is only a restriction if government-mandated, which is rare. Legislatures can, however, pass regulations that increase the price. Otherwise, price is an impact based on what clinics and hospitals and doctors determine.

Studies done in various ways suggest that higher monetary costs do indeed decrease abortion utilization (Gohman & Ohsfeldt, 1993; Medoff, 2007, 2008, 2012)

Parental Involvement

The natural experiment of parental involvement laws – ones requiring either parental notification or consent for minors, with a judicial bypass – allows for comparisons of abortion and birthrates immediately before and after laws go into effect.

The most commonly observed immediate impact is a drop in the first-trimester abortion rate among minors, but not among teenagers who are not minors (aged 18 and 19). This was found along with no increase in the birthrate for Minnesota (Rogers, Boruch, Stoms & DeMova, 1991) and Texas (Joyce, Kaestner & Colman, 2006) and state-level data from 1985-1996 (Levine, 2003). One analyst found in analyzing all state data that "A parental involvement law is associated with a significant reduction in a state's abortion ratio and the abortion rate of unintended pregnancies, which suggests that the law may have a behavioral modification effect" (Medoff, 2012).

Deborah Haas-Wilson (1996) finds with four ways of estimating involving several states, controlling for different variables, that parental involvement laws cause demand to drop 13 to 25% among minors, without considering birthrate. Ohsfeldt & Gohmann (1994) in doing state-level analysis from several states find a larger drop in the abortion rate and a smaller drop in the pregnancy rate.

In Massachusetts, researchers found the dramatic reduction in in-state abortions for minors was accounted for by the number who went to neighboring states, concluding the 1981 law had no immediate impact on pregnancy avoidance (Cartoof & Klerman, 1986). Massachusetts is a small state; if surrounding states did not have parental involvement laws, travel would be fairly easy.

In Arkansas, a legislative change from parental notification to parental consent appeared to make no difference (Joyce, 2010). In the hypothesis of behavior change, this is as would be expected; the inability to keep a pregnancy hidden from parents is the same in either case.

Colman, Joyce & Kaestner (2008) point out a possible misclassification bias: minors late in the year of being 17 may wait until they are 18 to have an abortion. They are counted in the reduction for minors, but included in the abortion rate for the older group to which it is being compared. A large portion of those who continue a pregnancy that started at age 17 do not give birth until they are 18, and many births among 18-year-olds come from pregnancies begun at age 17. Authors tried to resolve this utilizing data that included exact birth dates for the minor's age and gestational ages giving approximate conception times. They found that while the abortion rate did fall, the pregnancy rate had been under-counted. More childbirth was happening due to the abortion decline, but after minors were no longer minors. The level of intendedness of the pregnancy was not a variable in the analysis. This does show the importance of not simply comparing 15-17 year olds to 18-19 year-olds. Pregnancies last around nine months, after all. It is easy to achieve a one year difference in age during that time.

Bitler & Zavodny (2001) considered whether parental involvement laws statistically caused abortions to occur later in pregnancy. While *the portion* of second-trimester abortions increased, this was not due to a rise in absolute numbers. A reduction in first-trimester abortions made late-term abortions a higher percentage of the total.

Marshall Medoff asked whether the impact is long-term:

> Parental involvement laws reduced the likelihood of teen minor females (under 18 years of age) having unwanted pregnancies by altering their frequency of unprotected sexual activity or contraceptive use. This change in teen minors' pregnancy avoidance behavior is found to be perpetuated over adult women's childbearing span of 18-44 years of age. Parental involvement laws are estimated to account for approximately one-third of the decline in the abortion rates of adult women of childbearing age over the period 1982-2000. The empirical results remain robust even after controlling for outliers, interstate migration, regional effects, and the presence of a waiting period. (Medoff, 2010, p. 193)

Moving beyond the direct impact on abortion, Sabia & Rees (2012) used state-level data on suicides from 1987-2003. They found states with parental involvement laws were associated with an 11% to 21% *reduction* in suicides among females 15-17 years old, but had no impact on males in that age group or on older females.

Informed Consent and Waiting Periods

Laws requiring specific information be given to women as they make arrangements for an abortion are "informed consent" laws. These are sometimes accompanied by mandatory waiting periods to consider the information, ranging from as low as one hour to as high as 72 hours (three days); the most common period is 24 hours. These laws vary as to whether the information is delivered in-person or by other means, such as internet or telephone. When in person, two visits to the clinic are required. There are several countries that require this, but the differing laws in different states of the United States offer more of a possible natural experiment for making comparisons in roughly the same culture.

The Guttmacher Institute literature review of the impact of these laws identified 12 studies as of 2009 (Joyce, Henshaw, Dennis, Finer, & Blanchard, 2009). The clearest documentation showed that in the state of Mississippi, with a two-visit requirement, abortion rates fell. The number of women going out of state rose. Primarily, they found there was no measurable impact of the laws on reproductive outcomes, except perhaps for some delays. However, they found most of the studies were not well done in terms of completeness of data or controlling for other variables. Later, Medoff (2012) found no impact of mandatory counseling or a two-visit law on abortion either rate or ratio.

Klick (2010) asked the question of what impact waiting periods had on mental health, whether it was a protective cooling-off period or instead a possible source of additional stress. He used suicide rates of adult females at the state level as a proxy for mental health as a whole. The panel data analyses found the waiting periods associated with a statistically significant reduction of suicide rates of about 10 percent.

This is an area with considerably more variability than others. Whether funding is available or parental involvement for minors is required are simple yes-or-no variables. The nature of the information offered – say, a reluctant rendition of fetal development over the phone as opposed to bright colored photos of fetal development in person – could make a significant difference. Thus, the form that the informed consent takes is a more varying variable than other legal restrictions.

Pro-life researcher Michael J. New (2011, 2014) did find that "well-designed" informed consent laws have an impact, and pro-choice Marshall H. Medoff and Christopher Dennis (2014a, 2014b) disputed the findings. Both claimed errors in the other's methodology. At this writing, this is still a contentious empirical area.

Not Restrictions, But Assistance

How does public policy impact abortion decisions by way of providing economic supports to pregnant women?

One such mechanism is child support enforcement, a government arrangement which is firm about seeing that the father makes periodic payments to support the child. Cowley, Jagannathan and Falchettore (2012) collected data from 1978-2003 and found that child support enforcement effectiveness does decrease the abortion rate (abortions per 1,000 women), but not the abortion ratio (abortions per live birth).

As to the impact of other forms of assistance, attempts at empirical studies have been mired in disputes due to partisan political implications, so there is nothing solid yet to report.

Outright Legal Ban

The restrictions covered here will only prevent abortions in women whose desire to have an abortion is sufficiently ambivalent, or if the added inconvenience of procuring abortion puts the inconvenience of using a condom in a better light. Pregnant women who are determined to have an abortion will find funding, drive extra distances, tolerate information and waiting periods, and forge ahead. Only an outright legal ban makes abortion essentially unavailable. Even then, determined women will travel to where they are not banned or have them surreptitiously.

In previous decades abortion was more commonly banned in many countries. Studying the effect of a long-lasting ban encounters confounding variables involving other long-standing cultural assumptions. A sudden change in whether or not abortion is banned therefore makes a more workable study.

Two countries that have instituted legal bans after a period of fairly free availability are Poland in 1993 and Nicaragua in 2006. In both, the abortion rate went down (inasmuch as it was reported since it was banned), the maternal mortality rate went down, and indicators of maternal health went up.

However, there were simultaneous dramatic occurrences in both – a transition out of communism in Poland, and an assertive women's health-care campaign by the Nicaraguan government. These are sufficient to account for better maternal health statistics.

In the opposite direction, abortion legalization in South Africa, Ethiopia, and Nepal was also accompanied by better maternal health outcomes, and likely for similar reasons (Guttmacher Institute, 2012).

Mexico had a "natural experiment" as abortion was legalized in some of its 32 states but not others. Koch et al. (2015) tested whether there was an association with maternal mortality (from both aborted and continued pregnancies) after controlling for other variables such as clean water. Over ten years, they found states with less permissive laws had lower maternal mortality than states with more permissive laws. However, there were independent associations with female literacy, skilled attendance at birth, low birth weight, clean water, sanitation, and intimate partner violence, which in a regression accounted for most of the variance in maternal mortality. Authors conclude: "Although less permissive states exhibited consistently lower maternal mortality rates, this finding was not explained by abortion legislation itself. Rather, these differences were explained by other independent factors, which appeared to have a more favourable distribution in these states" (Koch et al. 2015, front page). The question of why less permissive abortion laws were associated with these other measures of benefit was beyond the scope of the study.

Conclusion

Empirical evidence on legislation's impact is currently quite meager. The primary focus has been on sheer numbers – abortion rates, birth rates, and sometimes other indicators – much coming from economists and political scientists inclined to think in those numerical terms.

Psychology research would delve more into the reasoning behind the numerical observations. Speculation about whether reductions in pregnancies are due to avoiding sex or better use of contraception, for example, are badly over-simplified. Is the avoided sex a form of male-privilege imposition, best avoided also on grounds of gender equality? Or is sex truly desired by both partners but avoided only due to fear? Both cases will exist, of course, and the distinction is not clear-cut, but what is the prevalence of each? The distinction can be important, as in the extreme case of the 14-year-old incest victim taken to a clinic who hoped to be able to divulge the situation and seek preventative intervention, but was instead advised on contraceptive methods and told to "be responsible."

In short, some preliminary studies have been done, primarily by people who have a policy-advocacy interest in the outcome. Yet there is a great need to design and implement studies that delve more deeply into the causes of any changes observed.

References

Bitler, M. & Zavodny, M. (2001). The effect of abortion restrictions on the timing of abortions. *Journal of Health Economics 20*, 1011–1032.

Boonstra, H. & Sonfield, A. (2000). Rights without access: Revisiting public funding of abortion for poor women. *The Guttmacher Report on Public Policy* 3(2). Retrieved from https://www.guttmacher.org/pubs/tgr/03/2/gr030208.html

Brown, R. W., Jewell R. T., & Rous J. J. (2001). Provider availability, race, and abortion demand. *Southern Economic Journal, 67*(3), 656-671. Retrieved from http://www.jstor.org/stable/1061456?seq=1#page_scan_tab_contents

Cartoof, V. & Klerman, L. (1986). Parental consent for abortion: Impact of the Massachusetts law. *American Journal of Public Health, 76*(4), 397-400.

Colman, S., Joyce, T., Kaestner, R., (2008). Misclassification bias and the estimated effect of parental involvement laws on adolescents' reproductive outcomes. *American Journal of Public Health 98*(10), 1881–1885.

Crowley, J. E., Jagannathan, R., & Falchettore, G. (2012). The effect of child support enforcement on abortion in the United States. *Social Science Quarterly, 93*(1), 152-172. Retrieved from http://www.ncbi.nlm.nih.gov/pubmed/22532964

David H. P., Dybrich Z., Matejcek Z., Schuller V. (Eds.). (1988). *Born unwanted: Development effects of denied abortion.* Prague: Avicenum-Czechoslovak Medical Press.

Gohmann, S. F., & Ohsfeldt, R. L. (1993). Effects of price and availability on abortion demand. *Contemporary Policy Issues, 11*(4). 42-55. doi: 10.1111/j.1465-7287.1993.tb00400.x

Grossman, D., Baum, S., Fuentes, L., White, K., Hopkins, K., Stevenson, A., & Potter, J. E. (2014). Change in abortion services after implementation of a restrictive law in Texas. *Contraception, 90*(5), 496-501.

Guttmacher Institute. (2012). Making abortion services accessible in the wake of legal reforms: A framework and six case studies. New York: Author. Retrieved from http://www.guttmacher.org/pubs/abortion-services-laws.pdf

Haas-Wilson, D. (1996). The impact of state abortion restrictions on minors' demand for abortions. *The Journal of Human Resources, 31*(1), 140-158. Retrieved from http://www.smith.edu/economics/documents/TheImpactofStateAbortionRestrictions.pdf

Henshaw, S. K., Joyce, T. J., Dennis, A., Finder, L. B., & Blanchard, K. (2009). Restrictions on Medicaid funding for abortions: A literature review. New York: Alan Guttmacher Institute. Retrieved from: http://www.guttmacher.org/ pubs/ MedicaidLitReview.pdf

Joyce, T. (2010). Parental consent for abortion and the judicial bypass option in Arkansas: effects and correlates. *Perspectives on Sexual and Reproductive Health 42*(3), 168-175. doi: 10.1363/4216810

Joyce, T. (2011). The supply-side economics of abortion. *New England Journal of Medicine, 365*(16), 1466-1469.

Joyce, T. J., Henshaw, S. K., Dennis, A., Finer, L. B., & Blanchard, K. (2009). Waiting period laws on abortion: A literature review. Guttmacher Institute. Retrieved from https://www.guttmacher.orgpubs/MandatoryCounseling.pdf

Joyce, T. J., Kaestner, R., Colman, S., (2006). Changes in abortions and births and the Texas parental notification law. *New England Journal of Medicine 354*(10),1031–1038.

Kane, T. J. & Staiger, D. (1996). Teen motherhood and abortion access. *The Quarterly Journal of Economics, 111*(2), 467-506.

Klick, J. (2006). Mandatory waiting periods for abortions and female mental health. *Health Matrix: Journal of Law-Medicine, 16*, 183-208. Retrieved from http://papers.ssrn.com/sol3/papers.cfm?abstract_id=821304##

Koch, E., Chireau, M., Pliego F., Stanford, J., Haddad, S., Cahoun, B., Aracena, P., Bravo, M., Gatica, S., & Thorp, J. (2015). Abortion legislation, maternal healthcare, fertility, female literacy, sanitation, violence against women and maternal deaths: a natural experiment in 32 Mexican states. *British Medical Journal Open Access*. Retrieved from http://bmjopen.bmj.com/content/5/2/e006013.full.pdf+html

Levine, P. B., Trainor, A. B., & Zimmerman, D. J. (1995). The effect of Medicaid abortion funding restrictions on abortions, pregnancies, and births. *Journal of Health Economics, 15*(5), 555–578.

Levine, P. B. (2003). Parental involvement laws and fertility behavior. *Journal of Health Economics 22*(5), 861–878.

Medoff, M. H. (2007). Price, restrictions and abortion demand. *Journal of Family and Economic Issues, 28*(4), 583–599.

Medoff, M. H. (2008). The response of abortion demand to changes in abortion costs. *Social Indicators Research, 87*(2), 329–346.

Medoff, M. H. (2010). State abortion policy and the long-term impact of parental involvement laws. *Politics and Policy, 38*(2), 193–221. doi: 10.1111/j.1747-1346.2010.00235.x

Medoff, M. H. (2012). Unintended pregnancies, restrictive abortion laws, and abortion demand. *International Scholarly Research Notices*. doi: 10.5402/2012/612081

Medoff, M. H., & Dennis, C. (2014a). A critical reexamination of the effect of antiabortion legislation in the post-Casey era. *State Policy & Politics Quarterly, 14*(3), 207-227. doi: 10.1177/1532440014534270

Medoff, M. H., & Dennis, C. (2014b). Another critical reexamination of the effect of antiabortion legislation in the post-Casey era. *State Policy & Politics Quarterly, 14*(3), 269-276. doi: 10.1177/1532440014535476

New, M. J. (2011). Analyzing the effect of anti-abortion U.S. state legislation in the post-*Casey* era. *State Policy & Politics Quarterly, 11*(1), 28-47. doi: 10.1177/1532440010387397

New, M. J. (2014). Analyzing the impact of U.S. antiabortion legislation in the post-*Casey* era: A reassessment. *State Policy & Politics Quarterly, 14*(3), 228-268. doi: 10.1177/1532440014535477

Ohsfeldt R. L., & Gohmann S. F. (1994). Do parental involvement laws reduce adolescent abortion rates? *Contemporary Economic Policy 12,* 65–76

Rogers, J., Boruch, R. F., Stoms, G. B., DeMoya, D. (1991). Impact of the Minnesota Parental Notification Law on abortion and birth. *American Journal of Public Health, 81,* 294–298. Retrieved from http://www.ncbi.nlm.nih.gov/pmc/articles/PMC1405024/

Sabia, J. J. & Rees, D. I., (2012). The effect of parental involvement laws on youth suicide. *Economic Inquiry, 51*(1), 620-636. doi: 10.1111/j.1465-7295.2011.00440.x

Shelton, J. D., Brann, E. A., & Schulz, K. F. (1976). Abortion utilization: Does travel distance matter? *Family Planning Perspectives, 8*(6), 260-262

Chapter 16

Pregnancy Prevention

by Rachel M. MacNair

Preventing abortion by preventing pregnancy is the most effective method and the most agreeable to all perspectives. When violence against women is the cause of pregnancy, as covered in Part 1, the best prevention is to stop the violence. Here we cover pregnancy prevention primarily outside of violence contexts.

Methods of Sexual Self-Discipline

The most commonly discussed methods of preventing pregnancy deal with the observation that sexual intercourse is its cause, and therefore focus on the act itself.

The Debate

The argument for contraceptive devices and chemicals is that their wider availability will prevent pregnancies – that being their purpose – and therefore prevent abortions. Abstinence is fine for those who wish, but for social policy, we must be realistic. Besides, many argue, sexual expressions are healthy and simply need to be done responsibly. If any people prefer Natural Family Planning (NFP), also known as Fertility Awareness Methods (FAM), this is fine; it is one of many options.

There is a counter-argument that programs to promote contraceptive devices or chemicals actually lead to *more* abortions. There is a failure rate. People may engage in more sexual activity when contraception is readily available, including circumstances where the sexual partner would not be a desirable co-parent. More pregnancies will occur under adverse circumstances. Also, people take the attitude that since they used contraception they are *entitled* to having no pregnancy, making a pregnancy more likely to be aborted. It is entirely unfair to the child to inform her that her very act of getting conceived constitutes a "failure."

Yet both views miss important points. Neither contraception nor abstinence work to prevent pregnancy if couples are unskilled in life planning, nor if a woman is depressed, intoxicated, or in an abusive relationship.

Here are three problems with either contraception or abstinence as the *sole* approach, from the abortion-as-violence perspective:

- Stating that preventing untimely pregnancies is the *only* way of stopping abortion is like saying preventing all conflict will stop war. While strictly accurate, it is not realistic. We need creative ways of dealing with unplanned pregnancy, just as we need constructive ways to deal with conflict.

- It is common for pregnant women to castigate themselves for the behavior that caused the condition. There is always a man who engaged in the same behavior, but blaming the woman is customary in our patriarchal society. A judgmental attitude on this point is unhelpful.

- If abortion is violence against unborn children, the children should not be required to avoid existing to be protected. Analogously, if undocumented immigrants were beaten, we would not say the beatings would be prevented if only they would remain in their own countries. People are entitled to protection from violence, period.

Empirical Evidence on Contraception
(Short-term and Long-lasting)

While there is much speculation and even computer simulations as to what might happen with greater access or better techniques, in psychology we are interested in the empirical evidence. There are two primary methods of study:

1. *Epidemiological.* Analyzes what happens to contraception rates related to abortion rates in wide geographic areas.

2. *Experimental.* Analyzes a before-and-after comparison of a specific intervention to determine its efficacy. This is done ideally with a comparison group where the experimental group receives the intervention and the comparison or control group receives an alternative or no intervention.

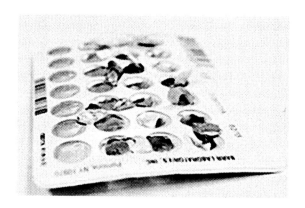

Epidemiological.

These countries had wider contraception availability associated with lower abortion rates: Kazakhstan; Kyrgyz Republic; Uzbekistan; Bulgaria; Turkey; Tunisia; and Switzerland (Marston & Cleland, 2003). These are cases where the prediction that more contraception means fewer abortions was accurate.

The first four are easily explained; abortion was readily available but contraception was not in the former Soviet Union and some Eastern European countries. The hypothesis of contraception causing greater sexual activity would no longer apply, since abortion as a birth-control method could have the same effect. Contraception's failure rate would be irrelevant; failure is always greater when not used at all.

Conversely, these countries had a *rise* in the abortion rate with the rise in contraception use: Cuba, Denmark, the Netherlands, the United States, Singapore, the Republic of Korea (Marston & Cleland, 2003), Spain (Dueñas, et al., 2011), and among adolescents in Sweden (Edgardh, 2002).

Correlation is not causation. If two things are correlated, called A and B, it could be that A causes B. It could be that B causes A. It could instead be that something else entirely, C, causes both A and B. This being the real world, it might not be so simple and there might be feedback loops with all three being true.

In the case where more contraception was associated with more abortion, there is one hypothesis that greater contraception causes more abortion because it leads to more sexual activity. There is instead the proposal that C causes both A and B:

> Rising contraceptive use results in reduced abortion incidence in settings where fertility itself is constant. The parallel rise in abortion and contraception in some countries occurred because increased contraceptive use alone was unable to meet the growing need for fertility regulation in situations where fertility was falling rapidly. (Marston & Cleland, 2003, p. 6)

With this reasoning, absence of contraception would have led to even more abortions. Falling fertility would have remained.

For the thesis that A causes B, however, there is epidemiological evidence for the concept of "risk compensation" or "behavioral adaptation." There are suggestions this interferes with prevention of HIV infection (Cassell, Halperin, Shelton, & Stanton, 2006) and condom use (Richens, Imrie & Copas, 2000). Richens et al. make an analogy to, of all things, seat belts:

> Condoms and car seat belts are applied to the human body to save lives. For both, there is an abundance of evidence of benefit to individuals directly exposed to risk. When evidence of benefit is sought at population level it becomes much harder to show beneficial effects. We look at evidence that suggests that the safety benefits of seat belts are offset by behavioural adaptation, and we ask whether condom promotion could also be undermined by unintended changes in sexual risk perception and behaviour. (Richens, et al., p. 400)

Seat belt laws succeeded in several countries in inducing more people to wear seat belts – but without impacting the statistics on injuries and fatalities. If someone who scrupulously follows the speed limit without a seat belt continues to do so after wearing one, then greater safety follows. If that person feels because of the seat belt it is now acceptable to drive much faster, this could counteract the benefit.

Another argument has been that results will depend on the type of contraception. Most methods depend on on-going self-discipline, which is why their failure rate under typical conditions is so much higher than the failure rate under ideal conditions (Trussel, 2011). However, Long-Acting Reversible Contraception (LARC), methods such as progestin implants and the intra-uterine device, require one medical visit and then no more action until the decision for another medical visit when pregnancy is desired. One study found an association of increased use of such methods due to a state program and a drop in the abortion numbers (Biggs, Rocca, Brindis,

Hirsch & Grossman, 2015) and another reported similar findings in Colorado (Ricketts, Klingler, & Schwalberg, 2014).

Interventions.

England offered an expensive three-year program to reduce teen pregnancy (as well as substance abuse and dropping out of school).Wiggins et al. (2009) studied its effectiveness by comparing participants with a control group getting standard treatment (n = 2,724). They found program participants were *more* likely to report becoming pregnant, 16% vs. 6%, an odds ratio of 3.55. This program appeared to be counter-productive.

Again, however, the type of contraception can make a difference. Secura, et al. (2014) studied an intervention in the U.S. city of St. Louis, Missouri (with no control group). They did a cohort study involving a large group of adolescents, in an effort to evaluate a program which made LARCs and other forms of contraception available for free, with emphasis on the benefits of LARCs. They followed the cohort for two to three years, and analyzed birth and abortion rates. They found a dramatic drop in both as compared to the US average: 9.7 abortions per 1,000, while in 2012 that rate was 29.4.

Dealing with physical side-effects of the LARCs was not one of the variables studied. This is important because adverse side-effects could be a cause of dropping use of the techniques and certainly of less satisfaction with outcomes. Immediate and long-term physical effects and impact on fertility are not minor matters to most young women – and these are techniques to be used only by the female half of the couple.

The intervention required parental consent for minors to participate, and minors knew they would get calls to monitor compliance. Authors acknowledged that each of those factors may have impacted the findings.

A New Zealand study of 510 women who were tracked for two years after abortions found that those who had used LARC had a significantly lower repeat abortion rate than those who did not (Rose & Lawton, 2012). There was no control group, and self-selection in terms of who did and did not use LARC when all women were offered it was not considered; still, if the goal is to reduce repeat abortions, then offering it as part of post-abortion counseling was shown to have that impact.

Planned Parenthood did a study with a cluster randomized trial: 20 of their clinics were the control group, and the other randomly-selected 20 clinics got more training on IUDs and implants (Harper, et al., 2015). As expected, the intervention group demonstrated an increase in the use of the LARCs, and those visiting to get family planning evidenced a lower pregnancy rate. However, contrary to the New Zealand study, pregnancy rates were not lower following post-abortion visits.

LARC has the advantage of being highly effective and avoiding the complication of being cancelled out by the risk compensation mechanism. Its disadvantages include being considerably more expensive, a requirement of trust in the medical care for reversal will be readily available, the chemical and mechanical impact on the female body which can lead to severe side-effects, and the fact that it is only the female body upon which it has such an impact. Men cannot be equal participants in the risks involved in the methods; they need not worry about uterine perforations or the IUD traveling to other organs.

An intervention can also operate in the other direction. A natural experiment comes from Texas, where Planned Parenthood facilities operated on a large scale. In 1999, five of its facilities closed; in 2001, seven more. Four more shut down later, so by 2008, none remained in the Texas Panhandle. Statistics on the teenage pregnancy rate in those counties show teen pregnancy rates dropped dramatically. The average rate in the 16 counties started at 43.7 per 1,000 in 1996 for those aged 13 to 17. By 2002, it was 28.6; by 2010, it had dropped to 24.1 per 1,000 (Texas Department, 2012).

Other Forms of Having Sex Without Pregnancy

Emergency Contraception.

Emergency contraception involves using pills after intercourse to make the female body inhospitable to sperm. Its primary use is when contraception was not used or failed, as when a condom breaks. It is also used to treat rape victims.

Empirical evidence is clear: as a program, providing emergency contraception has no impact on preventing unwanted pregnancy or abortion. Raymond, Trussel, & Polis (2007) reviewed 23 studies, from the US, Europe, and China. Despite their desire based on previous predictions to find pregnancy reduction, all studies are unambiguous. No such reduction occurs.

This covers general usage; women reporting rape may experience a different impact. From such women's viewpoint, medication that cuts the chance of pregnancy by even a small percent would be worth doing. These are individual cases, separate from a larger statistical impact.

Fertility Awareness Methods (FAM) / Natural Family Planning (NFP).

The Catholic Church has a position against "artificial" contraception, but not against family planning. The first foray into a "natural" method – relying on no devices or chemicals – was called *rhythm*. It was widely derided for its ineffectiveness. Women noted the most probable times they would be in a short fertile period in the middle of each menstrual cycle, using the calendar. If the woman's body did not abide by the calendar, pregnancy could result.

Currently, however, there are better methods to ascertain the woman's individual body fertility. There is already one computer app for fertility awareness, and there may be more available in the near future.

Such techniques are also especially useful for those who wish to *achieve* pregnancy. Adolescents can be taught techniques for practicing body awareness without implying that immediate sexual activity is expected.

Its widespread usefulness also requires secular reasoning. This is easily found in those who prefer natural to artificial in other realms, as shown in an article entitled "The Paradox of Crunchy Women and Chemical Birth Control":

> Eat the meat of a cow that has consumed synthetic hormones? No! Take them yourself via a highly concentrated white pill? Yes, please, but I can only wash them down with organic juice. Chemical free.
>
> The recent storm against GMOs are enough to make me think that if birth control didn't fall within the boundaries of "women's reproductive rights," it would have been banned long ago. Women would write letters until "Pharma" (birth control makes up a 2.8 billion dollar slice of the pharmaceutical pie) stopped making poison meant to be consumed by unsuspecting women. There is in fact a big label on any birth control, stating its synthetic nature and chemical name, along with its laundry list of side effects: weight gain, breast cancer, depression, blood clots, heart attacks, strokes – oh, and possible death. (Wing, 2014)

FAM and NFP require quite a bit of practice and discipline. In addition to daily observations, they include periodic abstinence at specified times – precisely when natural sex drive is highest. This also requires participation and discipline by the man, rather than it being the woman's responsibility alone.

Though they would be contrary to the Catholic position, barrier methods such as the condom or diaphragm can be added. This increases the effectiveness of both methods.

Empirical studies on effectiveness include a longitudinal study by Frank-Hermann et al. (2007) which followed a German cohort of 900 women. Findings were a pregnancy rate of 0.6 per hundred when the method was followed well; 1.8 per hundred pregnancies over-all, and 9.2 per hundred dropped out due to dissatisfaction with the method. These figures compare favorably with other methods.

Non-fertile Sexuality.

The Latin term *coitus interruptus* involves the man withdrawing before ejaculation. Its main advantage is its lack of special equipment. Its huge disadvantages are the need for extreme discipline and trust, and a situation that lends itself to ineffectiveness if not done with great caution. It is primarily of historical interest. While still used in some areas of the world, it does not have much institutional promotion.

The concept of "outercourse," a word-play on sexual "intercourse," does have some discussion in sexuality-education material. It involves forms of sexual expression between male and female that do not involve vaginal penetration. It still does require discipline and trust, and also creates a situation vulnerable to getting out of hand, but is more likely to prevent pregnancy than is *coitus interruptus.*

Masturbation has the advantage of requiring no equipment, being 100% effective against causing pregnancy, and avoiding relationship complications. There are people, however, who prefer the relationship complications.

Though there is some intuitive sense to the idea that sexual expressions in these ways might avoid sexual expressions in pregnancy-producing ways, no studies have been found on this point directly. Such studies would be difficult to design.

Sterilization.

There are two huge advantages to permanent sterilization for women or men who want no children or no more children. It does not require any self-discipline once the short initial procedure is completed, and it has near total effectiveness.

There is also a huge disadvantage: this very ease makes it readily available for coercion or deception. For example, here is the case of Fannie Lou Hamer, a prominent U.S. civil-rights activist and opponent of the American war in Vietnam:

> One day in 1961, Hamer entered the hospital to have "a knot on my stomach"—probably a benign uterine fibroid tumor—removed. She then returned to her family's shack on the plantation to recuperate. But in the big house, ominous tidings circulated. . . . Hamer had lost more than a tumor while unconscious—the surgeon removed her uterus, rendering Hamer sterile. . . .
>
> "I went to the doctor who did that to me and I asked him, 'Why? Why had he done that to me?' He didn't have to say nothing—and he didn't. . . ."
>
> But a lawsuit was out of the question, Hamer recalled. "At that time? Me? Getting a white lawyer against a white doctor? I would have been taking my hands and screwing tacks into my casket." (Washington, 2007, pp. 189-190)

Many people choose sterilization; when information is clear and it is properly done, it will be an effective pregnancy-prevention technique. When done by force or trickery on women or men who wish to have children, it becomes a vicious and possibly racist form of violence.

Social Psychological Components

Quality of Sexual Relationships

How well will a couple's pregnancy prevention plan work if the relationship is other than equal, gentle and sensitive? When only the woman is regarded as responsible, the man may blame her for a pregnancy. We covered intimate partner violence in Chapter 1, but male domination can be present without meeting the legal criteria for abuse. Nor need it be one-sided on gender; women are quite capable of keeping a relationship from being gentle.

Contraception sabotage.

The American Congress of Obstetricians and Gynecologists succinctly defined "contraception sabotage," suggesting solutions for their profession:

> Reproductive and sexual coercion involves behavior intended to maintain power and control in a relationship related to reproductive health by someone who is, was, or wishes to be involved in an intimate or dating relationship with an adult or adolescent. This behavior includes explicit attempts to impregnate a partner against her will, control outcomes of a pregnancy, coerce a partner to have unprotected sex, and interfere with contraceptive methods.
>
> Obstetrician-gynecologists are in a unique position to address reproductive and sexual coercion and provide screening and clinical interventions to improve health outcomes. Because of the known link between reproductive health and violence, health care providers should screen women and adolescent girls for intimate partner violence and reproductive and sexual coercion at periodic intervals . . . Interventions include education on the effect of reproductive and

sexual coercion and intimate partner violence on patients' health and choices, counseling on harm-reduction strategies, and prevention of unintended pregnancies by offering long-acting methods of contraception that are less detectable to partners. (Committee Opinion, 2013)

These solutions are short-term, as would be expected from physicians; their task is to address an individual's immediate needs. With hidden long-lasting contraception, they are providing a short-term solution for only one aspect of a male-dominated relationship over which those physicians have no control, while leaving that male domination in place with all its other negative aspects. Within the context of peace psychology, we would also be interested in society-wide efforts to prevent all forms of domination.

Intoxication.

Intoxication is another way the quality of the relationship can suffer. If a sober man has sex with an intoxicated woman, this is legally a sexual assault, because intoxication means lack of consent. Many men do not understand this and are startled to be accused and convicted. If an intoxicated man assaults a non-intoxicated woman, this is still a criminal offense. If both are intoxicated, the situation is muddled as to legal consequences – but not in the poor quality of the sexual relationship. Any programs successful in reducing the incidence of intoxication may also have an impact on preventing unwanted pregnancies.

Pedophilia.

Sexual relationships involving older men with minors is another area where we need to go to the root of the problem. If adults simply tell minors to use contraception, this might communicate they are expected to cooperate with the abuse, and miss an opportunity to intervene to prevent further abuse.

Adults arranging abortions for the under-aged assist in covering up the crime of statutory rape, thereby facilitating it to continue. This, in turn, could contribute to pregnancies occurring that would have been prevented had the adults instead arranged interventions.

The proposal that sexual abuse in childhood leads to more abortions in adolescence and adulthood does have some empirical support. Boden, Fergusson, and Horwood (2009) found this in a New Zealand longitudinal study.

Motivation

Many worry that minors who give birth have poorer prospects for escaping poverty. Others view wanted babies positively and think all mothers should be accommodated. Another perspective is both at once: take steps to discourage adolescent pregnancy, then make needed accommodations for those who become pregnant because they wish to.

What is the empirical evidence on motivation? Planned Parenthood's research arm, the Guttmacher Institute (1998), interviewed 187 women aged 15-18. The most common reasons for choosing motherhood were:

- Having dropped out of school, they felt it was time.

- They had positive role models of others their age with children.

- They wanted someone to love and who would love them; this was lacking in their own tumultuous families.

- They saw it as a way to become more mature, stable, and more likely to keep out of trouble.

- Some hoped for a better relationship with the baby's father. This seems mainly to have worked in the short term; 99.1% of the fathers were happy about the pregnancy.

This study was limited to mostly the less affluent. Still, it is one of the best for number of interviewees and a more objective gathering of themes.

Some suggest the young women be offered reasonable methods of solving their problems, and if reproductive choice genuinely means choice, we will respect that. Otherwise, the rhetoric of "choice" becomes simply intolerance by people who judge what they think the choice should be. Women in or near poverty often regard children as a great treasure.

Others say the cycle of poverty is perpetuated, that it is much healthier for women to wait until adulthood. Their situation should already be mature and stable when the baby comes, rather than having the baby help cause this – much more responsibility than a mere baby should have, and a huge problem for said baby if it does not work. Finding alternative solutions to the young women's problems would be much better for them.

Either way, additional contraception availability would not have any impact on the pregnancy rate in those women who are motivated to become pregnant. If other people regard their pregnancies as ill-timed and wish to persuade them so, those people need to promote programs to help the young women solve their problems in other ways.

Education

Methodology

A severe methodological problem in ascertaining the effectiveness of any form of education is that reports of sexual activity must rely on self-report. Scientists do not observe the behavior directly. Results such as pregnancy for women and sexually transmitted diseases for both sexes can indicate sex occurred, but their absence does not assure that it did not. Adolescents taught abstinence may report – indeed, honestly remember – less sex than occurred. Others might report more than occurred; sexual adventures are notorious for being exaggerated.

Kohler, Manhart and Lafferty (2008) analyzed data from 15-19 year-olds for the National Survey of Family Growth. They compared the adolescents who received formal sex education, either comprehensive or abstinence-only, and those who received none. They reported that those with the comprehensive version were less likely to report teen pregnancy than those who received none, with no significant difference between abstinence-only and none. However, whether teens would decline to report an aborted pregnancy was not considered. Therefore, actual pregnancy prevention was not accurately assessed – especially since there was no difference between groups in terms of incidence of sexually-transmitted diseases. Nor did they consider the quality of the programs. There are far more variables than a simple comprehensive/abstinence distinction.

Sexuality Education

These two points are generally covered in any form of sexuality education:

- Sex makes babies. Fertile people who have opposite-gender genital-contact sexual intercourse might make a baby. Using contraception or FAM reduces the chance of doing so. They do not remove it entirely.

- There are sexually-transmitted diseases that one should take care to avoid.

These points might also be considered as basic both for pregnancy prevention purposes as well as having their own merits:

- Having sex with someone without the consent of that person is rape, and is criminal, and is intolerable. Pressuring someone who does not wish to have sex may not be illegal, but is unethical.

- Sexual relationships should involve sensitivity, gentleness, and equality between the partners.

Sexuality education can be done in many ways – warm or cold, informative or scolding, with different levels of explicitness. Studies that do not take different forms into account may miss and/or misinterpret crucial findings.

The U.S.-based National Campaign to Prevent Teen and Unplanned Pregnancy (2012) has identified those factors that most contribute to effectiveness in pregnancy prevention programs:

- convincing teens that not having sex, or consistently and carefully using contraception, is the right thing to do

- carried out over enough time (more than a few weeks)

- taught by well-trained people who believe in their programs

- actively engage the participants, and individualize the information

- address problems of peer pressure

- teach communication skills

- are consistent with the age, the sexual experience, and the culture of participants

Abstinence-Only-Until-Marriage Education

Overviews of empirical studies vary from the Sexuality Information and Education Council of the United States (SIECUS, n.d.) which declares all studies reviewed to show programs to be ineffective or counterproductive, to the Heritage Foundation (Kim & Rector, 2008) finding most studies show positive impact. We will not attempt to settle the question here.

Two categories of people are failed by abstinence-only education: those unpersuaded, and those convinced but succumbing to temptation. For the unpersuaded, opponents argue, the missing education on contraception is harmful. The second group has been discouraged from making contraceptive preparation.

Proponents argue abstaining from sex is the only fool-proof method of avoiding pregnancy and sexually-transmitted diseases. It is helpful for young people who do not wish to have sex but where such activity is the norm; young women can find ways of "saying no without hurting the boy's feelings," so to speak, when this is what they wish.

The studies finding a positive impact nevertheless only find an impact. If it reduces sex outside of marriage, no one proposes it capable of eliminating it. Strong stigma in past centuries never succeeded in eliminating it. If abortion prevention is desired, the programs must take care not to increase stigma related to teen or unmarried pregnancy – a natural hazard of this approach.

Features of the program could make a major difference. Scolding or dogmatic assertions may be less effective than reasoning and helping with decision-making skills. Overviews of studies primarily do not yet make such distinctions, but they would seem rather important.

Life Skills Education

Life skills are behaviors enabling individuals to deal effectively with challenges of life -- how to communicate or make financial decisions, etc. Core life skills include the ability to:

- Make decisions
- Solve problems
- Think critically and creatively
- Clarify and analyze values
- Communicate and listen
- Build empathy
- Be assertive
- Negotiate
- Cope with emotions and stress
- Be self-aware

Additionally, practical skills and information that may be lacking in the home are taught.

Studies show many such programs are remarkably effective in avoiding several negative impacts, including dropping out of school, and positive impacts, such as maintaining physical health (UNICEF, 2000; CEDPA, 2001; United Nations, 2000) and specifically in pregnancy prevention (Philliber, 1997; Kirby, 2007).

Peace Education

Pregnancy prevention is seldom raised in discussions of peace education. One source from Ian Harris said:

> Peace educators, concerned about the violent behavior of youth, use violence prevention strategies to create street-safe kids, who know how to avoid bullying, weapons, crimes, alcohol, drugs, and pregnancy. There are many risk factors for violent behavior – family patterns of behavior; violent social environments; negative cultural models or peers; alcohol and/or drug abuse; and availability of weapons. Addressing some of these factors directly in school can help inoculate children against risky behaviors. (Harris, 2002, p. 22)

There is only a fine distinction between life-skills education and peace education; indeed, Life Skills could be regarded as one form of peace education. It is explicitly, for example, in Camp for Peace of Liberia (see http://campforpeace.org/programs/).

A focus on skills of conflict resolution and prevention of violence does have possibilities. All forms of crisis pregnancy resulting from male domination and violence will be prevented if the underlying violence is prevented, by whatever method, and peace education is designed for that purpose.

Conclusion

Preventing undesired pregnancy can directly reduce abortions inasmuch as no abortion occurs unless a pregnancy exists. Nevertheless, this is only a reduction strategy. Much as many people ache to have the entire problem solved this way, realistic people must admit unplanned pregnancies will still occur. Lower numbers will not go to zero.

The abortion-as-option perspective offers this as a reason abortion must always be available. The abortion-as-violence perspective notes this as a reason for offering nonviolent alternatives for meeting everyone's needs. Then women truly can have more options. *Choice* implies multiplicity, since "only one choice" and "no choice at all" are the same thing.

Therefore, arrangements, services, and society attitudes are necessary from both the pro-choice and the pro-life perspectives, and those in between. To this we turn in the next chapter.

References

Biggs, M. A., Rocca, C. H., Brindis, C. D., Hirsch, H. & Grossman, D. (2015). Did increasing use of highly effective contraception contribute to declining abortions in Iowa? *Contraception, 91*(2), 167-73. doi: 10.1016/j.contraception.2014.10.009

Boden, J. M., Fergusson, D. M., & Horwood, L. J. (2009). Experience of sexual abuse in childhood and abortion in adolescence and early adulthood . *Child Abuse & Neglect, 33*(12), 870-876. doi: 10.1016/j.chiabu.2009.04.006

Cassell, M. M., Halperin, D. T., Shelton, J. D., & Stanton, D. (2005). Risk compensation: the Achilles' heel of innovations in HIV prevention? *British Medical Journal, 332*(7541), 605–607.

CEDPA. (2001). *Adolescent girls in India choose a better future: An impact assessment.* Washington, DC: Author.

Committee Opinion. (2013, February). Reproductive and Sexual Coercion. *American Congress of Obstetricians and Gynecologists, 554.* Retrieved from http://www.acog.org/Resources-And-Publications/Committee-Opinions/Committee-on-Health-Care-for-Underserved-Women/Reproductive-and-Sexual-Coercion

Dueñas J. L., Lete I., Bermejo, R., Arbat, A., Pérez-Campos, E., Martínez-Salmeán, J., Serrano, I., Doval, J. L., & Coll, C. (2011). Trends in the use of contraceptive methods and voluntary interruption of pregnancy in the Spanish population during 1997-2007. *Contraception, 83*(1), 82-87. Retrieved from http://www.ncbi.nlm.nih.gov/pubmed/21134508

Edgardh, K. (2002). Adolescent sexual health in Sweden. *Sexually Transmitted Infections,* 78, 352-6; Retrieved from http://sti.bmjjournals.com/cgi/content/full/78/5/352

Frank-Hermann, P., Heil, J., Gnoth, C., Toledo, E., Baur, S. Pyper,C., Jenetzky, E., Strowitzki, T., & Freundl, G. (2007). The effectiveness of a fertility awareness based method to avoid pregnancy in relation to a couple's sexual behaviour during the fertile time: a prospective longitudinal study. *Human Reproduction,* 22(5), 1310-1319. Retrieved from http://humrep.oxfordjournals.org/content/22/5/1310.long

Guttmacher Institute. (1998). Teenagers' pregnancy intentions and decisions: A study of young women in California choosing to give birth. New York: Author. Retrieved from http://www.guttmacher.org/pubs/or_teen_preg_survey.html

Harper, C., Rocca, C., Thompson, K. M., Morfesis, J., Goodman, S., Damey, P. D., Westhoff, C. L., & Speidel, J. J. (2015). Reductions in pregnancy rates in the USA with long-acting reversible contraception: a cluster randomised trial. *The Lancet, 386*(9993), 562-568. doi: 10.1016/S0140-6736(14)62460-0

Marston, C. & Cleland, J. (2003). Relationships between contraception and abortion: A review of the evidence. *International Family Planning Perspectives, 29*(1), 6-13

Harris, I. (2002). Conceptual understandings of peace education. In G. Salomon & B. Nevo (Eds.). Peace education: The concept, principles, and practices around the world. Mahwah, NJ: Lawrence Erlbaum Associates.

Kim, C. C., & Rector, R. (2008). Abstinence education: Assessing the evidence. Heritage Foundation. Backgrounder 2126. Retrieved from http://www.heritage.org/Research/Welfare/bg2126.cfm.

Kirby, D. (2007). Emerging Answers 2007: New Research Findings on Programs to Reduce Teen Pregnancy —Full Report. Washington, DC: The National Campaign to Prevent Teen and Unplanned Pregnancy.

Kohler, P. K., Manhart, L. E., Lafferty, W. E. (2008). Abstinence-only and comprehensive sex education and the initiation of sexual activity and teen pregnancy. *Journal of Adolescent Health 42,* 344–351. doi:10.1016/j.jadohealth.2007.08.026

National Campaign to Prevent Teen and Unplanned Pregnancy. (2012). What works: Curriculum-based programs that help prevent teen pregnancy. Retrieved from https://thenationalcampaign.org/sites/default/files/resource-primary-download/WhatWorks.pdf

Philliber Research Associates. (1997). *Preventing teen pregnancy and academic failure: Experimental evaluation of a developmentally based approach.* Accord, NY: The Associate.

Richens, J., Imrie, J., & Copas, A. (2000). Condoms and seat belts: The parallels and the lessons. *The Lancet, 355*(9201). 400-403. doi: 10.1016/S0140-6736(99)09109-6

Ricketts, S., Klingler, G., & Schwalberg, R. (2014). Game change in Colorado: Widespread use of Long-Acting Reversible Contraceptives and rapid decline in births among young, low-income women. *Perspectives on Sexual and Reproductive Health, 46*(3), 125-132

Raymond E. G., Trussel, J., & Polis, C. B. (2007), Population effect of increased access to emergency contraceptive pills: A systematic review. *Obstetrics & Gynecology 109*(1), 181-8.

Rose, S. B., & Lawton, B. A. (2012). Impact of long-acting reversible contraception on return for repeat abortion. *American Journal of Obstetrics and Gynecology, 206*(1). doi: 10.1016/j.ajog.2011.06.102

Secura, G. M., Madden, T. McNicholas, C. Mullersman, J., Buckel, C. M., Zhao, Q. Z., Peipert, J. F. (2014). Provision of no-cost, long-acting contraception and teenage pregnancy. *New England Journal of Medicine, 371*, 1316-1323. doi: 10.1056/NEJMoa1400506

SIECUS. (n.d.)What the research aays: Abstinence-only-until-marriage programs. Retrieved from http://www.siecus.org/index.cfm?fuseaction=Page. ViewPage&PageID=1195

Texas Department of State Health Services. (2012). Table 14B: Reported pregnancies for women age 13-17. Retrieved from http://www.dshs.state.tx.us/chs/vstat/vs12/t14b.shtm

Trussell, J. (2011). Contraceptive failure in the United States. *Contraception, 83*(5), 397-404. doi: 10.1016/j.contraception.2011.01.021

UNICEF. (2000) *Skills-based health education to prevent HIV/AIDS.* New York: Author. Retrieved from www.unicef.org/programme/lifeskills/mainmenu.html

United Nations Joint Programme on HIV/AIDS (2000). *UNAIDS best practices in school AIDS education, the Zimbabwe case study.* New York: Author.

Washington, H. A. (2007). *Medical apartheid: The dark history of medical experimentation on Black Americans from colonial times to the present.* New York: Doubleday.

Wiggins, M., Bonell, C., Sawtell, M., Austerberry, H., Burchett, H. Allen, E., & Strange, V. (2009). Health outcomes of youth development programme in England: Prospective matched comparison study. *British Medical Journal, 339*(72). doi:10.1136/bmj.b2534

Wing, C. (2014, July 21). The paradox of crunchy women and chemical birth control. *Ethika Politika.* Retrieved from https://ethikapolitika.org/2014/07/21/paradox-crunchy-women-chemical-birth-control/

Chapter 17

Meeting the Needs of Pregnant Women, New Mothers, Children and Families

by Jennie E. Brightup
Licensed Clinical Marriage and Family Therapist

While pregnancy prevention is ideal because it avoids the question of abortion arising at all, once pregnancy occurs, this is no longer an option. As alternatives to abortion, what does a woman need as she seeks assistance in making a parenting or adoption choice? What is available, and what alternatives require further action (legislative and otherwise)? What research could help in ascertaining what is helpful?

Public Policy

Direct Governmental Assistance

In the United States, an example of a government agency that directly provides assistance is the Department of Health and Human Services. It has an arm of funding and services specifically directed toward children, youth and women of childbearing age. The Health Resources and Services Administration: Maternal and Child Health Department manages the Title V funding of over $5 billion annually for maternal and child health programs. Services include a large variety of medical, dental, and mental healthcare for pregnant adolescents and women, and children. Following delivery of a pregnancy, comprehensive services are available for a number of services that address needs such as but not limited to:

- Through free or reduced insurance, public policy provides for continuing services for medical/mental/dental health for the mother and child. There are also many community or local health departments that provide free or sliding scale fees for services.

- Income or cash/card supplements or vouchers for food and grocery items.

- Assistance in no/low income housing and shelters.

- Free assistance for completion of high school or GED, job training, and job opportunities.

- Early/Head Start Programs provide education concerning child development and infant mortality, continued development of cognitive, social and emotional development of children, or child care and home visiting services.

- Often federal and state government agencies partner with state or local non-profit or community based organizations to provide a greater reach of services to adolescents and women in need.

World-wide, governments in developed countries provide health care services directly to the population, and programs to help new mothers and children are widespread. Developing countries vary in the quality and quantity of services provided, and improvements here are an urgent matter for research and action.

Overwhelmed by Parenting

All U.S. states and several countries have enacted laws to protect mothers who are unable to continuing parenting. They allow women to take an infant to a "safe location" and relinquish parenting rights without retribution of criminal charges for child abuse. These laws vary in the number of days allowed, from three days to one year. They also vary in the physical locations a newborn or infant may be legally relinquished at facilities such as hospitals, medical facilities, fire or police stations or even places of worship. Any adult may bring in the child with anonymity. These laws are in place to assist adolescents and women of childbearing age that do not desire to parent, but have not been engaged in the decision until after delivery.

"Respite care" is another service offered to overwhelmed parents or caretakers. This is the opportunity to have a foster home care for a child anywhere from a limited number of hours, overnight, or limited periods of time. State and local agencies recognize that caretakers can be overwhelmed at times, and have programs in place to allow a parent the ability to have a "break" from parenting without a charge or penalty. Government entities have different services and how to access them.

Adoption

There are thousands of agencies working in the area of adoption – nonprofit charities, businesses, law firms, private lawyers or mental health care professionals. These different agencies assist in all manner of adoptions.

Adoption on a global scale has seen change in the past decade. A country such as China, which has had a "one-child policy," is a country of choice for intercountry adoptions. Due to this policy, families who do not make an abortion choice can be punished or fined by the government for having more than one child. There is also social or familial pressure for the child to be a male. Because of this policy, many children adopted from China are females, or children with special needs. Along with China, the countries of Russia, Ethiopia, and Ukraine have the highest rates of adoption (Bureau of Consular Affairs, 2014).

Families can choose to adopt "special needs" children. This can include physical or mental disabilities. There are many waiting for adoption who suffer from cognitive, social, psychological difficulties, as well as physical issues such as deformity, AIDS, Fetal Alcohol Syndrome, Autism, seizures, among others. Adoption of "special needs" children can be demanding, but also rewarding for the families.

Another reason for adoption is the trauma of war. War-torn countries have a large displacement of orphaned children, due to the death of parents or caretakers. There is also the stigma of pregnancy due to rape or forced sex work by women trapped in these circumstances. Often a pregnancy of mixed ethnicity can bring continuing shame to the mother or family. There are many social and physical barriers to these pregnancies or adoptions, each with a unique story.

Workplace Accommodation

For either a mother or father of newborn children, the family needs to have support both financially and in the workplace. Non-paid family leave is being engaged by many companies in the

United States; however, many employees do not know that it can be accessed by both father and mother. Paid leave by companies would encourage and support the family structure, in process facilitating parenting. Several countries do offer varying lengths of paid leave, along with other workplace accomodations for breastfeeding and of course the lengthier need for several years of childcare (International Labour Organization, 2014).

Addressing discrimination against pregnant women and new mothers is of prime importance. The United Nations' 1979 treaty, Convention on the Elimination of all Forms of Discrimination Against Women (CEDAW), forbids dismissal for pregnancy or maternity and ensures maternity leave or comparable social benefits. The same is done by the Maternity Protection Convention (International Labour Organization, 2000) which also covers matters of breastfeeding accommodations, leave for illness, and other matters of importance to employed mothers.

Child Support Enforcement

While greater paternal participation is desirable, the law in most places does require at a bare minimum that the father make payments according to the means of the parents and needs of the child. Locales vary in how well this is enforced, but greater enforcement does help meet the needs of the mothers and children.

Substance Abuse Treatment

Much of the medical discussion has moved away from punitive approaches to pregnant women engaged in various forms of substance abuse, and is moving toward understanding it as a treatable mental disorder, with pregnancy causing specific issues to be medically addressed (Lester & Twomey, 2008). The public policy need is that all pregnant women are able to access such care immediately, and not be put on waiting lists.

Private Agencies

Many faith-based agencies across the United States (and globally) have seen the opportunity to meet the needs of the adolescent or woman of childbearing age. It is clear to ministries and private agencies that a great need exists in support of a parenting decision. To this end, churches, synagogues, mosques, temples, and non-profits have stepped into the gap to provide a variety of services. Pregnancy Service Centers (PSC), also known as Pregnancy Resource Centers (PRC), can be found in every state in the United States, with nearly 2,000 centers in existence. Most pregnancy resource centers will be listed under the affiliation of Heartbeat International, Care Net Pregnancy Centers, or National Institute of Family and Life Advocates (NIFLA). These agencies are most often funded by private individuals, businesses, or churches in the community to offer assistance to any seeking services. Depending on the nature of the local center, a variety of services are available, usually at no cost to the clients. Services often can include but are not limited to:

- Limited medical care – pregnancy testing, ultrasound, prenatal vitamins, sexually transmitted disease testing and treatment, and/or limited pre-natal/OB care.

- Perinatal hospice services: ultrasound, natal end of life care, and counseling services for families.

- Mental health services.

- Educational opportunities concerning parenting skills, child development, financial skills, relationship skill building, job readiness, and a variety of other topics.

- Material supplies – items to help support infant/child such as diapers, formula, clothing, and toiletries for infants and children. At times differing agencies also have larger items such as car seats, cribs, or infant furniture.

- Various PRCs either offer temporary housing, or work in collaboration with other agencies to provide shelter for pregnant or newly delivered mothers who have housing/shelter needs.

- Adoption services and/or collaborations.

- Community referrals to collaborating organizations or agencies for continued services needed.

Caritas Internationalis is an international network of Catholic charities which operates in most nations and all dioceses, largely supported by the Catholic Church. These charities are also heavily invested in meeting the abortion alternative need, driven by their mandate to assist families out of poverty, and recognize women and adolescents of childbearing age to be among the most vulnerable to poverty. As a nationwide organization, Catholic Charities USA provides many of the same services the American PRCs provide: pregnancy care, limited pregnancy medical services, adoption services – both foster care or for individuals, shelter or housing for the vulnerable, referral for food assistance, educational classes for a variety of topics, and a full range of services for those who choose to parent.

In addition to these agencies listed above, there is a number of community or faith-based organizations that address physical needs that women and adolescents of childbearing ages might have. Major needs such as shelter or housing, in the short term or long term, can be high on the list for many. Domestic violence or substance abuse is present in many situations, putting both mother and child at physical health risks. Agencies such as the YMCA, Recovery Centers, or women's shelters are available on a limited basis.

Housing is always a strong need, often with many more seeking a place to stay than agencies have available beds for. Age is sometimes a barrier for shelters, as many are only funded to care for adolescents up to age 18, while others will be funded for up to age

21. Another barrier can be whether a child is present. Having an infant or young child can make it exponentially difficult to find shelter or housing.

Private non-profits also assist in providing items to furnish a home or infant furniture. These agencies not only assist women and children, but families in need. Families have access to items needed, at a free or reduced charge. These items can be big ticket pieces, such as beds, washer/dryer, couches, tables and chairs, microwaves and refrigerators. They can also be items such as clothes, linens, blankets, and other domestic needs to run a home.

Medical and mental health services can be found at a reduced rate or sliding scale fee in many cities. These clinics can be working in collaboration with religious entities; clinics connected to a college or university, or can be nonprofit businesses in their own right. Services are available for every type of medical or dental need. Mental health professionals provide services at a reduced rate, or patients can be seen at a university training facility, which benefits the patient with no/low cost services and patient contact hours for the training students.

Changing the Culture

While we have been discussing some practicalities, it is important to also conceptualize ideas to make more effective changes in this arena. The impact of changing attitudes on a local, national or global scale would bring about a new chapter in the discussion of needs.

- Changing the paradigm of "Services": A cultural shift is beginning with the understanding that long-term, relational investments in people's lives will ultimately have the greatest impact, creating lasting change. This shift is seen in the realization that "mentoring" or "coaching" relationships afford the most opportunities for growth and change. Embrace Grace is a faith based example of this model, engaging church members to become mentors for the pregnant/parenting women. Advocates do more than just offer material goods and service. They go to the next step, offering personal "mentoring and investing" in the day to day lives of women. Generation Her is a secular version of this model, also engaging mentoring and offering long-term investments in relationship to create change. These are examples of culture change in the distribution of services. It is a paradigm shift that can be adapted globally and implemented across nations.

- Making parenting more acceptable: Changing the attitudes of parenting will take many differing venues – as mentioned above, it includes policies such as paid family leave and against pregnancy discrimination. More generally, accommodations in the workplace will be an important cultural change – one that is just now starting to become a reality. These could be accommodations for children with disabilities, childcare opportunities onsite provided by companies or organizations, opportunities for "at home" work spaces or workload to allow for greater family interaction, just to include a few.

- Changing the male dominance/patriarchal worldview in society. This change in attitude can lift women and children into a higher plane of importance. This is a philosophical idea that could be a powerful agent of change in providing for the needs of the most vulnerable, children and women worldwide.

- Increased engagement in co-parenting. There are many factors that play into the lack of co-parenting. However, through education, information and engagement a cultural shift can take place that encourages fathers to step up to a stronger interactive parenting role, while providing opportunities for mothers to begin to assume role equality in co-parenting. This philosophy shift would encourage a more dynamic co-parenting relationship and shared responsibility for the various parties to enact together, without regard to the marital status of a relationship. Men, women and children all receive multiple benefits when healthy relationships are at play.

.

- Global micro loans to women – This new concept is sweeping the internet, allowing persons to make an incredible impact on the poverty level worldwide. Micro-loans allow women in underdeveloped countries to request funding for a small business loan, providing a business plan for the investors to see. People from all over the world have the capacity to "fund" even at very small levels. Once the fund has been matched, these women are given a loan with which to begin or increase their business reach. It is well documented that when women are given an income, they use this income to feed their children, further educational experiences, and invest in raising the family financial circumstances (Kristof and WuDunn, 2009). This in turn has the capacity to change the poverty level of a country.

Conclusion

There are many services offered to meet the needs of pregnant and parenting adolescents and women. Public policy and funding and a plethora of private agencies, both faith-based and community-based, work to assist or supplement public policy and services. Often private agencies can move into circumstances that the public funding might not be working in. Adoption is a viable option, with both public and private entities working to provide for the needs of both the birth mothers and fathers and the adoptive families. It is understood that there are complex needs, both nationally and globally, but collectively there is an opportunity to be a catalyst for change on the local, national, and global scale. For more information, several websites have been included below.

References

Bureau of Consular Affairs. (2014). Adoption statistics. Retrieved from http://travel.state.gov/content/adoptionsabroad/en/about-us/statistics.html

International Labour Organization. (2000). Maternity protection convention. Retrieved from http://www.ilo.org/dyn/normlex/en/f?p=NORMLEXPUB:12100:0::NO:: P12100_ILO_CODE:C183

International Labour Organization. (2014). *Maternity and paternity at work: Law and practice across the world.* Geneva: Author. Retrieved from https://fortunedotcom.files.wordpress.com/2014/05/wcms_242615.pdf

Kristof, N. D., WuDunn, S. (2009). *Half the sky: Turning oppression into opportunity for women worldwide.* New York: Knopf.

Lester, B. M. & Twomey, J. E. (2008). Treatment of substance abuse during pregnancy. *Women's Health, 4*(1), 67-77.

United Nations. (1979). Convention on the Elimination of all Forms of Discrimination Against Women. Retrieved from http://www.ohchr.org/EN/ProfessionalInterest/Pages/CEDAW.aspx

Recommended Web Sites

Feminists for Life

http://www.feministsforlife.org/cop - College Outreach Program and
http://www.feministsforlife.org/rkoas - Raising Kids on a Shoestring

The College Outreach Program includes resources available for college students to continue their education while parenting, and organizing on campus to make more resources available. The directory called Raising Kids on a Shoestring *offers information on a wide range of needs – housing, clothing, money management, transportation, education, recreation, and more.*

Pregnant on Campus

http://pregnantoncampus.studentsforlife.org

For the United States, the web page refers people to a wide range of pregnancy and parenting resources for their specific campus, including practical needs and peer support. This approach can also serve as a model for interested people in other countries.

U.S. Department of Health & Human Service:
Administration for Children & Families; Children's Bureau.

http://www.childwelfare.gov

Information concerning adoption, child welfare, foster care and Native American tribal information.

Centers for Disease Control and Prevention

http://www.cdc.gov/reproductivehealth/maternalinfanthealth/index.html
and
http://www.cdc.gov/reproductivehealth/unintendedpregnancy/qfp.htm

A variety of information concerning pre/post partum information and services available.

Lifeline Children's Services

http://lifelinechild.org/adoption/international/

An adoption agency working in both domestic and international countries.

CareNet

http://www.care-net.org/center-insights-blog

Non-profit agency providing support for pregnancy resource centers throughout the U.S.

Heartbeat International

https://www.heartbeatinternational.org/about/our-passion

Non-profit agency providing support to pregnancy resource centers domestic and international.

KIVA

http://www.kiva.org/

Non-profit organization with a mission to connect people through lending to alleviate poverty. Kiva uses the internet to provide microfinance options for people in poverty.

Half the Sky Movement

http://www.halftheskymovement.org/partners

A movement to advance women's rights worldwide, investing in women on a global scale.

Chapter 18

How We Get There From Here: Transforming the Debate over Abortion

by A. Marco Turk

Professor emeritus and director emeritus of the negotiation, conflict resolution and peacebuilding program at California State University Dominguez Hills.

Introduction

This chapter is unique in the ongoing heated abortion debate because we look at whether and how peace psychologists may be able to provide "helpful conflict transformation skills" to those on both sides of the issue: Believers that it is a matter of a woman's "option" on the one hand, while others are convinced it is "an act of violence against all concerned" (MacNair, 2013, p.3).

Historically, the abortion debate has been polarized between heated pro-life and pro-choice *positions* rather than the presentation of a reasoned expression of differing *points of view*, so the controversy has been politically charged oftentimes resulting in deadly violence. The aim of this chapter is to consider how to transform that heated discussion by developing the possibilities for successful conflict transformation in the society-wide political controversy and activist confrontations concerning the issue of abortion. There is a need as well as great potential for the design and implementation of an educational and applied program of conflict *transformation* that may provide a more peaceful and collaborative road through the abyss currently surrounding this issue.

Such a transformation must necessarily involve the asking of a different question than the historic one of whether pro-choice or pro-life is the "right" answer. The new question to be asked might be something such as what effect does abortion have on women both physically and emotionally, or is abortion something that comes within the category of violence against women? The idea would be to pose questions where the responses would require an open dialog that could bring pro-life and pro-choice proponents together to peacefully discuss possible answers and resulting ramifications, thereby reframing the underlying issues.

The *first step* is to understand that this issue primarily generates intense *emotions,* and the alternative would be to address the *concerns* (Fisher and Shapiro, 2005, p. 203). The way to the heart of the issue is to present the opportunity for constructive dialog rather than seeking to win the argument as to which position is right. It is necessary to understand that the difficult question posed for solution (pro-choice or pro-life) is in fact the *problem*, rather than the underlying issues of the effect on women and to what extent is abortion a violent act against them. The *second step* is to *humanize* rather than demonize the other point of view, acting with civility to form a consensus, and avoiding the "blame game." A necessary corollary is that there is no *right* or *wrong* solution here. The *third step* is to understand the difference between a negative rights-based approach to resolution of the conflict and how to construct a positive interests-based alternative, so the historically abrasive debate can be converted to *dialog* providing the opportunity for a mutually satisfactory result reached through collaboration and transformation (Cloke, 2001, p. 149).

~ 294 ~

It seems that over the long course of this increasingly polarized debate consisting of "mutually incompatible worldviews," we have seen the constant effort to achieve an "explicit compromise" (something that perhaps would have been best to avoid) degenerate into a "head to head" contest in the political arena (Burns, 2005, pp. 312-313). Whether one agrees or disagrees with the claim that *Roe v. Wade* is responsible for the passionate debate over abortion, we are nevertheless left with the challenge of how to succeed in uniting people on both sides so they can "live together with tolerance" (p. 314). It is time to abandon the contest over whether the *Roe* decision should be reversed, and instead seek something different (p. 314). If there is agreement with this statement, the question then becomes: How do we get there from here while maintaining social peace (p. 314)?

Guiding Principles of Conflict *Transformation*

The term "conflict transformation" was conceived by John Paul Lederach in the 1980s in response to his need to re-examine the use of "conflict resolution" and "conflict management" in the language of the field (Lederach, 2003, p. 3). He says the term imparts "constructive change efforts that include and go beyond the resolution of specific problems," because "conflict is normal in human relationships, and conflict is a motor of change" bringing "into focus the horizon toward which we journey – the building of healthy relationships and communities, locally and globally" requiring "real change in our current ways of relating [and] thinking" (p. 5).

Lederach believes this approach enables us to "envision and respond to the ebb and flow of social conflict as life-giving opportunities for creating constructive change processes that reduce violence, increase justice in direct interaction and social structures, and respond to real-life problems in human relationships" (2003, p. 22). The goals are to minimize the destructive effects of the conflict while maximizing our potential for growth and well-being; minimize poor communication and maximize human understanding; surface and deal with the fears and hopes related to emotions and interdependence; understand and address the root causes and social conditions that result in violence and like harmful expressions of conflict; pursue nonviolent mechanisms to reduce adversarial confrontation so that violence can be reduced and ultimately eliminated; seek to establish structures to produce "substantive justice" to meet basic human needs while at the same time encouraging maximum participation in "procedural justice" that affects the lives of those in conflict; comprehend what cultural patterns cause conflict to be expressed through violence; and, use the assets of a cultural setting for the constructive response to conflict (p. 27).

The "guiding question" is one that asks us to determine how we can put an end to what is undesirable and at the same time create what is worth having (Lederach, 2003, p. 30). For this, we must look to both the specific episode as well as the focal or center point of the conflict (p. 31). So it will be necessary to create a "map" of the conflict through the pursuit of three points of inquiry. The first of these presents the situation; the second envisions the future; and the third brings us to the change processes with their design and support creating an approach that is not simply negotiating a solution but rather something that provides a new way (pp. 34-38).

Transformation actually operates through the hyphenation of process and structure so the term now combines the independent characteristics of adaptability and purpose (Lederach, 2003, p. 40) Developing the capacity to accomplish the following personal practices will assist in effectively applying the concept of conflict transformation: The ability to present issues as windows; integrate multiple time frames; pose the energies of conflict as dilemmas; make a friend of complexity; and hear and engage the voices of identity (pp. 48-60). At the heart of transformation lies the capacity to "live with apparent contradictions and paradoxes" (p. 53). Rather than ignoring or talking away another's perception, make an attempt to understand its roots (p. 58).

So how do we apply the conflict transformation framework suggested by Lederach? He proposes the use of the following "lenses" (Lederach, 2003, pp. 62-67):

1. What do the lenses bring into focus?
   a. What is suggested about the episode?
   b. What is suggested about the epicenter?

2. What questions do the lenses raise?
   a. What do they suggest about the episode?
   b. What do they suggest about the epicenter?
   c. What does the dilemma ask?

3. What suggestions would come from a transformational platform?

The questions raised emphasize the potential for constructive change inherent in the conflict (Lederach, 2003, p. 68). This is something for which the narrow definition of conflict *resolution* does not provide, "the questions and inquiries necessary to spark the potential for broader change" (p. 68). Conflict *transformation* is interested in replacing the onset of increasing violence and coercion with "respect, creative problem-solving, individual and social capacities for dialog, and nonviolent systems for assuring human security and social change...guided by a transformational understanding of life and relationship" (pp.70-71).

A Capsulized View of the Controversy Presented by the Debate over Abortion

The debate over abortion predates *Roe v. Wade* by 170 years, the English Omnibus Crime Act (Lord Ellenborough's Act) having made abortion at any stage of the pregnancy a crime (Hull & Hoffer, 2010, pp. 334, 341). It is noteworthy that when President Nixon expanded Medicaid in 1972 to require all health care providers to offer contraception services or furnish referrals, the Catholic Church did not object and there is little evidence that such action was controversial (Murray & Luker, 2015, p. 627).

It seems the actions of legislatures in criminalizing abortion, citizen lawsuits, and courts interpreting anti-abortion statutes have since brought us to the abortion rights issue in its present form (Hull, Hoffer, & Hoffer, 2004, p. 332). And, while it is clear that lives of pregnant women are saved by legalized abortion, "making abortion criminal does not save the lives of large numbers of the unborn" (p. 333). A definitive resolution to the abortion rights controversy does not appear to be something that courts and judge-made law will be able to provide (p. 335). In this situation where we have the "clash of absolutes," we should be looking to a change in cultural values since this debate really may be one over the role of women in society where they "should not be viewed as carriers of the next generation unless they so choose" (pp. 336-337).

The problem is that we are facing a debate over moral precepts: For pro-choice forces, the right to choose has been a moral principle whose goal is "protecting the dignity, health, and autonomy of all women," whereas the pro-life groups insist that fetal life is a moral principle that reaches out to "the sacred memory of traditional families and motherhood as well as basic religious values" (Hull et al., 2004, p. 337). Unlike other controversies that have been resolved in our history as a nation, "the abortion/abortion rights debate does not show any signs of abating" (p. 337). And this proves interesting because recent polls indicate that "Americans are, for the most part, less strident than either of these positions suggests," even though "the debate over abortion continues to be as heated and emotional today as in the past" (Mooney, 2014, p. 8).

Next, let's look at the opportunities to move in the direction of abandoning the effort to "win an argument," and instead "open real discussion" concerning an "informed appraisal of where we have been, where we now stand, and where we are headed on this issue" (Judges, 1993, p. 294). We need to "get past the hostility and conflict-oriented approach of the abortion wars...searching for and listening to the lost voices" (Judges, 1993, p. 295). As John Stuart Mill said, it is important to consider opposing viewpoints because that is the "only way in which a human being can make some approach to knowing the whole of a subject "(Merino, 2014, p. 11). Only when we listen and truly hear will we appreciate the ideas of others, and objectively evaluate them, so we can determine their value for our consideration (Merino, 2014, p. 12). "Those with whom one disagrees should not be regarded as enemies but rather as people whose views deserve careful examination and may shed light on one's own" (p. 13).

Resolution of the debate will not come from "religion, science, judicial process, or legislative policy… [because] there is no one path, or one final answer, that can resolve the issue to everyone's liking" (Baker, 2015, p. x). Accepting this and acknowledging the complexity of the debate can move us "out of the abortion wars and toward peace" (p. xi). This will require using empathy rather than judgment, and dealing with others in the same manner we would like for ourselves, as advocated by the *pro-voice* movement (p. xi).

The *pro-voice* approach utilizes listening, storytelling, and "embracing gray areas" to get beyond the "rigid us-versus-them mentality…to generate new cultural norms" (Baker, 2015, p. xi). We need to seek a secure place for men and women to speak freely about their shared experiences (p. xi). The labels of "pro-choice and pro-life are not so cut and dry" (p. 111). Instead, listening to and appreciating personal stories is the recommended way to successfully accomplish *pro-voice* efforts (p. 128).

In Lederach's *Little Book* fashion, how would a reconstructed view see this controversy, and what might a platform for conflict transformation look like in response, as set forth below (2003, pp. 62-66)?

1. **What do our lenses bring into focus?**

Episode **lenses suggest the following concerns:**
- The morality of abortion.
- The impact of *Roe v. Wade.*
- The restriction of abortion rights.
- Medical and social concerns about abortion.

Epicenter **lenses suggest consideration of:**
- When does personhood (morally relevant life) begin?
- What rights does a woman have in relation to the fetus she carries?

- Did the Supreme Court commit error in providing a right to abortion?
- Was the decision in *Roe* the correct one?
- Has the Court allowed too many restrictions on this right?
- Where do we go now that the debate in this country appears to have shifted from overturning *Roe* to a controversy over the manner in which and when the right can be regulated and restricted?
- What are the medical and social concerns surrounding the right?

2. What questions do these lenses raise?

Episode suggests:
- Can we reconcile the "inherent value of human life" with the "integrity of a woman's moral will" (Merino, 2014, p. 56)?
- Can we get past condemning the Court for establishing the right to abortion, and reconcile those who believe it was correct with those who feel the Court has been too lenient in permitting restrictions on the right (Merino, 2014, p. 61)?
- Can we agree on the ways to regulate and restrict abortion (Merino, 2014, p. 101)?
- Can we agree on at least a portion of the issues having to do with the medical and social aspects of abortion (Merino, 2014, p. 130)?

Epicenter suggests:
- Can we discuss and develop a code of conduct concerning rights and responsibilities for all sides of the controversy that will prevent violence and promote reasoned discussion?
- Can we design a longer-term vision of what the respective interests and underlying needs are for all

sides of the controversy, setting this forth in a mission statement? And how can it be responsive to the peaceful discussion and consideration of the needs expressed by all sides?

- Can we establish a mechanism that provides all sides with a voice for their respective concerns, establishing regular and routine paths to constructive interaction?

Posing a dilemma asks:

- How can we deal with the issue of abortion *and at the same time* outline processes that facilitate a common vision for fairly and fully considering the various points of view?
- How can we deal with the feelings concerning the morality of abortion, *while at the same time* providing mechanisms for consideration of the needs that women have in relation to carrying a fetus?

3. **What would a transformational platform suggest?**

a. We need to create a motivation to achieve something that will encompass the entire problem. Hopefully, this will present an opportunity to explore the potential of what is good for the entire nation, searching beyond the current issues while keeping in mind the past years since *Roe.* These issues will be the key to a rational context providing a backdrop to this conflict, enabling a return to examine the design of processes as set forth below (Lederach, 2003, pp. 62-64).

b. These process responses should be both to the immediate issues and the longer-term agenda presented by all sides. The issues presented will provide a clear view into the nature of the repeated patterns, suggesting possible paths for what may be of future assistance, in considering multiple approaches, each with a different set of time frame requirements, but ones that are connected. Examples might include:

(1) A facilitated national forum to air grievances and clarify immediate needs and solutions.
(2) A facilitated national forum to discuss expectations for approaches to abortion.
(3) An initiative to develop regular exchanges and feedback between all sides of the controversy.
(4) An initiative to develop a long-range strategic plan for establishing a mission statement and guiding values for involving all sides.
(5) A plan to initiate a national advisory panel that creates specific ways in which all sides can consult and exchange their positive as well negative feelings.

Different types of support structures as well as time frames will be required in moving forward. In each case there may be a one-time event, for others an ongoing process, or perhaps a way to provide the basis for new national structures and resources. The goal is to accomplish change processes, and determine what will facilitate this in a constructive manner.

c. This presupposes a need to consider how to build a new and ongoing response mechanism for the "hot button" issues that abortion generates. For example, the advisory or facilitative group discussed above might initially pave the way to engage with the immediate process, but it also could become a facilitative device or platform encouraging an ongoing national response on longer-range issues. The idea is this: In the future, given the patterns of the past in dealing with the abortion issue, it will be important to anticipate new events. A plan that enables us to prepare and respond to a greater degree constructively will be necessary. Its purpose will be to bring together people from all points of view on both sides of the issues. An informed effort could be attempted that would subsequently become formalized if successful in dealing with situations as they arise.

d. A forum for current and future issues should be included, while at the same time care should be taken to avoid this as a "talk" arena. The future needs to be carefully planned so the interests and underlying needs of all sides will be constructively presented, considered and not allowed to become stale.

e. *Pro-voice* fits in perfectly with what Lederach advocates because it is "founded on a complete dedication to transformation" (Baker, 2015, p. 129). This puts oneself in the shoes of the other to experience the gray area through networking that is critical (pp. 130-131). Genuinely listening without judgment or assumptions, use of open-ended questions, employing engaging reflective language, validating personal experiences, participating in ethical storytelling fully exposing risks and benefits, utilizing gray areas, pursuing a "both/and approach" rather than one of "either/or," changing perspectives and practicing "self-care" (the art of "loving and respecting each other") is necessary to provide the maximum benefits from the pro-voice approach (pp. 156-163).

Conclusion

In the case of conflict *resolution,* we look for settlement of a *specific dispute.* However, when employing the conflict *transformation* approach, as amplified by the *pro-voice* movement, we are surveying the *larger picture,* setting our sights on changing how those in sharp disagreement deal with each other until they can reconstruct their relationship and arrive at an acceptable solution. This is so that, in the meantime, their continued incompatibility will be peaceful while they attempt to reconcile their differences. This should be the goal of both sides as the debate over abortion endures.

References

Baker, A. (2015). *Pro-voice: How to keep listening when the world wants a fight.* Oakland: Berrett-Koehler.

Burns, G. (2005). *The moral veto: Framing contraception, abortion, and cultural pluralism in the United States.* Cambridge: Cambridge University Press.

Cloke, K. (2001). *Mediating dangerously: The frontiers of conflict resolution.* San Francisco: Jossey-Bass.

Fisher, R., & Shapiro, D. (2005). *Beyond reason: Using emotions as you negotiate.* New York: Viking Penguin.

Hull, N., & Hoffer, P. (2010). *Roe v. Wade: The abortion rights controversy in American history.* (2nd Ed. Rev. & Exp.). Lawrence: University Press of Kansas.

Hull, N., Hoffer, W., & Hoffer, P. (Eds.). (2004). *The abortion rights controversy in America: A legal reader.* Chapel Hill: The University of North Carolina Press.

Judges, D. (1993). *Hard choices, lost voices: How the abortion conflict has divided America, disturbed constitutional rights, and damaged the courts.* Chicago: Ivan R. Dee.

Lederach, J. (2003). *The little book of conflict transformation.* Intercourse: Good Books.

MacNair, R. (2013). 2013 initiatives and presidential task forces. *PEACE Psychology, 22*(1), 3.

Merino, N. (Ed.). (2014). *Abortion: Opposing viewpoints.* Farmington Hills: Greenhaven Press.

Mooney, C. (2014). *Should abortion be legal?* San Diego: Reference Point Press.

Murray, M., & Luker, K. (2015). *Cases on reproductive rights and justice.* St. Paul: Foundation Press.

Chapter 19

Final Thoughts on Conflict Transformation

by Rachel M. MacNair

There is a small literature focused on fostering dialog on varying abortion perspectives (Goi, 2005; Herzig & Sahsin, 2006; Jacksteit & Kaufmann, 2011; LeBaron & Carstarphen, 1997; Schneider, 1996). Several attempts have occurred, such as a successful large conference held at Princeton October 15-16, 2010 (see http://uchv.princeton.edu/Life_Choice/), where people from both sides left their common echo chamber to see how their arguments sounded to the other side. While generally agreed to have been a worthwhile endeavor, there has been no follow-up.

People near the opposite ends of the continuum have similar problems with focusing entirely on only the common ground they share. For the pro-choice side, the points in common – as in all the chapters of Part 1 of this book – leave out any positive aspects of abortion. They must; anything positive would not be common ground. Yet there is a strong feeling of lack of balance that feels uncomfortable to many. Conversely, the legal status of abortion itself must be off the table, leaving many pro-lifers feeling that the exercise is simply a defense of the status quo.

As is customary in all heated conflicts, both sides fear that participation gives what they understand to be unworthy moral validation to the other side. Each is distressed by the non-common-ground activities the other continues to engage in, such as lobbying for restrictions on one side or raising money for low-income women's abortions on the other.

Understanding the Opponents of the Perspective

There has been only a little empirical examination of the proponents of differing views. These hypotheses have been pulled from the literature and from the rhetoric of advocates.

Abortion as Option: People who do not understand pregnancy termination as an option can be expected to have or be more likely to have: (a) an authoritarian personality; (b) an intolerance of ambiguity; (c) a punitive attitude, especially toward women; (d) conventional views of sexuality and sex roles.

Abortion as Violence: People who propose abortion as a problem-solver will share with other advocates of violence as a problem solver: (a) dehumanizing language; (b) distancing mechanisms including euphemisms; (c) discounting detrimental effects; (d) cognitive dissonance-induced belligerency.

In the case of the personality of abortion opponents, no specific literature was found on the authoritarian personality or intolerance of ambiguity. However, one study that considered personality variables as a whole in an exploratory manner have ascertained no personality differences that predict position differences on abortion or the death penalty (Lester, Hadley, & Lucas, 1990).

Kimberly Cook has been the primary researcher on the question of punitive attitudes, having found them in a set of interviews of a small number of individuals (Cook, 1998a) and a logistic regression on some other data (Cook, 1998b). However, a direct test of this with a measure for punitive attitude found that pro-lifers and pro-choicers did not differ on this, except among those who favored the death penalty. Among death penalty proponents, those who opposed abortion were less punitive and more saddened at executions compared to those who did not oppose abortion (MacNair, 2008). This study showed that more conventional views on sexuality do seem more prevalent among anti-abortion respondents, but the finding on sex roles shows no difference.

As for the abortion-as-violence perception of abortion-as-option people, William Brennan (1995) has documented extensive dehumanizing and euphemistic language in a variety of situations of violence against various groups of victims, including women, ethnic and religious minorities, people seen as enemies, those with disabilities, and unborn children. Yet this feature so clearly turns on whether or not abortion is in fact the killing of a child that it becomes practically tautological.

Projects and Legislation on which All Could Work Together

Are there projects that both sides could work on together, even if activists on each side continue taking actions objectionable to the other? Here are some possibilities:

- All effective programs, advocacy, and education that reduce domestic abuse, sex trafficking, intoxication, war and rape will be programs that both reduce abortions and give women more choices and control over our lives.

- Programs, advocacy, and education that increase the gentleness and sensitivity in gender relations will have a positive impact on preventing pregnancies and preventing those which do occur unintentionally from being perceived as crises.

- Programs, advocacy, and education giving positive information and attitudes toward any form a child may take – female, having disabilities, etc. – will help foster both life and choices.

- Public policy that helps pregnant women who choose to give birth can be lobbied for. In addition to such obvious services as financial assistance, this can include seeing to it that pregnant women suffering from addiction are never put on a waiting list but receive immediate medical services. Legislation allowing mothers impregnated by rape to block visitation or custody by the rapist has received strong support from all sides. There are undoubtedly many other possibilities along these lines, and people can work together on specific legislation even while they work against each other in other arenas.

- Private volunteering to help pregnant women who choose to give birth can be an especially inspiring program for groups of individuals (such as congregations or classes) who have had heated debates on the topic. Something as simple as donating diapers and baby clothes to a local pregnancy help center could be a project that everyone could participate in to ease the tensions of disputes.

References

Brennan, W. (1995). *Dehumanizing the vulnerable: When word games take lives.* Chicago, IL: Loyola University Press.

Cook, K. J. (1998a). *Divided passions: Public opinions on abortion and the death penalty.* Boston: Northeastern University Press.

Cook, K. J. (1998b). A passion to punish: Abortion opponents who favor the death penalty. *Justice Quarterly, 15,* 329-356.

Goi, S. (2005). Agonism, deliberation, and the politics of abortion. *Polity, 37*(1), 54-81. doi: 10.1177/08944393960140040l

Herzig, M. & Chasin, L. (2006). Fostering dialogue across divides. Retrieved from www.publicconversations.org/docs/resources/Jams_website.pdf

Jacksteit, M. & Kaufmann, A. (2011). *The common ground network for life and choice manual.* Retrieved from http://www.sfcg.org/programmes/usa/pdf/manual.pdf

LeBaron, M. & Carstarphen, N. (1997). Negotiating intractable conflict: The common ground dialogue process and abortion. *Negotiation Journal, 13*(4), 341-361. doi: 10.1111/j.1571-9979.1997.tb00138.x

Lester, D., Hadley, R. A., & Lucas, W. A. (1990). Personality and a Pro-death attitude. *Personality and Individual Differences, 11,* 1183-1185.

MacNair, R. M. (2008). Perceptions of connections. In R. M. MacNair R.M. & S. J. Zunes (Eds.). *Consistently opposing killing: From abortion to assisted suicide, the death penalty, and war* (pp. 87-104). Westport, CT: Praeger.

Schneider, S. M. (1996). Creating a democratic public sphere through political discussion: A case study of abortion conversation on the internet. *Social Science Computer Review, 14*(373), 373-393. doi: 10.1177/08944393960140040l

Index